THE A PLAYER

Josh,

Be the A Player!

Best,

Rick

6/3=23

Praise for *The A Player*

Very specific and very readable, *The A Player* is your strategic guide into transforming solid players into champions! The brilliance of Crossland's book is that it's for any employee who wants to be a top performer as well as any manager who wants to transform B or even C players into A players. It will help your organization achieve the performance you have versus the performance you want. Excellent!

—**Marshall Goldsmith**, World's Foremost
Executive Coach and Best-selling Author

Safelite AutoGlass is a company whose record-setting performance is fueled by our people. We strive to be a great place to work, with impactful leaders and talented individuals… the A Players. This book is a great catalyst to engage people to be their best. It offers a unique perspective on "what the CEO wants you to know." I recommend it to anyone wishing to be a high performer and challenge their teams to achieve new heights.

—**Tom Feeney**, President and CEO, Safelite AutoGlass

Topgrading is all about hiring only A Players, and Crossland's book is a wonderfully practical manual to guide A Players to remain A Players and for anyone aspiring to be an A Player to become one. Implicit in the book is a mini-MBA degree showing how As achieve great results. We at Topgrading, Inc. will use this book when coaching managers to move up to the A Player designation!

—**Brad Smart**, Founder and CEO of Topgrading and Best-selling Author

The A Player is a definitive book on creating a high-performance culture. It is a welcome addition to an already rich field of leadership literature, but is notable because it acts as a playbook and guide. If you are seeking a resource with specific actions and ideas, rather than concepts and theories, you will not be disappointed.

—**Brian Beitler**, Executive Vice President and CMO at Lane Bryant, Inc.

The A Player is a book you should read if you are committed to getting better. You'll get ideas for helping you and your team play at a higher level.

—**Mark Sanborn**, Best-selling Author, Renowned Public Speaker, and Leadership Expert

The A Player is more than just a leadership book: it is a game changer. In its pages, you will learn how to better yourself as an employee or leader, all while positively impacting your business. You will not only improve your personal productivity, but also the productivity of your direct reports and colleagues. You will be glad you invested the time to read this treasure chest of practical advice and insight.

—**Jeff Robinson**, VP Human Resources, BrightView

THE A PLAYER

The Definitive Playbook & Guide for Employees and Leaders
Who Want to Play and Perform at the Highest Level

RICK CROSSLAND

NEW YORK

NASHVILLE • MELBOURNE • VANCOUVER

THE A PLAYER

The Definitive Playbook and Guide for Employees and Leaders
Who Want to Play and Perform at the Highest Level

© 2017 **RICK CROSSLAND**.

Published in New York, New York, by Morgan James Publishing. Morgan James and The Entrepreneurial Publisher are trademarks of Morgan James, LLC.
www.MorganJamesPublishing.com

The Morgan James Speakers Group can bring authors to your live event. For more information or to book an event visit The Morgan James Speakers Group at www.TheMorganJamesSpeakersGroup.com.

Shelfie

A free eBook edition is available
with the purchase of this print book.

CLEARLY PRINT YOUR NAME ABOVE IN UPPER CASE

Instructions to claim your free eBook edition:
1. Download the Shelfie app for Android or iOS
2. Write your name in **UPPER CASE** above
3. Use the Shelfie app to submit a photo
4. Download your eBook to any device

ISBN 978-1-63047-992-3 paperback
ISBN 978-1-63047-993-0 eBook
ISBN 978-1-63047-994-7 hardcover
Library of Congress Control Number:
2016903411

Cover Design by:
Megan James

Interior Design by:
Bonnie Bushman
The Whole Caboodle Graphic Design

In an effort to support local communities, raise awareness and funds, Morgan James Publishing donates a percentage of all book sales for the life of each book to Habitat for Humanity Peninsula and Greater Williamsburg.

Get involved today! Visit
www.MorganJamesBuilds.com

For Jennifer, my ultimate A Player…

TABLE OF CONTENTS

A Play·er
/ ā plā-ər/
Noun

Also spelled A-Player

1. An employee who is in the top 10% of his or her profession on an industry wide basis for the salary paid
2. A person on your team whom you would enthusiastically rehire
3. The employees at an enterprise who drive all the profitability and growth
4. A person of high integrity who delivers on commitments
5. The employee that every organization covets

synonyms: awesome employee, top performer, high performer, rock star, all-star, superstar, team player, game changer

Story

THE ABCs OF BUSINESS

As Tom Feeney, the President and CEO of Safelite AutoGlass, approached the podium to address his top 300 executives at the National Leadership Meeting, he was astounded by what the company had achieved over the last 9 years. The nation's largest provider of vehicle glass repair and replacement services had transformed itself into a growth machine, nearly tripling its sales in that time period, and even more importantly, growing net profit 4 times over!

However, what Tom was most proud about was the dramatic cultural transformation that had occurred from inside the once staid company. In fact, he was most proud of the nearly 13,000 associates nationwide who were *not* at the meeting. These frontline team members had embraced and executed leadership at all levels to make these great results happen.

During the dark days of the "Great Recession," Safelite had to get a lot more customer-focused and efficient to move from "survive to thrive." They needed each and every employee to step up to the plate and become an A Player. They named this culture of 100% A Players "People Powered, Customer Driven." In this culture each employee had to exhibit, and live out three attributes on a daily basis: Service Mindset, Can Do Attitude, and Caring Heart.

Tom had been amazed by how well his team responded to the challenge to be their absolute best every single day. It was hard work, and many employees had to learn new skills and step out of their comfort zones to achieve the necessary results. Not everyone made the journey. Those that had an entitlement mentality about their jobs soon found out that the new culture no longer tolerated people who simply wanted to "punch the clock" and watch others do the work. Those that did not have a mindset of ownership, accountability, and responsibility soon found Safelite to be a culture not suitable to them.

For the majority, however, the new culture provided challenge and a breath of fresh air. They loved that blame, excuses, and denial were no longer allowed and instead were replaced by positive attitudes, caring for one another, and a celebration for results. To protect this culture of high performers, Safelite instituted rigorous hiring and interview techniques including half and full-day job assessments. By being very selective in their hiring process, and establishing world-class interview techniques, Safelite was able to ensure that the new people joining their team not only had the requisite skills, but also fully bought into Safelite's core values. In other words, Safelite could virtually guarantee with a high degree of confidence that their new team members were A Players.

The results of these high-performing employees were amazing. In addition to the revenue and profit growth, employee engagement reached an all-time high of 80%. Safelite employees were aligned, engaged, and motivated to the company vision and purpose. In addition, Safelite employed the Net Promoter Score (NPS) methodology—a measure of how many customers would enthusiastically recommend Safelite's services to a friend or relative, net of any detractors. This score improved by thirteen points to 86%! This meant that Safelite's services and customer experience rated considerably higher than other respected power brands like Apple, Southwest Airlines, and Disney. Finally, the increased profits generated from the business enabled significant job growth, promotions, and financial incentives for the team members who had contributed to these outstanding results. It also enabled Safelite to invest in innovation, technology, leadership development, improved employee benefits, and brand building initiatives.

As Tom stood before his high-performing leadership team, they were all genuinely excited by what they had achieved and by the company's bright future. The cultural and performance transformation that occurred was nothing short of amazing. His team was more accountable than ever, and was working with passion and drive. Tom attributed this to the absolute commitment of everyone on the team being "People Powered, Customer Driven." Most of all, by creating a culture where people come first, associates understood their value and their role in the big picture; they worked with a greater sense of purpose—to really make a difference and bring unexpected happiness to people's everyday lives. The work they did mattered!

As Tom savored the moment, he thought about how remarkable A Players were, and he pondered the qualities, skills, and attitudes that went into making these extraordinary employees. This was a formula that needed to be shared…

Chapter 1

THE MAGIC OF *A* PLAYERS

"You Win with People"
—**Woody Hayes**, former Ohio State football coach

*I*f you have ever worked on a team project and had your "A" grade dragged down to a lower grade by B or C Players who did not pull their weight, then you can immediately grasp the A Player concept and the importance of only having A Players on your team. In any endeavor, being a great team member on a fantastic team is the recipe for success. People have understood this concept in the world of academics and sports for decades. For some reason, however, we have too long tolerated B and C Players in the workforce. This is baffling, for unlike school and sports (unless you are a pro-athlete), at work we are now playing for our own livelihood. The stakes are much higher so to speak. If you stop to think about it, this is actually staggering, as your job and career prospects are directly linked to your organization's performance. If your company is tolerating B and C underperformers, then by definition the company could be performing better, which hurts both the immediate and long-term compensation, benefits, and growth you and the other top performers should be receiving. With this revelation, there is no successful argument for why we should have B and C Players on a team.

So what is an A Player? A Players are defined as employees who are in the top 10% of their industry for the salary offered.[1] A Players are the employees that would be *enthusiastically* rehired by their employers. If you think about it a moment, defining A Players as the top 10% of the industry is actually very liberating to an organization, as there is no constraint to force rank people on the team. Since we are evaluating from an industry-wide vantage point, the very exciting possibility of creating an entire All-Star team of A Players in our own organizations becomes a reality. Therefore, our teams can be comprised of 100% A Players.

A Players are aligned in their careers and absolutely shine in their roles. They are the employees who make all the goodness in an organization happen. Their performance and great attitudes are almost magical. If you are reading this book, you are either an employee who aspires to be an A Player, or one who has already achieved A Player status and knows he or she can be even better. Or, you may be an executive leader looking for an essential playbook designed for companies who want to build an A Player Culture. *The A Player* offers employees and teams the roadmap to help get them there. Outstanding employees drive great companies, and in turn great companies provide amazing career opportunities for those employees who align with their mission and purpose. It is truly a two-way street. Great companies are inherently vested in your success.

However, just like All-Stars are annually voted on in professional sports, achieving and then maintaining A Player status requires continual effort. We can lose it just as quickly as we receive it. We cannot rest on our laurels. The expectations increase as we reach higher levels in our careers.

Why are A Players so important? Most people are not thrilled to have surgery performed by a B Player heart surgeon; or fly on an airplane piloted by a B Player pilot. Obviously these are mission critical occupations, and there is no room for B or C Players to be at the helm in such sensitive situations.

Similarly, the work you do is important. You are mission critical to your employer and your customers. Thus, there is no room for the mediocrity that

---

1   As defined by Dr. Brad Smart in *Topgrading*.

a B or C Player offers. On average, an A Player produces at least two to three times the quality and volume of work of the B Player, which is why A Players are so greatly coveted. We don't settle for B or C Player surgeons or airline pilots, so why should an employer settle for less than the absolute best in their specific industry? The reality is that they should not.

Likewise, if you are a leader who manages people, you cannot settle for underperformers who will drag down the overall performance of your team. This book will give you the tools to shape your team into a group of high performers. It will help you identify, lead, coach, and develop A Players, as well as become a better leader yourself. In fact, leaders need to understand A Player acumen better than anyone else. Remember, the rest of the organization rises or falls to your level of leadership competency, so you need to model the way.

These aforementioned tools will help you serve your organization at the highest possible level, while also achieving your personal best. Being an A Player helps you achieve *excellence*, which produces a more long-term and altruistic impact for a much larger constituency than just yourself.

When you do your best, you become more personally satisfied, your company's leadership is also more satisfied, and the organization flourishes. Everybody wins. Being an A Player employee will not guarantee you job security, but will guarantee you career security, as the services of the "best" employees are always in high demand.

Everyone wants to know what it takes to be an A Player. You will soon discover the proven mindsets, behaviors, and actions that these elite performers have in their DNA. A Players not only drive better performance, but also create a more professional and collegial work environment. A Players are beneficial, wholesome, and helpful people to have around. The truth is that powerful things occur when a team of 100% A Players come together to create a fantastic environment. There is no denying that A Players are at the center of every great endeavor. Thus, being an A Player is the straightforward, simple, and practically universal goal for us all.

Now, you may be thinking: Am I an A Player? And if not, what happens to me? Let's answer that important question this way: everybody deserves the opportunity to be an A Player *somewhere*. The goal is to help you become that top performer at your current organization. This book will show you what it takes.

So, what if you already consider yourself an A Player? Most people, even high performers, have some B and C Player tendencies that need to be purged. Everyone in your organization needs to fully understand what it means to be an A Player, and then recognize the mindsets, behaviors, and actions required to achieve and maintain that status. Simultaneously, you will also learn how to recognize *A Player* performance and how to hold yourself and others accountable for achieving it. In fact, having your entire workgroup read and apply the principles of *The A Player* will create the biggest gains for your organization. Think about how wonderful life will be when you fully respect the work ethic and results of all of your coworkers. On top of that, you get the joy of working with the best in your business—your own All-Star team. The results are limitless.

The payoff for being an A Player is huge. If you are a leader, becoming an A Player will yield even more respect and high performance from your team. They will follow you because of who you are, not because of your title. If you are an employee, becoming an A Player means you are contributing at a very high level to the success of the organization. This means your employer will enthusiastically rehire you, support your development, and put you in positions of increasing responsibility. This also means that you are in high demand and are employable, no matter the circumstances of your business.

There is also an even bigger societal benefit at play here. Businesses that have teams of 100% A Players create companies that thrive. They are able to offer better opportunities, and more stable environments; they also grow with the needs of their team members. Beyond that, the company is better positioned to share that prosperity in terms of a greater purpose by providing incredible products and services that truly help people, as well as by providing amazing benefits and growth opportunities for its employees. Many of these companies also use this prosperity to fund meaningful social responsibility work such as improving the working conditions in their supply base. Think Apple here, as Apple was founded on the principle of 100% A Players.

Becoming an A Player requires a higher level of strategic thinking than most employees consider. *The A Player* focuses on strategic issues that will endear you to high-performing managers, leaders, and companies. By focusing at this strategic level, it will open up your horizons to ever-increasing levels of responsibility and success—wherever you are. It will also require that you raise your levels of leadership, accountability, and business acumen. The bigger impact is that you will attract others just like you, and recognize enormous results to culture, performance, and happiness. As Daniel Pink summarizes in the book *Drive*, "We are motivated by our innate need to direct our own lives, to learn and create new things and to do better for ourselves and our world." These motivations are precisely aligned with how the A Player's mindset operates. We play for bigger stakes than just a paycheck.

Everybody has the opportunity to be an A Player *somewhere*. The question is: do you have what it takes to be an A Player employee in your current organization? Your employer has the right to create a team of 100% A Players. If you are not currently performing as an A, you either need to make the attitudinal shifts and additional effort to get there, or find an organization where the demands of being an A Player are less challenging. However, keep in mind that just like in investments, the more risk you take, the greater the returns and potential benefits. If you play at a less demanding level, you may be happier, albeit likely for less compensation than you were making on the bigger stage. We'll leave that decision up to you, as the important thing is that you find a place where you can thrive and align your purpose with the organization's.

Congratulations on your journey to becoming an A Player! The pages that follow contain the experiences, strategies, and advice of proven A Players, CEOs, and other executive leaders—this is all included so you can thrive in your career and create an unbelievable culture within your team. This book's aim is to fundamentality change the way people approach work, and to create the magic in your organization that happens when people are aligned and play with passion, drive, and purpose. There is no theory within, only methods proven to work in the real world. Taking this information to heart and using it can literally be life changing. Please keep an open mind. The results will astound you.

Chapter 2

DEFINING THE *A* PLAYER

"Talent is God given. Be humble. Fame is man-given. Be grateful. Conceit is self-given. Be careful."
      —**John Wooden**, Hall of Fame Basketball Coach

*A*s you can imagine, the term A Player carries a very specific definition. Many business leaders enjoy touting how their business is differentiated by their team of great people. However, when asked the critical question: "How many people on your team would you enthusiastically rehire?" Their response is usually surprisingly, that they would only rehire less than 50% of their current "dream team." What was once a strong group of team members is now less than half what they would enthusiastically rehire! How is that possible?

Obviously, the operative word here is enthusiastically. This exercise proved very effective at challenging leaders to upgrade their teams. It was as if a light bulb went off as the answer to the question rambled off their tongues. Since employee payroll is likely the largest fixed expense of every business or organization, putting up with employees who are not high performers in terms of bottom-line results, attitudes, and cultural fit will cause the business to jeopardize performance and make the lives of everyone who has to deal with them pretty miserable. If the business is not functioning at its peak performance, you are literally subsidizing those who are unwilling to work at their peak potential. If that's the case, the business is literally leaving money on the table—money that should be in the pocket of an A Player in terms of a bonus or profit sharing.

In Dr. Brad Smart's Topgrading® work, he defines an A Player as an individual that is part of the top 10% of talent available in the market for the salary paid. Notice we say the overall market and not the company. This mitigates the in-fighting all too common in many corporate cultures to grab the top spot. In an A Player Culture, it's an All-Star team, so everyone can win. A Players are the employees that get *enthusiastically* rehired. They have great attitudes, work ethics, and abide well with company cultural values. Don't confuse A Players with Type-A personalities, as they may or may not be more assertive, but are clearly driven and maintain strong core values, making them great team players. For this excellence, A Players are typically compensated at the top of the salary range for the position and may command a higher salary premium versus B Player talent; and rightfully so—they are worth it.

In fact, they are the driving force of company productivity because a workforce of 100% A Players is much more productive than the average team, as far fewer employees can produce far greater output. A Players produce between two to three times more results and productivity than their non-A counterparts. Hiring fewer and better candidates is a recipe for business success and happiness. In addition, teams of A Players drive additional efficiency because a manager can easily manage twice as many A Players as B and C Players. The manager with Bs and Cs on the team may only be able to manage say six employees, whereas with 100% A Players that span can easily go to twelve or more.

In his excellent book *Scaling Up*, business expert Verne Harnish has a fantastic shorthand test to define the A Player. He states that A Players:

1. Fit the company culture.
2. Don't need to be managed.
3. Regularly wow the team with their output and insights.

The A Player employee's performance is magical, but not mythical! So much happens in the daily whirlwind of business that it is impossible for a manager to prescribe every move an employee should make. In fact, to do so entails micromanaging, which is counterproductive for both the employee and the manager. This is where the A Player comes in. Their combination of strong business acumen, great attitude, work ethic, and uncanny ability to recognize and forecast needs make them indispensable to organizations.

Here is a useful definition between A, B, and C Players:

Instant A Player Assessment: Overall

A Player	B Player	C Player
Almost Perfect	Basic	Corrosive/Detrimental

But What About Everyone Else?

In my interviews with CEOs on the subject of A Players, these leaders consistently marvel at the ability of A Players to anticipate and fill in the gaps, even before the need arises. Most CEOs stare at me wide-eyed and with a beaming smile as they describe their top performers. Their descriptions are effortless and easy. But when the conversation shifts to everyone else, CEOs hesitate and begin to pause in their responses. That being said, it is the B and C Players that remain the largest concern. We'll address how to handle B and C Players right now.

The B Players represent the next 25%; these folks have trouble meeting or beating goals and deadlines with regularity. They also tend to push back on initiatives. They bring problems and not solutions and mistakenly feel they are adding value by being the "devil's advocate." Finally, a B Player manager cannot lead an A Player employee. In fact, you cannot be an A Player manager if you have B or C Players on your team. In short, the B Player dazzles you with mediocrity.

C Players represent all those below the top 35%. Think of them as an even worse version of the B Player. These are people who are either simply not cutting it in their jobs, or attitudinally are so difficult to work with that they are either actively or passively aggressive on pushing back on initiatives. C Players only work for money and survival. They do not work for a greater purpose or mission.

As their name implies, C Players like to *complain*. They chronically miss goals and deadlines and tend to spend most of their time making excuses. They have a particularly annoying habit of trying to reverse delegate! They also tend to have a substantial entitlement mentality and are virtually nonresponsive to feedback and coaching. They are adept at avoiding accountability. The C Players are easily identified by the fact you really wish they would quit rather than remain your teammate. In summary, C Players are A Player repellent!

As a leader or teammate, the goal is to inspire B and C Players to elevate their game and grow into A Players. Of course, they have to have the desire and drive to improve. Working with B and C Players represents the danger zone of executive coaching and investment. If they are earnest in improving themselves and make a commitment, it is worth a try to invest in them to see if they can become A Players. It is possible to work with B and C Players and get them to become full-fledged A Players. Once, a D Player[2] even made it all the way to become an A! However, please be aware that the odds are lower with these, so proceed with caution. In reality, your best investment is in getting the A to an even higher level of performance. The next best investment is getting an earnest B Player to become an A. Keep in mind if your Bs and Cs are not earnest there is really not much that can be done for them to improve their performance. It is their responsibility to take ownership for wanting to improve, not yours. In any case, don't invest time and resources in people who are unwilling to invest and commit in themselves, as you'll never get them where you want them to be if they do not want it as well.

Through a combination of being coached and his or her resultant performance, every employee has the opportunity to become an A Player. The time frame for improving to an A should be 6-9 months, depending on your specific situation. If you are a B Player or C Player reading this book and are earnest about taking the steps to become an A Player, there is definitely a chance you can improve to this level. Based on personal experience, about 50% of the B Players become As and about 25% of C Players become As. If you have the drive, skill, will and mindset to become an A, this book will give you the tools needed

---

2   In some organizations there are employees who are even more detrimental than a C Player. Since they are so bad, this book will not devote any attention to D, E, and F Players.

to get there. However, keep in mind your actions and results must be immediate and significant to change the perceptions of your leadership and teammates.

Also of significant note, moving a C Player to a B Player is not a win. While the movement is promising, a C Player needs to move all the way to an A to be considered a success. Don't settle with only getting halfway there!

But It's All About The *A* Players

Now back to the A Players. When people talk about A Players, one pushback often heard from executives is that they say they do not want teams of 100% A Players. Really, you don't want the best talent available for your team? One executive even commented that he liked the notion of building a team of A Players, but he could never have a team filled with them. Really???

It's possible these executives are thinking about Type-A personalities rather than A talent. They may even be mistaken about having top-heavy organizations with too many executive leaders. In each case, nothing could be further from the truth. Look at it like this: think of your 100% A Player team as more of an All-Star team. An All-Star team is comprised of 100% superstar players that are often position specific. As you look at the composition of the All-Star team, you find it is comprised of varying types of players. If it's baseball there are pitchers, first basemen, outfielders, etc. If it's basketball then there are guards, forwards, and centers. Each of the skills and abilities needed for each of these positions is very different. Additionally, salaries vary by position even at the All-Star team level. A Pro-Bowl lineman earns much less than a Pro-Bowl quarterback. However, both roles are vital and are uniquely different. Of course, no matter how good that Pro-Bowl quarterback is they can never replace the value the lineman provides and vice-versa, no matter how much money you throw at them. Bottom-line, each unique role is critical.

Likewise, your team has a number of unique roles. For example, you have the CEO, the other executive suite officers, the vice presidents, the directors, the managers, the coordinators, the analysts, and the administrative assistants among many others. The notion of a 100% A Player team is that you have A Players in each of these positions. Remember this: A Players are available for each role. It's up to you as an A Player leader to attract this A Player talent. A wise person once shared that you get who you deserve as a leader. With better role definition and robust recruiting systems, A Players can be found in abundance. A Players deserve a reasonable salary premium for their talents. This is only fair and right. Typically this premium runs, as a rule, in the 5% to 10% range for the salary band. For example, if a competitive salary for a production manager is $100,000, then an A Player should probably garner a salary in the $105,000 to $110,000 range. Deservingly so, these salary premiums will put A Players at or near the top of the salary range for their respective positions. Please remember two things related to this:

1. As A Players drawing A Player compensation, we need to produce A Player results with A Player attitudes.
2. That our employers hate to be held hostage to constant compensation discussions.

This is why companies should pay A Players like A Players, demand A Player quality results of them, and then tie any additional compensation to company performance and the direct contributions of those A Players. Think here of performance bonuses and profit sharing. So please don't walk into your boss's office tomorrow demanding a raise. It won't go over very well. A better strategy is to discuss a performance bonus when you deliver tangible results that drive financial performance. A Players ask in this way, "what value do I need to provide to be worth…?"

A Players Are Team Players. A Player employees have a significant responsibility to the organization to deliver a high level of performance results. Unlike the B and C Players, A Players do not get involved in office politics and gossip, and do not second-guess the management team. The job of the A Player is to align with leadership on strategy and then execute on time, under budget and over goal. A Players hold their talents with humility. They are definitely not prima donnas, nor are they one-man teams. Instead they are the ultimate team players, modeling leadership at all levels and helping teammates out in any way possible. As Leo Burnett North American CEO Rich Stoddart remarked, "The A Player hungers to be in the presence of other high performers." They are not threatened by other high performers on the team, but instead relish the opportunity to hone their craft and get even better. One aspect of A Players that is unparalleled is the joy of working with other great, committed employees on a daily basis.

A Players Carry Strong Core Values. A Players possess both very high performance and moral character attributes. They are focused on results but not at the expense of ethical standards. They not only do the right things, but they also do things right. In summary, A Players are top performers. They are more reliable and more resourceful, they are more innovative, they produce more with less, produce better strategies, deliver higher-quality work, and bring solutions to problems. Much of this is because they are morally centered and grounded in who they are and what they strive to accomplish. In addition, they have better business acumen and a keener focus of what really matters to the company or organization in terms of key drivers of success. They understand that all revenue and company existence come from customers and thus typically have a much keener customer focus. Finally, they are also better team members and are more supportive of management and leadership. It is no wonder why A Players are so highly sought out for their contributions to organizations.

A Players Are Clearly Differentiated from Bs and Cs

With that said, it is crucial to have a clear understanding of the difference between the As, Bs, and Cs. With the right guidelines, the differences between A, B and C Players becomes clear. Therefore, below is a summary of A, B and C Player characteristics from an employer perspective. Please use this chart as a tool to guide your A Player behaviors and purge B and C Player tendencies.

Summary of A, B, and C Player Characteristics as Seen Through the Eyes of an Employer:

A Players

✓ A Players are employees that are considered by their organizations to be the "best" employees. These employees are committed to being in the top 10% of their profession. They are aligned in their careers and absolutely shine in what they do. They love their jobs and are committed to continual learning and personal growth.

✓ A Players have great attitudes, high accountability and deliver "WOW!" customer service.

✓ A Players deliver 2-3 times the productivity and results of B Players for similar compensation. Many excellent companies contend one great A Player can replace three average B Player employees.

✓ A Players routinely meet or beat goals.

✓ A Players can easily quantify their value to the organization.

✓ A Players don't need to be managed. They simply need to be led by providing goals, vision, purpose and values.

✓ A Players are aligned to the goals, vision, purpose and values of the organization.

✓ A Players have a growth, not a fixed, mindset.

✓ A Players are committed to continual learning and personal growth.

✓ A Players achieve success by helping others become successful.

✓ A Players fit, value and abide by the company culture.

✓ A Players practice Ownership Thinking.

✓ A Players put others' needs before their own.

✓ A Players love their jobs.

✓ A Players are happy.

✓ A Players delight customers.

✓ A Players want to be in the presence of other high performers.

✓ A Players regularly "WOW!" the team with their insights and output.[3]

✓ A Players are resilient; they handle setbacks because they have faith in something bigger than themselves.

✓ Appropriately placed individuals who are highly productive, but are not immediately promotable, can also be A Players.

✓ A manager cannot be an A Player if he or she has Bs and Cs reporting to him or her. In other words, you must have a team of 100% A Players to be one yourself.

✓ If you would enthusiastically rehire the employee, they are an A Player.

3   From *Scaling Up*.

B Players

✓ Are the next 25% of employees in an average organization. Unlike, the A Player, you would not enthusiastically rehire these individuals, due to a combination of performance that is only average, cultural misalignment, variable attitude and/or high maintenance tendencies.

✓ B Players tend to push back on initiatives and practice selective accountability. They are a third to half as productive as A Players. If you put a lot of time and effort into them you can temporarily "inflate"[4] them to produce results, but don't let them fool you, you are doing the work, not them!

✓ They bring problems and not solutions and mistakenly feel they are adding value by being the "Devil's advocate." Nobody actually invited the Devil to the meeting, so this adds little to no value.

✓ B Players have a huge "I Know" quotient, yet repeatedly make mistakes for missing goals.

✓ B Players resist reading books and continual learning.

✓ B Players are self-centered and "me" centric. They tend to approach work as if the world revolves around them.

✓ Finally, a B Player manager cannot lead an A Player employee. In fact, you cannot be an A Player manager if you harbor B or C Players on your team.

✓ B Players need to move all the way to A Player performance and attitudes within 6-9 months. Only about 50% of B Players become A Players.

✓ In short, the B Player dazzles you with mediocrity. You tend to tolerate them far too long because they do produce some occasional useful work and may in fact be people that you like personally, but not professionally. When you finally let them go you lament "I wish I had done that sooner!"

C Players

✓ The employees in the organization that are below the top 35%. They need to constantly be told what to do. They do not take the initiative on their own.

---

4   I refer to this concept as the "Inflatable A"

✓ C Players only work for money. They do not work for a greater purpose or mission. As their name implies, C Players like to complain.

✓ They also are adroit at trying to reverse delegate. They are A Player repellant, as A Players do not want to be part of an organization that fosters C Players.

✓ They chronically miss goals and deadlines and tend to spend most of their time making excuses.

✓ They also tend to have a substantial entitlement mentality and are virtually nonresponsive to feedback and coaching. They are adept at avoiding accountability.

✓ C Players kill initiatives even faster than B Players. They need to move all the way to A Player performance and attitudes within 6-9 months. Do not be satisfied if they only improve to a B Player. Only about 25% of C Players become A Players.

✓ If they do not commit to becoming A Players, you need to immediately free up their employment options so they have the potential opportunity to become an A Player somewhere else.

Here is a simple way to remember the above summary of A, B and C Players:

Instant A Player Assessment: Overall Summary of A, B and C Players

A Player	B Player	C Player
Awesome	Basic	Can't Wait to Get You Off the Team

So with that said, you should now feel comfortable with not only the definition of an A Player, but also with the striking difference A Players, B Players, and C Players contribute to success. Using these different classifications on a daily basis, as well as the skills and descriptions above, you'll find yourself in a strong position to make the decisions that benefit your organization the most.

Now is an excellent time to confirm where you stand in terms of being an A, B, or C Player by taking the A Player Assessment located in Appendix 1. This assessment will help you pinpoint opportunities in your developmental plan on the road to fulfilling your A Player status.

After you take the assessment, start by ensuring you are now performing as an A Player. If you want those around you to be A Players, you need to make the first move to become one yourself. Ask your manager where you stand.[5] Work on making immediate improvements to your game based on his or her feedback. Frederick Douglass said, "Man's greatness consists in his ability to do and the proper application of his powers to things needed to be done." A Players are "doers." They have an uncanny ability to take the right actions to get results in a manner that aligns with the organization's core purpose, all while enhancing the culture around them. We will now explore what this commitment looks like.

---

5   When asking your manager for feedback, do not lead them by asking them if you are an A Player. Instead, ask as an open-ended question. If his or her feedback is less than an A Player for you, ask them what behaviors and steps you need to take to become one.

Chapter 3

MAKE A DECISION

"I studied the lives of great men and famous women, and I found that the men and women who got to the top were those who did the jobs they had in hand, with everything they had of energy and enthusiasm and hard work."
—**Harry Truman**, 33rd President of the United States

Hopefully you have had a chance to take the self-assessment in Appendix 1 to determine whether you are an A, B, or C Player. If you haven't yet, now would be an excellent time to do so. Did you find the results surprising? If so, don't worry—this book will help you elevate your game. Since we tend to grade ourselves easier than others, be sure to verify your status with your boss and coworkers alike. You never know where your blind spots are until you take a look at things from a different angle.

So now it's decision time. If you have verified you are an A Player, are you committed to continuing to deliver A Player results this quarter? Next year? For years to come? If you are either a B or C Player, have you made the decision to become an A Player? If so, when will you begin to make this substantial shift? You know what I am going to say—obviously, the sooner the better.

So here is the decision: Are you committed to being in the top 10% of your profession and having the discipline to become and remain an A Player?

Most people would like to be or think they are A Players, but few actually make the commitment to pay the price and endure the sacrifice necessary to achieve this goal. Here is what best-selling business author and leadership expert Robin Sharma says on this topic: "If you want to get the same results the top 5% do, then you have to do things only people in the top 5% do. This means you need to think, act and produce like the top 5%." Robin alludes to the top 5%. Our definition of an A player is actually the top 10%, but obviously we work with many A Players who are actually in the top 5%, 2% or even top 1% of what they do! We refer to these top percentile people as "Ultra As."

However, for our purposes, this decision is the starting point for transforming into an A Player. Throughout this book you'll learn more about the mindset, values, and behavior of the A Player. Ultimately, you will have to decide if you are willing to pay the price! It is possible for both B Players and C Players to become A Players, and those that succeed do so because of continued commitment. There is a key difference between making a decision and making a commitment. Decisions are made in the short term, while commitments to the decision are the follow-throughs made and etched in stone in the long term. Yes, you have to live with decisions, but commitment is the harder action of the two because it is usually in the commitment phase where the pain and hardship come in; it is really where you feel the burn. But the sweetest successes are the result of challenge, struggle and perseverance, not immediate gratification. If it were easy, everybody would do it. As NBA superstar LeBron James says, "earned, not given."

Depending on your specific situation and mindset, the transition to A Player status may require several adjustments, or it may be a radical reprogramming and overhaul of your values, beliefs, skills, and behaviors to create dramatically different results. It may also mean you need to cleanse or purge yourself of some B and C Player tendencies that limit your ability to excel. Regardless of whether or not these changes are relatively easy or hard for you, your effort will be well worth it in becoming an A Player. If you are an A Player, it is also well worth it to keep your A Player standing, as not even All-Stars can rest on their laurels.

An *A* Player at What?

"You can't find happiness without meaning and you cannot have meaning without happiness."
—**Marshall Goldsmith**, World renowned
executive coach and bestselling author

So with that said, have you made the decision and pledged your commitment? You can become an A Player at a whole host of things. It may not even be limited to your career. Now, let's discuss the importance of determining exactly where you want to pinpoint your success.

Marshall Goldsmith is one of the superstar A Players I had the pleasure of interviewing for this book. He is the world's foremost executive coach and has worked with CEOs from some of the world's largest corporations. Goldsmith is the author or editor of 32 books, including New York Times best-seller, *What Got You Here Won't Get You There* and one of my personal favorites, *Mojo: How to Get It, How to Keep It, How to Get It Back If You Lose It.*

Over the last several years, Marshall has been a mentor of mine and is passionate on the topic of peak performance. Marshall loves people and is always willing to offer a helping hand, but he is also a stickler about personal responsibility and is quick to point out when an executive is self-sabotaging his or her self. In our interview, I inquired of Marshall to share those characteristics that distinguish A Players from B and C Players. Firstly, Marshall described that A Players love what they do. Despite whatever level of wealth or success they've attained, A Players don't work for money. Marshall went on to share that A Players love the process of work and find meaning in the process itself. Then he went on to share something that strikes home at the essence of the A Player. He said, "You can't find happiness without meaning and you cannot have meaning without happiness." According to Marshall, the A Player is doing something that is meaningful and marketable that makes them happy.

I next asked Marshall what he would tell a B or C Player that needed to change to become an A Player. His quick and pointed answer somewhat surprised me: He said, "An A Player at what?" What struck me about his response is the clarity with which an A Player needs to operate. Ask yourself this question: What are you an A Player at? What specific skill or contribution puts you in the top 10% of the world at what you do? Marshall illustrated this point by having me Google the term "helping successful leaders." Of the first 500 results that popped up on Google, Marshall Goldsmith appears in over 450! He then asked me to Google "fixing hopeless losers." Would you believe he didn't show up once in the first 500 searches! What's the moral of the story? Discover and define what you are an A Player at!

Take the time to answer the following questions to help focus your journey and hone in on your desired results:

A Player Exercise: An A Player at What?

Please take a moment to write down the answer to the following questions:

1. *What you are an A Player at?*

2. *What specific skill or contribution puts you in the top 10% of the world at what you do?*

The answers you provided should be very revealing. If you struggled with providing specific responses, then you likely need to spend more time defining your goals in the days and weeks ahead. What are you truly top 10% in the world at? Specificity wins here. Perhaps you are among the best 10% of Internet marketers in the world in the resort industry. Or maybe you are part of the top 10% of process engineers in craft brewing. Remember, the guideline here is to make your endeavor something that is meaningful, marketable (relevant to others), and that makes you happy. Understanding this is the key element to defining your success as an A Player. Be sure to ensure that what you define is relevant to others and is marketable. Marshall shared with me the story of a promising young man with whom he drove out to Dartmouth College in hopes of an Ivy League education, but instead watched as this young man dedicated his life to being an A Player of videogames. When I asked Marshall what became of this young man and how Dartmouth turned out, he said with a disappointed tone, "He drove out to Dartmouth, but he was an A Player in *World of Warcraft*." Make sure you endeavor to be an A Player in something meaningful in creating value to others!

What Drives *A* Players?

A key insight that manifested like a blinding flash of light before my eyes during my conversation with Marshall regarding A Players is the notion that A Players are driven by accomplishments, not money. They are motivated by excellence and a passion for the process, and the top compensation that comes from this excellence is just a by-product of doing really outstanding work.

If you define your specific area of expertise but are still performing as a B or C Player, Marshall suggests you look to your:

1. Motivation. Is it an issue of your motivation? Remember, it is your responsibility (and not anyone else's) to get yourself motivated and inspired. This comes from within. Don't forget: Motivation lasts days, inspiration lasts a lifetime.

2. Ability. Do you have the abilities and skills to be an A Player in the particular role you are in? Do you have the will to develop the skills? I define this along with root motivation as:

Will → Skill ← Will

In other words, you need to have motivation or will in the first place. Beyond this, do you have the will to develop your skill? Don't wait for others to develop it for you.

On the other extreme, there are cases where there are real limitations to where our skills will take us. When I watch my beloved Duke Blue Devil basketball team, I dream of being able to hammer dunk the ball. But because of a lack of skill (well technically also age) it's simply not going to happen at this point of my life. Instead, I focus on sports such as skiing, tennis, and golf where my physical gifts and passion to improve are more aligned.

3. Understanding. Do you have the know-how to get the job done? Again, as an A Player, it's your responsibility to locate and hone these skills.

4. Confidence. Do you have the confidence of those around you? Interestingly, this is closely linked to a huge finding in my research of CEOs and other top executives who explained that they trusted A Players more. Why? A Players are more accountable to deliver results with no issues. Trust leads to more confidence, which then leads to greater autonomy. What are you doing to increase your trustworthiness?

5. Support. Do you have the support of those around you? If not, it may be time to take the necessary steps to obtain it. I have found that teammates and leaders have a lot of support for people who are earnestly working to improve themselves and their performance. What can you do now to increase support of those around you?

6. Relevance. Are you relevant to the organization's mission? Do your actions fit the needs of the environment? If not, you need to align with the mission or the organization, or switch to a team that needs what you provide.

7. Alignment. This is my addition to Marshall's list, as it is directly related to relevance. Are you aligned with your leadership team and doing the work that truly matters to an organization? Are you doing what the organization needs, or what you prefer to do?

Take a look at the following chart to see the difference in alignment between A, B, and C Players:

Instant A Player Assessment: Alignment

A Player	B Player	C Player
Aligned	Self-centered	Clueless

Marshall offers us a powerful list of what truly motivates A Players, as well as what separates them from the B and C Players. Review this list and determine those categories at which you excel, and those at which you need to improve. Then begin the shift. As you begin this transition to higher ground, make yourself a promise—one you are willing to keep and one to which you are capable of dedicating your time and effort.

Ask yourself the following questions on a daily basis:

Six Daily Questions to Fulfill Your A Player Promise:
To help assess on a daily basis how we are doing to fulfill our promise to be A Players, Marshall Goldsmith shared these six questions from his latest book *Triggers*. Each is to be scaled from 1-10 with 10 being high.

Daily Question	Score
1. Did I do my best to set clear goals?	
2. Did I do my best to make progress towards goal achievement?	
3. Did I do my best to be happy?	
4. Did I do my best to find meaning?	
5. Did I do my best to build positive relationships?	
6. Did I do my best to be fully engaged?	

Courtesy: Dr. Marshall Goldsmith

Marshall's six daily questions provide a tremendous tool for calibrating and then moving towards A Player excellence. In addition to a daily check-in, I use these questions with my leadership teams to reflect on both quarterly and annual assessments on how well we have done or not done towards achieving A Player status. In fact, it is possible for an A Player to have a non-A Player quarter or other period of time. Usually the A Player is the first to recognize the slump and works to immediately restore him or herself to full A Player performance.

Being an A Player is an honor that is earned on a day-by-day, month-by-month, quarter-by-quarter and year-by-year basis. There is no tenured professorship for A Players. We are only as good as our last performance.

As ten-time NCAA national basketball championship coach and Hall of Famer John Wooden of UCLA so eloquently reminds us: "Make each day your masterpiece."

A Player Tip: Knowing Your Passions and Talents and Why They Matter to Your Organization

A Player employees are very self-aware. They do not stretch for assignments they are not passionate about or do not have the skills or capacity to handle. In his useful book *Traction*, Gino Wickman describes this as the GWC filter. GWC stands for Get It, Want It, and Capacity to Do It. All three elements of GWC must be in place for an employee to function as an A Player. *Get It* means that the employee understands their role, how they contribute value, and how they enhance the culture of the organization. *Want It* means the employee is truly passionate about the role and likes it. In other words, they like it intrinsically and not just the compensation it provides. *Capacity to Do It* means they have the right intellectual capacity, skills, experience, and commitment to get the job done. This phenomenon is akin to what authors Catherine Nomura, Julia Waller and Shannon Waller describe as Unique Ability® in a book by the same name. We all have a Unique Ability® and it is the responsibility of the A Player to figure out how to serve the organization. The result is that work does not feel like work at all. A Players naturally seek constant self-improvement; work is fun, rewarding, and energizing. They have an intrinsic, natural passion that drives them more than anyone else can. When they find the right opportunity to display these talents and passions, they create value for others, and a positive upward spiral of greater opportunities and rewards occurs. This is what Jim Collins describes as the right person on the right seat on the right bus.

Chapter 4

HOW CEOS AND SENIOR LEADERS VIEW *A* PLAYERS

"Somebody once said that in looking for people to hire, you look for three qualities: integrity, intelligence, and energy. And if you don't have the first, the other two will kill you. You think about it; it's true. If you hire somebody without [integrity], you really want them to be dumb and lazy."

—Warren Buffet

The reality is that viewing yourself as an A Player is not enough. Heck, it is not even close to enough. It is important to maintain confidence in your ability and maintain positive self-talk, but it's the CEOs, senior leadership, and your manager who determine who are the A, B, and C Players. This is reflected in who gets promoted and who is getting the rewards. So most A Players are completely aware of how C-Suite management and their immediate leaders view their progression and their place in the business.

A key aspect to creating this book was to directly capture insights about what constitutes A Players from the perspective of leaders who run some of the most sophisticated, successful, and in some cases, largest enterprises in the world. What is particularly interesting from these interviews is how CEOs, COOs and other senior leaders viscerally value the contributions made by A Player employees.

In fact, even in organizations where the term "A Player" is not common vernacular, within seconds of starting the research interviews, CEOs, COOs and other senior leaders immediately adopted the terminology and started talking about their own "best employees" in a combination of marvel and near reverence.

When interviewing Battelle Memorial Institute COO Martin Inglis about the difference A Players make versus Bs and Cs, he quickly indicated the most substantial determining factor is "Impact!" As one of the nation's leading scientific institutions, Battelle is in the business of innovation. In fact, they have contributed to some of the most famous innovations of the last century, including xerography, CD-ROMs, and fuel cells to name just a few. Therefore, the need for Battelle employees to make breakthrough impacts is critical to their overall goals and mission.

Inglis speaks of the almost magical ability for A Players to "take the agenda forward, faster and better than you expected." Such a notion speaks to the demand for autonomy in today's electron fast speed of business. There is no way for any leader, no matter how good, to choreograph the specific decisions and actions of any individual employee. In fact, to do so would constitute micromanagement. Instead, the A Player has excellent listening and strategic skills and (like the autopilot control on an airplane) makes infinite course adjustments, decisions, and actions en route to achieving goals and making a three-point landing.

The senior leaders' experience of leading A Players is one of intense satisfaction; much like the coach of an elite sports team watching his players execute a play to perfection. In fact, many senior leaders remarked what a joy it is to watch A Players at work. The following chart should give you some idea as to the difference amongst the As, Bs, and Cs:

Instant A Player Assessment: Leading

A Player	B Player	C Player
Joyful	Fatiguing	Drudgery

Speaking of teamwork, A Players recognize that business is a team sport and not an individual one. As the April 22, 2014, *Fortune* magazine article pointed out: Ford Motor Company CEO Alan Mulally's major contribution to the company was cultural: "Forcing the automaker and its top executives to simplify the company's business strategy and to work in harmony with one another. A relentlessly positive figure, Mulally represented a breath of fresh air at a place known for its vicious internal politics and tumultuous executive rivalries."

As an alumnus of this storied company, I can attest that literally hundreds of billions of dollars (if not trillions) are wasted in organizations by unhealthy internal rivalries and infighting. CEOs prize teamwork and alignment in one direction because it focuses energy, effort, and manpower where it matters most: in delighting the customer and outperforming the competition. In today's organizations, there is simply no room for an individual who cannot work well with others. No one person is valuable enough to an organization to tolerate his or her negative behavior. Besides, an adept organization that attracts and values A Players will create a pipeline of both internal and external candidates to fill a non-team player's shoes.

Rich Stoddart, CEO of Leo Burnett, the famous advertising agency, believes leadership is the distinguishing factor that creates A Players. Stoddart explains that leadership is an emotional maturity that transcends age or seniority.

He goes on to explain that the A Player does not accept the status quo, but instead is able to push and galvanize the organization by utilizing both IQ and EQ[6] skills to achieve goals without leaving a trail of dead bodies in his or her wake. Like Inglis, Stoddart speaks of the speed at which A Players operate. He went on to describe that when there is a lack of A Players on a team, "It feels like something is broken." His solution: reset the talent on the team. In a tone of near wonderment, Stoddart says, "It's amazing how *fast* it changes…It's like the sun comes up!" I've seen this exact phenomenon firsthand in companies I've worked with. In a matter of a few short months a company can literally be turned around when the right A Players are in place.

Improvement at the Speed of Light

On the topic of speed, it's also amazing how quickly A Players assimilate into work environments and produce results. I recently worked with a team of high

---

6   Intelligence Quotient and Emotional Quotient. Covered in Chapter 21: A Player EQ/EI: Putting Emotional Intelligence to Use.

performers where, just two days after joining the company, an A Player approved a major initiative to streamline operations between India and the United States. Another made dramatic improvements to production efficiencies within a week of arriving. Yet another reshaped the entire HR function within a month.

One of my client's formulas is to take one month to recruit the A Player and one month to on-board him or her. Within weeks, her A Players are producing meaningful results and melding into the culture like they had been there for years. I've literally had CEOs so amazed by the results of their new A Players that they cannot remember the names of the B Players they replaced just a couple of weeks before! This is a testament to how quickly A Player employees can impact not only the performance, but also the positive culture of organizations.

Another key element of speed is the swiftness at which A Players align with their managers on important initiatives. They have an almost innate sense of what is important, and they take immediate action on priorities and projects. As Brian Tracy likes to advise: "Whatever your boss gives you to do, do it quickly and do it well. Then go and ask for more responsibility." A Players never ask for more responsibility or bigger jobs without first performing and delivering results on current assignments. Remember, delivering on your current responsibilities and commitments, and providing an increased level of value to an organization precedes increased compensation.

Sadly, most organizations are very lax on timeliness and follow-up. Think about how often peers or departments miss deadlines. Candidly, even if you are an A Player, you likely know in your heart you still have additional opportunity to improve your integrity and execution in committing to timing, taking prompt action, and hitting deadlines. Too many employees hedge and waiver on making and meeting commitments. The true A Player employee makes thoughtful, yet bold commitments and then delivers the results.

A Player Integrity

In fact, in an excellent article posted on the Harvard Business Review blog in April 2014, entitled *The Behaviors That Define A-Players*, Jack Zenger and Joseph Folkman found that among 4,158 individuals studied through 360-degree peer ratings, the highest competency of high performers "go far beyond the others in their scrupulous practice of always doing what they say they will do." This is the definition of integrity. In short, the best performers are dramatically more productive than average performers. From the perspective of the outstanding CEOs and senior leaders interviewed for this book, this vast performance and productivity difference between A Players and everyone else in the organization leaves no tolerance for B or C Player performance. While weaker leaders and managers make the excuse of tolerating Bs and Cs as a natural Gaussian distribution, exemplary leaders know that harboring Bs and Cs is actually unfair to top performers and the organization as a whole, as the company's performance is by definition compromised by subsidizing underperformers.

WHAT MAKES AN INDIVIDUAL PERFORMER STAND OUT?
The best are dramatically more productive than the average.

PRODUCTIVITY PERCENTILE RATING

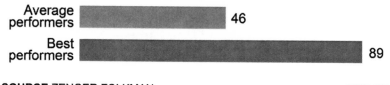

SOURCE ZENGER FOLKMAN   HBR.ORG

The study concludes the competency trait of integrity received the highest scores among the highest performers. In other words, integrity for committing to and producing results is the #1 hallmark of the A Player. Taking this a step further, A Players set high goals, commit to them, and then follow through on their commitments by doing what they said they would do.

So what differentiates the good from the great and defines the A Player that leads to extraordinary performance? Here are the full findings in rank order from Zenger and Folkman's excellent study:

1. Set stretch goals and adopt high standards for themselves.
2. Work collaboratively.
3. Volunteer to represent the group.

4. Embrace change, rather than resisting it.
5. Take initiative.
6. Walk the talk.
7. Use good judgment.
8. Display personal resilience.
9. Give honest feedback.

These findings are completely consistent with the input CEOs and senior leaders provided in the interviews conducted in conjunction with the development of this book. The ensuing chapters cover in detail the mindsets and skills A Players use to excel in these and other areas to truly be exemplary employees and human beings. As Zenger and Folkman point out, improving your proficiency in one or two of the behaviors most relevant to your current assignment is an excellent personal development plan that will pay dividends.

A Player Tip: A Player Integrity

Lack of true integrity between what people say and what they do is one of the biggest issues organizations face. Too often, average organizations allow an employee to articulate something that sounds like a commitment, only to let them slip out of it. This is chronic B and C Player behavior, not just for the employee, but also for the organization's culture. Zenger and Folkman point out in their study (see quote below) that integrity is the biggest single score high-performing A Players received, and how they believe that lack of integrity is *dishonest behavior.* Adopting these strict criteria in your own behavior and your organizations will improve performance.

It's easy for some people to casually agree to do something and then let it slip their minds. Most people would say that this is mere forgetfulness. We disagree. *We believe it is dishonest behavior.* If you commit to doing something, barring some event truly beyond your control, you should follow through. The best individual contributors are careful not to say one thing and do another. They are excellent role models for others. This is the competency for which the collective group of 4,158 individuals we studied received highest scores. That means, essentially, that following through on commitments is table stakes. But exceptional individual contributors go far beyond the others in their scrupulous practice of always doing what they say they will do.

You can see from this excerpt how rare and extraordinary A Player integrity is in typical organizations. It is one of the key reasons A Players make enormous impacts to a company's success and why they are so valuable to the organization. In the next few chapters we will explore how when your company prospers, not only do you also prosper as an A Player, but your organization can also serve a greater purpose that is bigger than either you or the organization itself. This greater purpose, which is funded by profits, creates a powerful force for good in the world. Understanding how all this works and how you fit in as the A Player will require understanding the language of business, which is finance. Mastering financial acumen and translating profits into purpose is the purview of the A Player.

Chapter 5

PURPOSE BEYOND PROFITS

"I believe that most of the greatest companies in the world also have great purposes... Having a deeper, more transcendent purpose is highly energizing for all of the various interdependent stakeholders, including the customers, employees, investors, suppliers, and the larger communities in which the business participates."
—**John Mackey**, CEO, Whole Foods Market

What would you say if I were to ask you what the purpose is of a business? Is it to make money? Is it to produce a good or service in which customers find value? Is it to make proceeds from the sales of a good or service that can be directly donated to a social cause? You are not alone if you are confused by the question of purpose within business. Most business people, CEOs, and other senior business leaders also wrestle with this question and the simultaneous and often conflicting tradeoffs of achieving both profit and purpose. In fact, as someone desiring to be an A Player, let me challenge you for a moment: Are you at your current company for solely your own personal profit, or are you at your organization to fulfill a purpose beyond yourself? You see, the same rules that apply to business also apply to you.

My goal for these next several chapters is very ambitious. I plan to share some cutting edge thinking in the area of profits versus purpose that is based on some very altruistic principles, and hopefully make some breakthrough contributions to the way employees understand and contribute to profits as the key *enabler of* purpose.

A Story of Purpose and Profits

A young man joined Ford Motor Company out of Duke University's MBA program back in 1992. Despite a pretty severe recession at the outset of the 1990s, this young man's job prospects were very good. He possessed a technical undergraduate degree in chemistry and had fortified his business acumen over his two-year master's degree with a heavy mix of marketing, finance, quantitative analysis, and leadership courses. Despite larger offers from companies in industries considered safer and with more upside than the automobile industry, this young man really wanted to join a U.S. based carmaker because he had a deep seated belief that America and American workers should be able to always produce goods of the highest standard in the world, and that a vibrant United States manufacturing base was needed to ensure a healthy U.S. economy.

Although companies like Toyota, Honda and Nissan were talking a good game about American jobs with their new U.S. [trans] plants, it did not seem like the cars were really American cars since they were designed overseas, they imported engines from Asia, and most of the senior jobs were held by foreign executives. What really got this young man's ire was the commonly held perception by Americans that the Japanese produced far superior cars than that of their American counterparts.

This young man's noble purpose was to get in the thick of the action, and do what he could do to help make American designed and built vehicles as good as any in the world. He wanted to get as close to product design as he could to help make the vehicles not only meet, but exceed the quality and appeal of the Japanese vehicles. He wanted to be at the frontlines of creating exciting, high quality vehicles that would delight customers and run reliably for years. The culture and rich history of Ford Motor Company very much appealed to him. He liked the people and they seemed earnest in turning things around. Only one set of questions nagged at him even after all of the business and financial training he received with his MBA:

How was Ford going to pay his salary given the significant losses they had incurred in the prior years? Where was the money coming from?

If you haven't figured it out yet, that young man was me! Truly understanding the impacts of financials is not an uncommon problem, even for those with formal business and even specialized financial training. The good news is that they can be understood by learning to think and act as if you owned the business yourself. In fact, business finances behave exactly like your own personal finances do, which makes them not only possible to comprehend, but also possible for you to personally control. By understanding the impact that profits have on business, you can make a much bigger influence not only to yourself, but also to a purpose greater than yourself.

Widespread Financial Illiteracy

Over my nearly 30 year career as a business executive, executive business coach, and A Player talent expert, I have become convinced that we have done a fairly poor job of teaching employees about the need for profits and more specifically about the symbiotic relationship between profits and purpose. I find both employees and leadership are often confounded with how to reconcile generating profits alongside fulfilling the purpose of the business. Said another way: is the purpose of the business to produce a profit or is it something entirely different?

This is an important evaluation because simultaneously optimizing both of these outcomes is actually not covered in the curriculum of even the top business schools. Specifically, I'm talking about the amount of profits that need to be generated to sustain a healthy business that can actually give back to both its employees and support a larger purpose beyond the business itself. Now, before the dean of every major business school sends me hate mail, let me illustrate this widespread illiteracy with a simple test you can administer with your team: Ask your team members what the net pre-tax profit of your business needs to be to sustain healthy operations and growth. How many of them can answer that? I'd be impressed if very few outside of the finance department actually knows what constitutes a healthy net pre-tax profit target for the business.

Typically, this net pre-tax profit needs to be 10% of revenue or higher in any business to generate the investment needed to produce the sustainable growth necessary for your company to fulfill its purpose. We'll get into the why and how of this later in this chapter, but for now we need to come to the realization that the vast amount of employees in general have no clue as to the baseline profits needed to sustain company operations, so the company can accomplish its larger purpose (or purposes). To further put an exclamation point on the need for this financial clarity, I asked my friend, who is the CFO of a multimillion dollar venture capital fund, this same question to determine the profit level needed to sustain the purpose of a company. He said, "Rick, I don't know how to answer that!" My friend is an extremely sharp and gifted finance professional. My point is this information is simply not taught from this perspective! It is taught from an after the fact analysis perspective, rather than one centered on how to drive the variables that create prosperity. In other words, students are taught how to analyze profits rather than how to create them. This is where A Players learning about how to create the *profits* needed to produce *prosperity* really comes in.

Conventional Wisdom

Many employees are very confused regarding the purpose of the business. For many of them, particularly the B and C Players, the company is just there to provide a paycheck and be a source of healthcare benefits. Many bristle at the notion that the company is there to produce a profit. Much of the current emphasis on increasing shareholder value as the primary objective stems from the work of Milton Friedman, the famed University of Chicago economist. Friedman's quote in his book *Capitalism and Freedom*, written in 1962, which was re-quoted in the *New York Times Magazine* in 1970, directs all of the social responsibility of business towards profits:

> There is one and only one social responsibility of business—to use its resources and engage in activities designed to increase its profits so long as it stays within the rules of the game, which is to say, engages in open and free competition without deception or fraud.

I am not here to discredit the Nobel Prize laureate who advised Ronald Reagan to policies that propelled the United States through a period of strong economic growth in the 1980s, but I do want to point out that this notion of "profits for profit's sake" has created confusion and friction between the goals of profits versus purpose for generations of employees.

As author Jen Lawrence points out in her blog Engage the Fox: "The thing is, Friedman was not against corporations doing socially responsible things. He was against corporations doing socially responsible things for the sake of social responsibility." Friedman clarified his point further:

> The executive is exercising a distinct "social responsibility," rather than serving as an agent of the stockholders or the customers or the employees, only if he spends the money in a different way than they would have spent it.

In fact, I do think that Freidman had greater motives than profits for profit's sake. But the issue is that his words have been used out of context by CEOs, shareholders, and employees alike to drive a profit-only strategy.

Is the Solution Caring Capitalism?

Several of my friends like TOMS shoes. If you are not familiar with TOMS, they produce simple slip-on canvas slippers with rubber soles than cost about $50 and are modeled after the *alpargatas* worn by Argentine farmers. One reason people really like TOMS is their One for One™ business model. For each pair of TOMS shoes purchased, the TOMS company donates a pair of shoes free of charge to the shoeless youth of Argentina and other developing countries around the world. This even includes parts of the United States. In fact, the name TOMS is derived from word "tomorrow" and is derived from the company's original mission of "Shoes for Tomorrow Project." TOMS is an example of a *Caring Capitalism* company.

Many people like TOMS because they feel good about buying shoes from a company that is doing social good. While they may not publically admit it, they also like the social statement that wearing TOMS shoes makes about them. Wearing TOMS announces that you are hip and socially responsible.

As of 2012, TOMS had donated over one million pairs of shoes around the world. One effect of these donations is that donations become a business expense that lowers the amount of profit TOMS makes and the taxes they need to pay the U.S. Government. I point this out because there is a case to be made that TOMS may actually make an even bigger social impact if they made more profit and donated cash instead of shoes. In addition, paying as much tax as possible through increased profits does help our country in the long run.

While everyone is pretty much in agreement that TOMS is trying to do good, not everyone agrees the program is making a meaningful difference:

Vox.com's Amanda Taub writes:

But the truth is that while that kind of messaging is evidently a great way to sell trendy shoes, or to otherwise raise money, it's not a very good way to do charity. At best, it's inefficient: It focuses on programs that waste your hard-earned cash by failing to do the most good per dollar. At worst, it promotes a view of the world's poor as helpless, ineffective people passively waiting for trinkets from shoe-buying Americans. While the shoes themselves probably won't lead to any kind of disaster, that worldview can lead to bad policies and real, serious harm.

Adele Chapin of racked.com reports:

Here's the evidence that shoe donations from TOMS might not be helping children in need: an outside research team reported that the shoes weren't making a noticeable difference in kids' lives, according to Vox.com. "The bad news is that there is no evidence that the shoes exhibit any kind of life-changing impact, except for potentially making them feel somewhat more reliant on external aid," professor Bruce Wydick wrote in a blog post this spring, after studying the TOMS shoe donation program in El Salvador.

The team also found "a small negative impact on local markets" caused by the TOMS giveaways, in which local shoe vendors sold just a few less shoes because of the donations. Taub suggests that TOMS efforts aren't getting to the root of the poverty problem, and consumers would be better off donating cash as a more effective way to help.

I should say that professor Wydick and others do have extremely positive things to say about the TOMS organization, particularly around their transparency, openness to criticism, and their extreme sincerity to responding to ways to better their program. For example, one additional criticism they received was that jobs were needed even more than the shoes in the countries that received the shoe donations, but the TOMS shoes were actually manufactured in China, and not in those needy areas. In addition, there were other concerns about the poor labor workforce conditions of the Chinese laborers. TOMS is responding to this by relocating at least one-third of the shoe manufacturing to the countries that received the shoes.

TOMS is an example of a company that practices Caring Capitalism, in which pursuit of social responsibility is apparently its primary stated goal. Firms like Ben & Jerry's ice cream and Burt's Bees skin care are other illustrations. As a matter of fact, by virtue of purchasing this book, you are practicing Caring Capitalism, as a portion of the proceeds go directly to Habitat for Humanity. What is clear with Caring Capitalism firms are that the companies have pure, altruistic motives to help people and society. In the case of TOMS, it is through their One for One™ shoe donation program. It also seems apparent that this brand of Caring Capitalism is very attractive to TOMS' customers as well as attracting employees who buy into this purpose of helping others; in this case children who need shoes. What is unclear with Caring Capitalism companies like TOMS is how well they do at serving other stakeholders like employees and shareholders. Also, TOMS is a privately held company, which is owned by founder Blake Mycoskie (50%), and by venture capital firm Bain Capital (50%). Since it is privately held, their financial performance is not public knowledge. Their intent to help others is extremely laudable. But perhaps there is even a deeper and more effective way to integrate purpose and profits to benefit employees, create fantastic products, ensure social responsibility, and protect shareholders.

As altruistic as Caring Capitalism companies like TOMS and others are, I believe there is an even better and more effective way to drive purpose beyond profits. For one, you as the A Player are the pivotal part in making purpose beyond profits happen. A Players need to participate and partake firsthand in the purpose of the business. I call this better method the *Prosperity Principles*®: It takes the altruistic ethos of Caring Capitalism and combines it with a culture that focuses on the well-being of the A Player employees first, with the accountability that financial acumen provides, to create a very powerful force for good.

Chapter 6

THE PROSPERITY PRINCIPLES

"Making money is a lot more fun when you are helping the people around you become successful."
—**Kip Tindell**, CEO, The Container Store

A Key Purpose:
Creating a Culture Where *A* Player Employees Thrive

One of the constituents that the Caring Capitalist companies could certainly more specifically address is their purpose in supporting the well-being of their employees. Call me old fashioned, but as my mother always likes to say, "charity begins at home." For me, this means making life abundant for our A Player employees. Some companies are doing some very innovative things to support employees. Most of these cutting edge initiatives include developing people's capabilities through training and leadership building so employees are ready to grow into increasing roles and responsibilities. This is the proverbial teaching a man to fish, rather than just giving him one fish to eat.

Another thing the cutting edge companies do is directly support the employees' charities of choice by directly matching their volunteerism and donations. These programs turn out to be very effective in motivating A Player employees because these A Players appreciate their company directly supporting causes they are involved in and care about personally. They also work extremely well because everyone has skin in the game. The more the employee is involved, the more the company contributes. This is a great example of holistically integrating the whole well-being of employees. They deeply value working for a company whose values are aligned with their own.

However, many companies that talk a great game of social responsibility usually don't include enough specifics on what they are doing to promote the well-being of their employees. For example, Starbucks has a reputation as a socially responsible company, primarily via their fair trade program to third-world coffee farmers, but is their social responsibility statement specific enough in putting their people first?

> So it is our vision that together we will elevate our partners, customers, suppliers and neighbors to create positive change. To be innovators, leaders and contributors to an inclusive society and a healthy environment so that Starbucks and everyone we touch can endure and thrive.

Nice words to be sure, I just point out that a $16-billion company as abundant as Starbucks may have even more opportunity by being even more intentional and specific in ways their employees can win, particularly for the hard-working baristas who are the front line face of the operation. They can build on the educational reimbursement program they have in play to be even more focused on the people who make their operation possible. Why not actually put the employees first?

Speaking of employees, *Conscious Capitalism*® is moving in the direction of making a great livelihood for employees through building on the altruistic principles of Caring Capitalism by listing out the synergies and interdependencies between all of the stakeholders, including employees. Founded by John Mackey (co-founder & co-CEO of Whole Foods Market), the *Conscious Capitalism* movement aims to do this by formally linking purpose beyond profit.

Conscious Capitalism recognizes that every business has a purpose that includes, but is more than, making money. Both Mackey and Kip Tindell (The Container Store CEO) are trustees of Conscious Capitalism Inc., a nonprofit organization supporting these values. What is intriguing about both of these *Conscious Capitalism* companies is how well they perform both financially and in supporting their purpose. Both also put tangible and defined programs that support the entire well-being and growth of employees into play. In addition to these two companies; Southwest Airlines, Costco, Trader Joe's and Chick-fil-A also follow *Conscious Capitalism* principles and also achieve wonderful results for a wide range of constituents including their employees, charities and their communities. Tindell defines *Conscious Capitalism* as a business where everyone associated with it can thrive—its employees, customers, vendors, communities and shareholders.

Building on this, in my work with developing cultures of 100% A Players, I have become convinced that taking awesome care of A Player employees should actually be a company's first and primary purpose. This is a specific enhancement of *Conscious Capitalism* called an *Employee First* culture that was innovated by Kip Tindell. It has worked extremely well for his company as evidenced by their over 37 years of 21% compounded annualized growth rate! To make an *Employee First* culture work The Container Store only hires A Players. Here is what Tindell has to say about the *Employee First* culture:

> But here's the twist: Treating your employees with affection and respect is not only the right thing to do, it also happens to be the fastest road to success. In fact, it's much more successful than any other business methodology. We've found if you really and truly take better care of the employees than anybody else, your employees will truly take care of your customers.
>
> In short, if these two groups of people—your employees and your customers—are ecstatic, then wonderfully and ironically, your shareholders are going to be ecstatic as well.

An *Employee First* culture relies on a team of 100% A Players. A Players understand all of this, while B and C Players do not. A Players have a deeper sense of purpose and gratitude for their employers and the company's mission. The more they are rewarded for being great employees, the deeper and more strategic their bond with the company becomes. In fact, when Kip Tindell was asked how to prevent employees from abusing and taking advantage of an *Employee First* culture, he immediately responded that the A Players at the company realize that they have a great thing, and if B and C Players are trying to take advantage of the *Employee First* culture by either freeloading or bringing a jaundiced attitude, the A Players self-police them out. In fact, this phenomenon is common at many companies, as a strong team of A Players will coach the Bs and Cs up or out on their own. This is akin to white blood cells fighting cancer cells that try to infiltrate your body.

With A Players, because of their extremely high productivity, and great alignment in the mutual success of the company and themselves, you can have an *Employee First* culture and reward them with superior compensation and benefits. An *Employee First* culture is anything but a charity free-for-all for the employees. Like anything truly great in life, the amazing care for the total well-being of employees in the *Employee First* culture is earned, not given; it is a two-way street. "To whom much is given, much is expected." B and C Players who try to freeload off of this benevolent culture are not tolerated.

When people are compensated well for their performance, you are actually giving them far more than a paycheck. You are empowering them to actually think, act and be rewarded like an owner of the business. Earned rewards do so much more for one's self-esteem than compensation and benefits that are not truly earned. When compensation is earned, you inspire employees to want to achieve even higher levels of greatness. Besides that, when people have their own prosperity and abundance, they can make their own decisions about which charities and social causes they would like to support with their own donations. This too is empowering. A Players not only get, but also embrace these concepts.

So now we will take the notions of *Conscious Capitalism* and *Employee First* culture even further with the *Prosperity Principles*®, where we will learn about the constituent alignment and financial performance needed to create this prosperity engine.

A Better Way: The Prosperity Principles®

Now that we have a good grounding in *Conscious Capitalism* and an *Employee First* culture, we are ready to go deeper into how to generate prosperity. These principles take both a holistic and realistic view of the many constituents of a business that are needed to create mutually beneficial outcomes. When declaring a noble purpose beyond profits, it is very important to specifically identify those constituents. Here is a comprehensive list of a business's constituents:

1. Employees
2. Customers
3. Company
4. Suppliers and Vendors
5. Investors and Shareholders
6. The Environment
7. The Community
8. Social Responsibility

It is also important that we are very specific and intentional on the purpose we are going to deliver with our prosperity for each of these groups, so let's take a deeper look at the particular needs of each of these constituents:

Stakeholder	Primary Needs	Additional Considerations
Employees	• Purpose • Good, fair paying jobs • Personal growth and development • Strong company culture and sense of community and place	• Raises • Promotions • Share in the company's success—bonuses and profit sharing • Benefits including health insurance

Stakeholder	Primary Needs	Additional Considerations
Customers	• Great products and services that fulfill a purpose • Quality, value, dependability and longevity • Great customer service	• Companies they purchase from are environmentally and socially responsible
Company	• Profitable for sustained operations	• Capital safety net fully capitalized with cash equal to two month's expenses to handle emergency situations • Low to no debt • Strong balance sheet
Suppliers and Vendors	• Mutual profits • Long-term strategic relationship with company • Timely payments	• Provide best product innovations to company • Symbiotic relationship
Investors and Shareholders	• Return on their investment • Return commensurate with the risk and other investment opportunities	• Payback on their investment • Reinvestment for future growth
The Environment	• No environmental harm	• Leave the environment better than you found it
The Community	• Facilities and footprint enhance the community • Job creation • Tax base	• Good esthetics and upkeep of buildings and grounds • Support and invest in the community infrastructure need to support the facility • Community can enjoy the company's facilities
Social Responsibility	• Company becomes a platform for giving	• Cash and job creation have the biggest impacts

Each of these benefits comes from a prosperous company. Profits are the engine of this prosperity. As the chart above illustrates, there are numerous demands for a company's purpose that require cash. But profits are the only sustainable source of that cash. Profits allow for a company to produce products and services that are vital to peoples' lives; they fuel growth and expansion, they enable job creation, and they support social responsibility, to emphasize just a few great things that profits provide. A healthy company also does not carry too much in debt from borrowing. The smaller the amount of debt the better, with the ideal being no debt at all. Note that profits are the only source of cash to pay back these loans and reduce or eliminate debt. If a company is too much in debt, they cannot do the altruistic actions listed above.

In the past, it has been very challenging for companies, their leadership and employees to reconcile generating profits alongside fulfilling the purpose of the business. As we saw above, there are a lot of competing priories and purposes for the business.

To drive home this quandary of profits versus purpose, let me share with you an example that is likely familiar to you—the development of mission statements. When developing company mission statements, the issue of whether to include a profit metric often arises. While the mission statement definitely contains the company's purpose, the question remains: should we put a profit metric in there for the entire world to see? After all, isn't that a little trite after pouring out our noble purpose of all of the great things our company and products contribute to society? Besides, won't including the profit goals possibly make us seem greedy? In reviewing these statements, what if our best customer sees that our profit targets are actually higher than theirs? Will they come back to us for price concessions? Finally, if we do decide to include profit metrics, do our employees really care about them and understand them anyway? These are real issues we have all seen time and time again.

The resolution to this apparent conflict between purpose and profit is resolved with the simple and incredibly powerful phrase:

Profits exist so we can fulfill our Purpose.

Conscious Capitalism calls this Purpose Beyond Profit. A net sum game is often wrongly assumed. I have found that people are really fond of saying you can have one, but not the other. Of course, the real magic is in delivering both! The better way of thinking about profits is that healthy profits allow us to continue to sustain the fun of delivering our ultimate purpose. CEO Kip Tindell has an excellent phrase to drive this point home:

> On the other hand, creating profits with a powerful purpose creates an incredibly powerful force for good. Our company does not exist to make a profit; it makes a profit so it can exist. And it exists to bring prosperity and happiness to every life we touch. That way, in the end, everybody wins.

A reasonable baseline of profitability is needed to make this prosperity dynamic occur: Employees need to realize that this net pre-tax profit number needs to be 10% of revenue or better to sustain the business's noble purpose. You should be aware as an A Player that very few people are actually trained in knowing the level of net pre-tax profit needed to generate prosperity in a business. Many know how to analyze profitability, but A Players know how to drive this vital number.

One way we have resolved this in the companies in which I am involved is through giving profits the prominence they are due by creating an equally important document that stands alongside the mission statement. We call this document the *Prosperity Principles*®. The *Prosperity Principles* outline the profit and financial parameters required to fulfill the purpose of the organization, while also outlining those prosperity factors (purpose, promotions, raises, social causes and more) that appeal most to employees. Imagine this document standing alongside your Vision, Purpose, Mission, and Values documents as a tool to align everyone in your company to what needs to happen to have a prosperous company. It works wonders to align and excite A Player employees on the right actions to take. Here is an example of what the *Prosperity Principles* document for a specific company can look like:

Prosperity Principles®

To achieve our Purpose beyond Profits, our Net Pretax Profit goal is 10% of Revenue. For 2016 this translates into $20 million dollars profit on revenues of $200 million

The following company Purposes will be served from this Prosperity:

1. **Fulfill our Employee First Culture through: Raises, Promotions, Training and Personal Growth Opportunities. Sustain Healthcare and Benefits plan. Create $5 million Profit Sharing pool.**
2. **Product Leadership: Invest 10% of profit back into R&D to sustain #1 position in industry**
3. **Growth: Set aside $3 million for capital expansion**
4. **Social Responsibility: Donate $2 million to Children's Hospital.**

We have had tremendous success in engaging employees with this approach, particularly the extremely purpose driven Millennial generation. They appreciate the transparency the *Prosperity Principles* provides regarding the connection of the profits to the purpose of the organization. It is really liberating to give profits and prosperity their own page so to speak. It lays out the rules of the game. These become the baseline profit objectives for the organization to rally behind to create the prosperity engine needed to drive purpose. It also goes far beyond the relatively vague mission statements most socially conscious companies have. For example, the *Caring Capitalism* ice cream maker Ben & Jerry's is:

Our Social Mission compels us to use our Company in innovative ways to make the world a better place. To operate the company in a way that actively recognizes the central role that business plays in society by initiating innovative ways to improve the quality of life locally, nationally and internationally.

Not only does having a concrete number make this mission a lot more tangible and exciting for employees to get behind, but stating the number and what needs to happen to achieve this holds everyone involved accountable to achieving it.

How 10% Net Income Drives Prosperity

As mentioned at the outset of this chapter, there is too much financial illiteracy in companies. This is a real shame, as even an introductory knowledge of financial acumen goes a long way in business. Remember that *finance is the language of business*, so as A Players it behooves us to increase our literacy in this critical area.

Employees want things like a strong mission and purpose for the business, as well as for the company to produce great products and services that customers value, along with regular raises, promotions, bonuses, profit sharing, capital investments, hiring more employees, and much more. You may also possibly want your company to accomplish social good by directly supporting the communities it does business in or through direct donations to charitable causes.

These are all great things. The awesome thing is they are all possible with the right financial returns. Let me now show you how a 10% net profit return drives the *Prosperity Principles*.

My friend and colleague Greg Crabtree, CPA and author of the fantastic financial book *Simple Numbers, Straight Talk, Big Profits!*, innovated the practice of a 10% baseline net profit as the standard for a healthy, sustainable company. Greg's book is excellent reading for A Players looking to strengthen their financial acumen. As I mentioned earlier in this chapter, even MBAs from top business schools are not taught what a strong baseline level of profitability that drives prosperity needs to be.

It turns out that baseline level for net pre-tax profit turns out to be at least 10% of revenue. 10% percent happens to be the magic level because at 10% and greater, enough profit is generated even after about 40% of that profit is paid as taxes to the government to start reinvesting in the business and its constituents.

Now, let's start getting our hands dirty and familiarize ourselves with the power of the financials. Look at what this 10% net pre-tax profit goal looks like on the income statement of a $200 million revenue business:

Income Statement: 10% Net Pre-tax Profit on $200 million Revenue			
Revenue		$200,000,000	
-Variable Costs	$120,000,000		
Gross Profit		$80,000,000	40%
-Payroll	$40,000,000		20%
-Non-Payroll Expenses	$20,000,000		10%
Total Fixed Expenses		$60,000,000	
Net Pre-tax Profit		$20,000,000	10%

Just as a way of an overview to these financials, this represents a nice, healthy business making a 10% net pre-tax profit on a 200 million dollar revenue base. This translates to 20 million dollars that can be used for paying profit sharing, offering raises and promotions in the following year, buying equipment, investing in research and development, paying taxes, and supporting the company's social responsibility causes. Profits are important because they represent sustainability. As I advise the employees of clients: "we'll pay you bonuses and promotions out of profits, but not out of owner's equity or debt."

Going after a profit target like this is very liberating. Instead of trying to reconcile whether we should go after profits or purpose, this approach declares the amount of profits needed to sustain all of this fun. Stating the *Prosperity Principles* is like acknowledging the elephant in the room, rather than tiptoeing around the issue of profits. This helps to employ the "magic of both." As we discussed, profits are the prosperity engine of any enterprise.

There is another huge advantage of this approach. By declaring the 10% net pre-tax profit target, we can easily derive our affordable variable cost, as well as payroll and non-payroll costs. In other words, we set benchmarks for how much we can afford on each of these areas. As payroll, or salaries, is usually one of the biggest expenses, we need to set a "salary cap" on how many people are on the team, and how much we can pay the team in total. Crabtree reminds us that this is exactly what the National Football League (NFL) does. I love his term of the building "the best [A Player] team money can buy." In this case, we have a salary cap of 20 percent of revenue on payroll, and a 10 percent cap on non-payroll expenses.

Now, suppose that unfortunately your company forecasts only $180 million in revenue. What happens to profitability if you don't adjust your payroll and non-payroll expenses in line with this new reality and your caps?

Income Statement: Impact on Net Pre-tax Profit on Lower $180 million Revenue without Adjusting Payroll or Non-Payroll Costs			
Revenue		$180,000,000	
-Variable Costs	$108,000,000		
Gross Profit		$72,000,000	40%
-Payroll	$40,000,000		22%
-Non-Payroll Expenses	$20,000,000		11%
Total Fixed Expenses		$60,000,000	
Net Pre-tax Profit		$12,000,000	6.7%

Well, if you do not adjust the size of your payroll and non-payroll costs, then your net pre-tax profit drops from twenty million dollars to twelve million dollars or only 6.7%. This means there is not adequate money to reinvest in employee bonuses, offer promotions and raises, invest in products, and support the social causes. Traditional companies would accept this as fate. To A Players and their companies, this is unacceptable, as the prosperity engine has been compromised. Think of this as hurting the goose that lays the golden egg.

Instead, the company of A Players would set their salary caps around the new lower revenue target to keep the 10% net pre-tax profit. The simplest way to do this is keep them at the same percentage of revenue as our initial example. If you recall, these were 20% of revenue for payroll and 10% of revenue for non-payroll.

Income Statement: Impact on Net Pretax Profit on Lower $180 million Revenue by Maintaining Salary and Expense Caps			
Revenue		$180,000,000	
-Variable Costs	$108,000,000		
Gross Profit		$72,000,000	40%

-Payroll	$36,000,000		20%
-Non-Payroll Expenses	$18,000,000		10%
Total Fixed Expenses		$54,000,000	
Net Pre-tax Profit		$18,000,000	10%

Employing good financial acumen like this means making hard choices and maintaining discipline. Challenging to do at times, but look at the payoff: versus the prior example, despite being down $20 million in revenue, we are down just $2 million in profit! Although nobody likes getting a haircut, this business is in far better financial shape ($18 million in profit versus $12 million) than the example above it, and the employees and other constituents will most likely share in the prosperity that this 10% net pre-tax profit creates. This is because it is far better to make a higher percentage profit on a lower revenue number, as it is still a more efficient operation. In most cases, when a company hits its target percent net margin, things like bonuses, profit sharing and promotions are awarded on a pro-rata basis because the company is still operating efficiently and is pound for pound as profitable.

Some of you may be asking how did we make the hard trade-offs that allowed us to reduce our payroll and non-payroll expenses? Rather than hurt your A Players, start by eliminating underperforming C and B Players. Let those underperformers explore free agency. Also a good old-fashioned belt tightening on expenses goes a long way. Keep an eye on unproductive marketing, unnecessary travel and equipment upgrades, and other extraneous expenses. While these cutbacks will cause you some minor short-term discomfort, they will ensure the long-term financial health of your company.

As I mentioned at the outset, if your company already performs at a higher pre-tax net profit percentage than 10%, then use this higher figure for your targets. Many firms aim to increase their pre-tax net profit efficiency by a few points each year. Let's look at the prosperity impact of a higher pre-tax net profit percentage of 15 percent on the original $200 million dollar company.

Income Statement: 15% Net Pretax Profit on $200 Million Revenue			
Revenue		$200,000,000	
-Variable Costs	$117,000,000		
Gross Profit		$84,000,000	42.5%
-Payroll	$36,000,000		18.3%
-Non-Payroll Expenses	$18,000,000		9.2%
Total Fixed Expenses		$54,000,000	
Net Pre-tax Profit		$30,000,000	15%

As you can see from the example, increasing the net pre-tax profit margin from 10% to 15% has a huge impact on the profitability of this business. Achieving these levels would most likely require a balanced attack on variable costs, nonproductive payroll, and other non-payroll costs over the course of several years. But, as you can see, the positive effects on profits and the prosperity you can generate is enormous from the original $20 million turning into $30 million! A Player contributors would certainly enjoy the benefits in terms of growing into bigger jobs and profit sharing.

A Player Tip: Embrace Financial Mastery

Finance is the language of business. As an A Player, embrace the financials of the business regardless of your functional position within the company. Far too often I see people either getting intimidated by the financials, or saying they do not believe the numbers. Getting familiar with your company's financials and using financial data to make decisions is one of the quickest ways to improve the business. Befriend your colleagues in the finance department. They are usually more than willing to partner with you to provide, explain, and help you improve the financial data. Supplement this information through reading and educating yourself to ensure you can understand and crunch the numbers once they come your way. Finally, treat the revenue and expenses as if you owned the company.

This chapter was either a breeze or challenging for you depending on your level of financial training and education. My experience as an executive, coach, and A Player talent expert is that building a direct link between the prosperity that profits provide and the purpose of a business is usually sorely lacking, and that a deeper dive in this area whether you are a novice or an expert always yields massive results. Healthy profits allow for giving back. Many companies have one, but not the other. Documenting and aligning with clear-cut *Prosperity Principles* is an excellent way to provide this within your team and achieve the magic of both.

Using the *Prosperity Principles*, align with your team on the pre-tax net profit target needed to sustain a prosperous business. Learn how to construct and interpret income statements as illustrated above. Also outline the specific purposes of your business as you do this. Remember your key constituencies are employees, customers, company, investors and shareholders, the environment, the community, and social responsibility. Set out specific budgets for giving in each of these areas. Remember, for a prosperous, sustainable business, this pre-tax net profit number typically needs to be greater than 10% of revenue. The advantage of this approach is that it is very easy for you to figure out your salary and budget caps for all areas of your business by solving for 10% or better net pre-tax profit. As an A Player, figure out how you contribute to driving the key numbers. Typical businesses try for any profit they can get. A Player businesses are very purposeful in how they achieve profit to achieve prosperity for a greater purpose.

Chapter 7

HOW BUSINESS REALLY WORKS: BECOMING A PROSPERITY CENTER!

"Profit is the applause you get for taking care of your customers and creating a motivating environment for your people."
—**Ken Blanchard**, leadership expert and author

*I*n the last chapter, we learned about the *Prosperity Principles* and how businesses should link profits to purpose. There, we explored how the whole business prospered. In this chapter we will dig deeper into how each employee needs to become his or her own individual prosperity center, and will show you how you plug in with your own individual level of contribution.

As a matter of fact, your company or organization hired you to *improve* the profitability and efficiency of the operation. Yes, that's right, your leaders have collectively agreed that they forecast they will be better off and more profitable with you on the team. Now it is your job not to disappoint them! And that is at least partially why becoming an A Player is so important. Top-notch performers generate top-notch profit. Those that contribute the most value get the most autonomy, rewards, and growth. This is how prosperity works.

As we covered in the last chapter, profits are a good thing! Trust me, it is far better for you to work for a company with strong profits than weaker ones or even those operating at a loss. Companies that operate with weak profits or at a loss will soon be out of business, or at best limp around in a zombie-like existence. Remember, all the things you want as an employee are provided only through the generation of strong profits: Innovative products, strong research and development, stock growth, promotions, bonus plans, benefits, and giving back socially to name just a few.

As I mentioned, I had the opportunity to see The Container Store CEO Kip Tindell speak at a Fortune Growth Summit. One interesting thing among many about The Container Store is that they pay their employees a significant premium above the prevailing average wage within their industry[7]. This is the *Employee First* culture at work. What is also interesting is that The Container Store only hires A Players, choosing one great employee to replace what three good employees would typically do. They call this principle: 1 Great Person = 3 Good People[SM]. This formula is a win for everyone involved in the equation: A Players earn a salary premium, A Players get the joy of working with other A Player coworkers on an All-Star team, customers are then served by only excellent employees, and employee productivity is 150-200 percent better than competitors, which then drives excellent profitability to shareholders and additional profit sharing for employees. Interestingly enough, this prosperity and abundance also translates to the suppliers of The Container Store, whose goal under *Conscious Capitalism* is to ensure mutual profitability and long-term relationships with their vendors.

Often when working with new clients, I am disappointed with how many employees fail to see the connection between their compensation and overall company performance. I'll never forget the entitlement mentality I received from one employee who was grumbling about being underpaid. When I asked her what value and return on investment (ROI) she contributed to the organization, her response was something to the fact that she was paid to polish her seat with her backside. I just shook my head and walked away! This is the classic "show up and work for work's sake" mentality. It is a defining C Player characteristic.

---

7   The Container Store is a retailer and pays a 50% to 100% premium versus an average retail wage of $10 per hour. Their employees also undergo 9 intensive interviews before hire and receive over 260 hours of training—30 times the industry average. Only 3% of applicants are accepted.

Sadly, this entitlement trait is far too pervasive in organizations. Contrary to popular opinion, you are not paid simply to fill a spot on the organizational chart. In fact, the organization is looking to make a multiple from their investment in your salary. This axiom holds true for both profit and not-for-profit organizations.

It doesn't matter if your annual compensation is $30,000, $75,000, $100,000, $250,000 or more, as your organization is making an investment with the intent of seeing a return on that same investment (ROI) from your abilities. In fact, the bigger your compensation, the bigger the expected return. This is exactly akin to the risk and reward thinking in financial investments.

This is worth exploring further. Say you are the newly minted marketing manager of a company with a $100,000 base salary. How much revenue and profit does the organization expect to make in return for your services? Have you actually ever thought about your employment this way? As an A Player employee, I highly encourage you to think in this regard. The measure is called Profit per Employee, or as I like to call it PPE. In the 2007 McKinsey Quarterly, entitled *The New Metric for Corporate Performance-Profit per Employee*, author Lowell L. Bryan shared that in his study of the world's 30 largest corporations, net profit per employee improved from $35,000 to $83,000 in the period from 1995 to 2005. Note this is the bottom-line net profit per employee, which takes into account all overheads, so the implied gross profit expectation for a $100,000 employee would be a minimum of $300,000. Remember, that variable costs and fixed costs will need to be deducted from the implied revenue for which your position is responsible.

A Player Tip: Gross Profit vs. Net Profit

Gross Profit and Net Profit are two of the most powerful numbers in business for an A Player to understand. Both are critical not only in driving the overall prosperity of the company, but also for calculating your specific ROI in terms of Profit per Employee.

Simply stated, these are two specific areas where profit is evaluated with differing levels of expense taken out.

Gross Profit is defined as: Revenue - Variable Costs=Gross Profit

Net Profit is defined as: Gross Profit - Fixed Costs=Net Profit

As you can see, Net Profit is derived from Gross Profit. Gross Profit is the cost of the goods you are selling minus the direct (variable) costs to produce it. Net Profit then takes out the fixed overheads like payroll, rent, marketing costs, and employee benefits that don't directly fluctuate with the amount of goods produced. Net Profit is the Bottom Line!

It is important that A Players understand the formula for return on investment (ROI)[8] in any given position:

Employee ROI=

(Revenue attached to your Position
x
Gross Profit % of the Products/Services of your Business)
-
Investment in Your Salary

Investment in Your Salary

Knowing this formula is critical to knowing the value you bring to the organization, and that you provide enough value to cover both the direct and indirect costs of your position.

My point is that you need to provide "line of sight" into the real economic value your position contributes to the organization. The last thing you want to be is part of the costly "overhead" of any business.

Greg Crabtree, who we introduced in the last chapter, has very similar metrics for measuring employee profitability. He refers to them as Labor Efficiency Ratios. These ratios are a finer cut of the payroll expenses we explored

---

8   Gross Profit is used in the calculation because the addition of an incremental employee does not necessitate the need to expand facilities or fixed cost overheads.

in the last chapter. Crabtree breaks down the income statement and calculates the Labor Efficiency Ratio through (Gross Profit/Direct Labor $s), Management Efficiency Ratio (Contribution Margin/Management and Admin Labor $s) and Sales Efficiency Ratio (Contribution Margin/Sales Labor $s)[9]. An overall Labor Efficiency Ratio for your company or division can also be calculated by dividing (Gross Profit/Total Payroll $s). This overall LER shows the gross profit earned for each labor dollar invested.

These ratios are useful because they highlight productivity across different areas of the company. The fastest way for a company to become more profitable is to increase its labor efficiency ratios and to then add more gross profit (revenue - cost of goods sold) without adding more people or labor dollars. As we touched on, Crabtree compares this to the salary caps mandated in the NFL. Even though all NFL teams have the same salary caps, some elite teams consistently make the playoffs, while others flounder. They focus on better labor efficiency. This is exactly the same concept espoused in the well-known book, and movie by the same name, *Moneyball*. Your company or organization has only so much money to allot to salaries. They can spend the money on B and C Players and have poor Labor Efficiency Ratios, or they can stack the team with 100% A Players and flourish with bottom-line results. Therefore, for the same money, we want to build the "best team money can buy." As an A Player, you understand that when you win, your company wins, and when your company wins, you win back in return.

As an A Player employee, I recommend that you shoot for at least tripling your salary in terms of the profitability you generate for the company. Labor Efficiency Ratios for a healthy company are better than a multiple of 2 for the entire organization, so 3 for an A Player has you leading your team. For example, if you are in marketing, then your activities should be generating return on investments that average more than 300%. Said another way, the return on investment generated by your marketing activities in relationship to your budget should be three times your salary.[10] Likewise, if you are in sales, you are expected to sell revenue levels several factors beyond your salary. In fact, based on

---

9   Contribution Margin = Gross Profit - Direct Labor
10   A 300% ROI is the same as a 3 times return on investment.

experience with my clients, it is quite common for salespeople with $100,000 in total compensation to produce in excess of $1 to 4 million of sales revenue and $300,000 to $1,200,000 in gross margin, across a range of industries.

Sales and marketing organizations are typically held to the highest accountability to return on investment, largely because they are revenue-generating organizations. Sadly, many marketers do not hold themselves accountable to ROI, which is a key reason why the position of Chief Marketing Officer (CMO) has the highest turnover of any office found in the C-level suite. They simply have trouble quantifying the value of what they are doing.[11] Other organizations fall into the same fate and those are usually the ones that get cut when belt-tightening measures come around. My challenge to you is to measure everything and know your specific value to the organization, measured in terms of ROI. If you are in engineering, know the value of your quality improvement and cost reduction initiatives. Perhaps you are making the product more appealing, which will increase sales. If you are in customer service, measure your impact on customer retention. If you are in finance, see that you are enabling key financial targets to be met. Consistently ask: What is the tangible value, measured in ROI, that you and your function are providing the organization? With a little help from your finance team, they can provide you with the gross profit and total department payroll needed so you can easily calculate these numbers and set targets for your team.

Why do I point this out? In even the largest and most sophisticated of organizations, including those found within the Fortune 500, we frequently encounter employees at all levels that have no concept of the tangible value they need to provide to the organization relative to their compensation. Whether you are in legal, accounting, manufacturing, customer service or engineering, you need to be able to show your value in terms of return on investment, or at least as an avoided opportunity cost versus the next best option. In today's environment of outsourcing work, at least be able to show that you provide more value than if your function was outsourced. As one senior executive at a major insurance company whom I coach bemoaned during a coaching session: "It's like some people work here for their own amusement!" I've shared this story with

---

11   For the record the best marketers can and do show the quantifiable value of their work.

many other executives over the years, and they laugh and nod with the knowing recognition that they've seen this problem time and time again. Let's just hope they are not referring to you!

A Player Tip: Be Better Than the Outsourced Option

One of the biggest trends in business is outsourcing. Why? It is both tremendously effective and efficient. Effective in the sense that in many cases outsourcing the function provides better quality at a lower price. In many cases, businesses can hire specialists who can do things better, faster, and cheaper than internal employees. A Players are always better than the outsourced option, which makes them A Players in the first place.

Contrary to popular opinion, and consistent with *Conscious Capitalism*, the primary role of organizations is not to provide jobs. That's a popular tag line for politicians, but not for business owners and shareholders. Instead, the primary role is to provide economic value and a return to the owners and shareholders through the production of a good or service that adds value to customers. Besides, why would any organization want to employ people with whom they were not thrilled? Of course, if more great jobs are created as the result of company growth, then that is a terrific outcome and allows the company to benefit even more people.

However, realistically speaking, an organization will always opt to produce more work with less people; that is simply the definition of efficiency. The only reason you currently have a job or are being interviewed for a new job is that the leadership of the company is making an investment in your talents for the forecasted payout of a combination of more revenue and/or reduced expenses, therefore yielding more profit. If you work for a nonprofit organization, the goal is to provide more services delivered per employee than they were doing before they hired you.

If this is not the case, then you have simply become an expense center, and not a profit or prosperity center. As one of my CEO clients likes to point out:

"If you're on the revenue side of the equation, you're in good shape. If you're on the expense side, you're in trouble!" If this is the case then you'll find yourself expendable. As an A Player employee, it is incumbent on you to figure this out before your management team does. Take the initiative to develop a plan that will reconfigure your role to become profitable to the company. Always having this Profit per Employee mindset will ensure that you are always adding value to your organization. Even if you are in a function that has traditionally been viewed as a staff function or an expense center like customer service, finance, accounting, or warranty, find ways to change this traditional view by linking your function back to customer loyalty, cost reduction, or improved efficiency. Interestingly, in the nonprofit world, where the organizations usually have an outwardly altruistic persona, on the inside they run even more lean and mean than for-profit enterprises due to limited funds.

Again, congratulations on being a prosperity center! Remember, when a company generates profits, prosperity for those involved ensues. When you act, think, and perform as a profit center you unleash an entrepreneurial spirit and ownership mentality that will propel you in your profession. A profitable business that satisfies customer needs is the only kind that succeeds. You will go far if you do this on an individual level that is aligned with your organization's goals. Enjoy the journey!

Chapter 8

WHAT YOUR BUSINESS OWNERS WANT YOU TO KNOW

"Whenever you see a successful business, someone once made a courageous decision."

—Peter F. Drucker

In the previous chapter we discussed the importance of every employee in your business being a prosperity center. Intrinsically knowing your worth to the company provides huge value to both you and your organization. What we are really aspiring to do here is to create prosperity for everyone involved in the organization. Thinking and acting like an owner of the business are what drives those awesome results. With that in mind, this chapter will go deeper into the idea of Ownership Thinking.

Ownership Thinking is the mindset of the owner of the business. For larger businesses this often translates into many shareholders. Make no mistake—every organization has owners, shareholders, and/or stakeholders. If you have direct interaction with the owner or CEO in a smaller or midsized company, view Ownership Thinking as the way that owner/CEO would like you to think and act on his or her behalf. In the same way, if you are part of either a privately or publicly held larger organization, Ownership Thinking is the way either the owners or the shareholders would like you to invest and protect their money. At the employee level, Ownership Thinking is of great importance to your owners and leaders, and should be at the forefront of A Players' minds. You may not own the company, but you do own the results of your immediate workgroup. Ownership Thinking also turns out to be the highest and most prized form of personal accountability, which we will cover in greater detail in *Chapter 16*. So, let's take a look at some of the key strategic items of Ownership Thinking that owners think about on a daily basis:

1. **Fulfilling the noble purpose of the business or organization.**
2. **Considering questions like: What is the next best move for the business?**
3. **Thinking about issues like: Is it prudent to invest now? Can I bet on the growth we are predicting? When should I add additional employees?**
4. **Inquire as to the actual return on investment on an action.**
5. **Consider how the business grows.**
6. **Always evaluate: How is the consistency of the customer pipeline?**
7. **Ask important questions like: Is the efficiency of the organization improving?**
8. **How can I help my employees and teammates be more successful?**
9. **Results: Who owns this? Will my teammates deliver?**
10. **And finally: Am I providing follow-up versus micromanagement?**

Throughout this chapter we will assess and discuss each of these questions to better understand the notion of Ownership Thinking.

1. Fulfilling the purpose of the business or organization

A Players know and are aligned to the *Purpose* of an organization. As an A Player, this should be the real reason you joined the organization. Business expert Roy Spence defines purpose as "The organization's reason for being; it goes beyond making money and it almost always results in making more money than you ever thought possible." Spence should know; he has worked with some of the world's best companies including Southwest Airlines. For context, I have paraphrased how he describes the interaction between Purpose, Mission, and Vision. For completeness, I have added Values and the *Prosperity Principles* to make 5 critical guiding principles of an organization:

Purpose:	The difference you are making.
Mission:	Is how you do it.
Vision:	Is how the world is different after you have done your Purpose and Mission.
Values:	The operating principles that drive behaviors and your business. If violated would cease either employment or the business practice.
Prosperity Principles:	The profit and financial parameters required to fulfill the purpose of the organization, with specific plans for this prosperity.

A critical difference between A Players and Bs and Cs is that A Players work for Purpose (and Mission, Vision, Values, and Prosperity), while B and C Players only work for money.

The organization's Purpose should be altruistic and beneficial to customers outside the organization. It also can stop far short of earth-changing events such as solving world hunger or achieving world peace. You simply need to make somebody else's life better in a meaningful way or solve a basic humanistic problem.

For example, Callaway Golf's purpose statement is:

Through an unwavering commitment to innovation, Callaway Golf Company creates products and services designed to deliver serious performance and serious fun for every golfer. We are a global leader in advanced golf technology, and for 30 years we have consistently found new ways to empower golfers of all abilities.

Not some fluffy statement about some lofty goal they cannot possibly fulfill, but very relevant to golfers who want to enjoy their pastime more.

A Players align with the organization's purpose. Fulfilling that joint and aligned purpose drives them to excellence. In his best-selling book *Drive*, author

Daniel Pink concludes that people want to be connected to others and want meaning in their lives. A Player employees deeply understand their purpose within an organization and in turn deeply align and execute the organization's purpose as they connect to improve customer's lives. As author and customer service expert Ron Kaufman, who helped Singapore Airlines achieve preeminence in the airline industry for outstanding service, says: "There are two basic types of people in life. One that has the attitude of 'what's in it for me' and the other that says 'what can I do for you?'" Which one are you? Are you in it for yourself or are you here to serve others? I call this "service before self." Think about which mindset yields far greater results in the long run.

To the A Player, the money, fame, and acclaim that follow are merely by-products. The real fuel that drives A Players are the "thank-you's" they receive from customers, as well as the satisfaction from doing something well and increasingly better every time. Oh, and just in case you are wondering, the money does follow! Oh yes it follows, much more than if you focused on the money alone. Management experts Jim Collins and Jerry Porrass, who authored both *Built to Last* and *Good to Great*, found that purpose- and value-driven organizations outperformed the market by 15:1, and outperformed their competition by 6:1. Those sound like A Player numbers to me!

To obtain these results, the A Player needs to have two simultaneous foci. As the famous author F. Scott Fitzgerald once said: "The test of a first-rate intelligence is the ability to hold two opposed ideas in mind at the same time and still retain the ability to function." These two areas include:

1. ***Fulfilling the purpose of the organization.***
2. ***Achievement of organizational goals.***

I like to think of this in the context of *The Inner Game of Work* model championed by best-selling author and consultant Timothy Gallwey, who first wrote *The Inner Game of Tennis*, and followed up with *The Inner Game of Work*. In *The Inner Game of Tennis*, Gallwey revolutionized the coaching of the sport by suggesting the player simply study the motion of the ball as they approached and after it was hit. In short, this provided intense focus on the important elements of moving the body and racquet to squarely hit the ball, as well as observe the results of the hit by studying the flight of the returned ball. So to continue the tennis analogy, the player focuses on the pureness of contact of the strings to the ball and the flight of the ball, and simultaneously focuses on the end result of a well-placed winning shot. Both of these factors are important and necessary.

Likewise, the A Player first focuses on the organization's core purpose, which usually centers on producing a superior product or service and helping customers succeed. Simultaneously, the A Player also focuses on the organization's goals and targets, including financial objectives. In the process of focusing on organizational goals, the A Player also translates these goals into personal goals.

This focus on both the customer and organizational goals is Jim Collins' "Magic of And," and like Fitzgerald, he contends this is the test of first-rate intelligence, ability, and greatness. B and C Players complain about this paradox. They will say, "Which way do you want it?" as an excuse concerning their priorities. This is where A Players truly stand out. They fully understand that fulfilling purpose and achieving organizational goals are not only harmonious, but also essential to success. Think of the *Prosperity Principles* here; in essence, they have one eye on the customer and the other eye on the goal.

A Player employees have a purpose that is 100% aligned with their employer. Having a purpose gives more meaning to your job, which in turn gives more meaning to your life, which in turn leads to more effectiveness, which in turn leads to more happiness.

So with that said, you will also find A Player leaders, including yourself, asking some very specific Ownership Thinking questions to demonstrate forward thinking and future result oriented actions:

2. What is the next best move for the business?

Owners are always thinking about what they should do next for the good of the business. Typically, these options are at a strategic level and involve major investments in product development, plant capacity, or personnel capacity through hiring and expansion. As an A Player, you should be thinking about the same things. Your insightful thinking will add value to your leadership team.

Periodically engage your boss or leadership on their thoughts on strategic issues, including issues on growth.

**A Player Tip: How to Engage Your
Leadership Team on Strategic Issues:**

It is always best to engage your leadership team via a well-thought-out question rather than an opinion. A well-thought-out question actually shows your insight more than an opinion would. Ask a well-thought-out question and you will be rewarded by your leadership by being asked for your thoughts on this and future topics. An A Player employee always asks and does not tell, unless asked in the first place. Remember the interrogative form of speech is more powerful than the declarative.

A Player Action Step: Practice powerful, insightful questions.

---

3. Is it prudent to invest now? Can I bet on the growth we are predicting? When should I add additional employees?

Ownership constantly tries to ascertain if it is prudent to invest. Investment can come in either the form of product development, increasing plant capacity, expanding to new cities, or adding additional team members. The thought process going through ownership's head is squarely based on how to increase company capacity without adding overhead that will sit idle too long, draining profitability.

In almost every case, including adding a new employee, the investment needs to be made long before the new asset becomes productive. Keep in mind that improving gross and net profit margins and profit per employee are the key measures that define productivity and efficiency; and that ownership always wants these factors improving, thus ensuring a better, more efficient company or organization. You should want that too. In other words, at some point, ownership wants to enjoy the harvest of their investments and not always spend for the future without a reasonable return occurring today. You'd want the same as an investor.

The key question going through ownership and leadership's mind is: "Is the business better and more profitable if the investment is made?" The technical way to look at this is through a discounted cash flow analysis, where all of the cash outflows and inflows are put on a time line and discounted back to today's value using the cost of capital[12]. In reality, the higher the value, the more attractive the investment opportunity. This is a great analysis to make sure we are spending wisely on investments that will truly pay off. If one knew for certain that the projections would be delivered, they would certainly add the investments mentioned above. However, nothing in business is certain, so the task for A Players is to take as much risk out of the equation for the leadership team as possible. One of the key hallmarks of an A Player is producing predictable results that the company can literally take to the bank.

When it comes to adding team members, remember that it is usually a minimum of 30-90 days after a new employee is hired that they start to become productive. Before they are fully up-to-speed, they are essentially a liability. As an A Player, you will want to understand this dynamic and be productive to your organization immediately. In many cases, this means studying the training assets the company has in your own time. A Player employees should contribute immediately from Day #1.

4. What is the return on investment on an action?

The next strategic question is related to the return of an investment. It is world-class Ownership Thinking of A Players to consider the return of every business action they take (big or small). On a personal level, think about business decisions that you have a lot of influence over. For example, next time you request travel for work, or requisition for a faster computer with two large screens, ask yourself: "What is the return of investment on this action?" If the payout is not crystal clear, it is likely that that money could be better invested elsewhere. Likewise, on larger level department or divisional actions, work out the business case on a *pro forma* basis and actually calculate the return on

---

12 Very similar in concept to the annual interest rate on a loan. Future cash flows are
     discounted to current values using the time value of money principle.

investment, in terms of dollars flowing in versus investment flowing out. This is A Player thinking that will not only endear you to your financial team, but also will simply make you a more efficient and well-rounded business person. You will find that these principles also carry over very well to your personal financial life as well.

In short, think of every action as an investment and condition yourself to calculate the return on investment of that action. This is how A Players think and act!

5. How does the business grow?

A Players are aware of the need for growth. They understand how it works and consider what they can do to accelerate growth. A business is exactly like a tree. It naturally needs to keep growing. The same is true for a nonprofit organization. It also needs to grow. If an organization is not growing, it is by nature dying. How so you may ask? To use our tree analogy, if a tree is not growing, it is constantly under attack by adverse weather conditions, insects, and disease, to name just a few. Only a growing tree can withstand and thrive against these threats. Likewise, your organization is always under inflationary and competitive threats. Therefore, the owner or shareholders, or Board of Directors in the case of a nonprofit, are always looking for ways to grow and get more efficient.

Your leadership is always looking for the best and healthiest ways to grow. They are constantly asking questions like: Should the organization grow organically? If so, what are the best ways to grow? How successful are the marketing investments and the sales team in generating predictable growth? Or, should the organization look to grow by acquiring another organization?

Also, your leadership is looking for the right rate of growth. Slow growth may lead to missed critical opportunities. Fast growth within the organization can cause it to spin out of control, leaving your customer base unsatisfied, as you cannot keep up with your product or service delivery. Perhaps even worse, organizations that grow too fast may "grow broke" by spending more cash on growth than they are taking in.

As an A Player, remain dialed into your leadership's growth strategies and ensure that your activities are aligned with these strategies. Doing so will make sure that your activities are directly benefiting the growth of the organization. You will find that when you are aligned to this growth, approvals of your initiatives will come faster and with a very enthusiastic response.

6. How is the customer pipeline?

A Players are constantly aware of the customer pipeline. The strength of the customer pipeline is one of the critical lead indicators of success for your organization. Again, this concept is universal for both the for-profit and nonprofit worlds. The reason why is that an organization's customer pipeline represents its future potential revenue stream. The customer pipeline has two dimensions. The first dimension is its depth, or how many customers are estimated to be in line to buy your goods or services (or to donate to your nonprofit). The second dimension is the probability that these customers will actually buy, and the pipeline is not a pipe dream! Think of the second dimension as the actual conversion rate of the pipeline. The more we know about the potential customers and their unique needs, the higher the likelihood that they will actually convert.

Why does an owner concern him or herself so much with the customer pipeline? This is because most leaders don't wake up in the middle of the night worrying about how to produce the goods or services your company provides. Believe it or not, most companies have a pretty good handle on that. What they don't have a good handle on is if customer orders are going to keep your plants open or if customer order centers are busy enough to be considered profit centers. Visibility into the customer pipeline allows transparency to the predictable organizational growth detailed above. In short, leadership will give their approval on both capital and personnel investments based on their confidence in both the depth and quality of the customer pipeline. As an A Player employee, it is therefore important that you align yourself to this thinking to best support your owner and/or shareholders and coordinate your actions appropriately.

I recently had the opportunity to learn firsthand from billionaire Mark Cuban, the owner of the Dallas Mavericks, who also invests in over 140 companies. One of Mark's first comments was that everyone in the organization needs to be involved in knowing about their customers on an intimate basis. Everyone needs to be involved in selling, not just the sales people. When you focus on helping your customer solve their needs, everything changes for the better!

7. Is the efficiency of the organization improving?

The next question to ask concerning Ownership Thinking is related to the efficiency of a business. One of the most important aspects of a business or organization is its relative efficiency over time. Bigger is not always better, but being a more lean and efficient organization always wins. How does this work? Organizationally speaking, efficiency in your business is the return it keeps for the investment made. *Two of the most important categories of efficiency metrics are:*

1. *Net Profit*
2. *Profit Per Employee (PPE) and Labor Efficiency Ratio (LER)*

Let's take a look at each:

Net profit is also known as net income or operating income. This is literally the "Bottom Line" of the income statement. Remember, for most healthy companies this number is at least in the 10 to 15% range. Competitive net profit numbers are available for your industry from annual reports or websites like bizstats.com. What net profit shows is how efficient an organization is at converting sales into profits. Put another way, if the net profit is 12%, for every $1 dollar in sales the company makes, you put 12 cents in your pocket from every dollar you generate. Net profit takes into account the entire variable and fixed expenses required by the organization to produce and sell its goods and services. To state the obvious, as employees we want to fight for every point of net profit, as twelve percent is twenty percent more profitable than a ten percent net profit company.

There is a huge advantage to a business that can improve the percentage of net profits it keeps. In fact, it benefits everyone from employees to shareholders. Bonuses and other special employee compensation come from only one place, and that is net profit! In addition, profits are the source of fuel for investments that facilitate future growth. A company with a growing net profit can plow that money back into the company to fund organic growth in the form of exciting products and geographical expansion. As a company grows, leadership wants to make sure the net profit margin is growing as well, as this is a key indicator that the organization is running efficiently and its value is growing.

Profit Per Employee (PPE) and Labor Efficiency Ratio (LER), which we covered in the prior chapter, are two of the most accurate measures of both overall company and people efficiency. This is because salary and payroll expenses are typically the largest expense category in the income statement by a wide margin. This is where the expense of you as an employee is accounted for. Analyzing both PPE and LER will show if the business is getting more or less efficient from period to period with the team we are employing. We need to field the best team money can buy. Having a business that is getting more efficient on a per employee (PPE) or per labor dollar (LER) basis is one of the most important drivers of success in any enterprise.

As an A Player, you should be focused on making your organization more efficient. This is one huge reason why A Players are so great; they are so productive they produce more for less. This is how businesses prosper. Don't worry; they are also well compensated for their efforts, usually at the top of the pay scales for their respective fields. A Players also have the satisfaction of doing their personal best. There is always career security for the best and most efficient!

8. How can I help my employees and teammates be more successful?

At the end of the day, being a leader calls for you to constantly work to improve those you lead. As owners and leaders look around the organization, they are always assessing who is really producing results and who is also aligned with organization objectives. Often candidly, leaders scratch their heads when an employee or teammate does not "get it" or buy into the vision. Contrary to popular belief, leaders are not looking to make employees' lives miserable. To do so would actually be counterproductive, as they would be sabotaging the results they are looking for.

The goal is to maintain a healthy ownership perspective. That sounds like: "How can I help my employees be more successful?" This question transcends into the even deeper questions such as: "What does my employee want out of life?" or "What is their *purpose* on planet Earth?" and "*Who* do they want to become?"

Any rational owner or leader relies on the success of their employees both on the job and in life. Can leaders and owners improve their leadership skills? Absolutely! Nearly 100% of the time! However, an even bigger opportunity is for employees to realize the opportunities afforded to them by their leadership and organization. Instead of perpetuating the "Us versus Them" complex, as author and consultant Quint Studer calls it, look for the opportunities leadership is serving up for your benefit and success. Are you stepping up to the plate? For instance, are you getting aligned to leadership initiatives, programs, and training opportunities available? Again, it should be in leadership's best interest to care about your success. However, much of the time they are scratching their heads trying to figure out what makes you tick and how to get you to actually respond to the opportunities available for you to shine. Here's a tip: Put yourself in their shoes. What performance expectations do they have for your role? Looking at your role through your manager's lens can produce some revealing insights.

Success is a two-way street. This is called employee engagement. A Player employees actively seek feedback and participate with their leadership to become even more successful. Try not to leave them guessing!

A Player Tip: More on "Us versus Them"

A hallmark of A Player employees is they take ownership for decisions and policies made by company leadership. When another employee or third-party challenges a decision or policy, the A Player never deflects the blame to the leadership team by referring to the leadership team as "Them." Instead, they internalize the ownership for these decisions and policies by owning them with the word "Us." Similar to a cohesive family unit, A Players never air our internal dirty laundry to the outside world. Another important insight is if you blame decisions on "Them," you have disempowered yourself.

9. Results: Who owns this? Will my teammates deliver?

The next question to consider is: Who owns the initiative? Who owns the result? Often, owners and leaders are left wondering whether their employees and teammates will deliver on commitments and assignments. There are many reasons for this, with the root cause typically being lack of accountability, poor communication, and little feedback on the part of the employee. Employees frequently mistake empowerment with a "leave me alone" attitude. While empowerment gives employees the freedom from minute-to-minute micromanagement, it is still incumbent upon the employee to keep ownership and leadership informed of their activities and results. As CEO of Bry-Air Inc., a manufacturer of environmental control systems, Mel Meyers says, "my need for information is inversely related to you [the employee] hitting the goal."

Often during the course of a challenging deliverable, employees frequently evade reporting to leadership in order to avoid challenging and uncomfortable questions about their status. This only creates a situation where they can "run but not hide." In fact, it perpetuates a continual problem. You will be far better off facing the music immediately when there is still time to correct the situation if you are behind schedule or over budget. Avoiding accountability while the matter festers is a recipe for disaster. It is far better to take constructive criticism while there is still time for corrective measures than to take the full blame of a failed or missed deliverable. Another one of billionaire Mark Cuban's insights is he asks his employees to report bad news first. His expectation is for his employees to deliver good news. He wants to hear the bad news so he is not blindsided and countermeasures can be employed. Beware if you don't give Mark the bad news, as you will be fired if he finds out from someone other than you!

As A Player employees it is your responsibility to keep your leadership in the loop on your activities and deliverables. Don't leave your management in the dark about whether we will deliver on a commitment or not. Instead, provide leadership with frequent status reports that allow them to know that projects and results will be predictably delivered. This is what we want from our peers, and direct reports and this practice will absolutely endear you to management and provide for a much more efficient organization.

10. Am I providing follow-up versus micromanagement?

Often at the heart of culture, performance, and communication issues between employees and their leadership team is the issue of "Micromanagement." This is a very common problem in almost every organization, and one I frequently work with leadership teams on improving.

Merriam-Webster's dictionary defines micromanagement as: To manage especially with excessive control or attention to details. In practice, I find the issue of "micromanagement" incidents occurring more frequently with B and C Players. These employees have lower technical and leadership skills and therefore typically lack the specific actions and results necessary to satisfy management's interest in important projects. As a result, their knee-jerk reaction is to blame their management team with "micromanagement" instead of looking at their own follow-up mechanisms to keep their bosses informed. Management has the right to be kept informed on projects on a very frequent basis. For projects approaching a critical deadline, or that have huge immediate consequences, follow-ups and status updates may even approach an hour-by-hour or minute-by-minute basis. It is incumbent on employees to keep their leadership team informed. If management keeps coming to you for updates that is a clear signal that you are not meeting their information needs, and that you need to improve your follow-up and status reports. Trust me; leaders do not want to do your job! Any good leader or manager loathes having to micromanage.

Timely and appropriate feedback on the part of the employee (or leader) is the secret to not only avoiding micromanagement, but also to avoiding root conflicts generated by the lack of communication. Feedback is defined as people getting the information necessary to keep their efforts on track. This concept comes from the process of Systems Thinking[13] where the exchange of data is necessary, as one part of data that is off track can throw off the rest of the system. Therefore, being integral to the success of the system, each player in the organization needs to provide status on how they are doing so that any part heading off course can be improved before it is too late.

In organizations, the vast majority of executional problems, misunderstandings, customer service issues, and the like stem from a breakdown in communication. Plain and simple, poor communication occurred, bad assumptions were made, and a lack of information existed to make the appropriate decisions. Usually, the root cause of poor communication is a bad or missing feedback mechanism. For example, the reason a manager keeps asking about the status and resolution on a customer's service problem is not that they want to micromanage you, or do your job for you. Rather, it purely is a critical element to the organization's success, and they are following up to ensure the corrective actions have been completed. Providing timely feedback to your organization as to the status is incumbent upon the employee.

Take the lead in keeping your management satisfied with updates and they will happily leave you alone! You will feel more empowerment and experience more success with this approach.

---

13 Systems Thinking is an approach to problem solving that views "problems" in the context of the total overall system, rather than reacting to only a specific part, outcome, or event in isolation. This is a useful problem solving tool when viewing manager and employee interactions, as it shows all of the impacts of either missing feedback or excessive micromanagement and prevents the unintended consequences of misdiagnosing an isolated situation.

Chapter 9

EVERYTHING HAS A BUSINESS CASE—
PUT YOUR PLAN IN WRITING

"Writing is called a "psycho-neuro-motor activity." The act of writing forces you to think and concentrate. It forces you to choose what is more important to you and your future. As a result, when you write down your goal, you impress it into your subconscious mind, which then goes to work twenty-four hours a day to bring your goal to reality."
—**Brian Tracy**, Business Expert and Best-selling Author

Recently, during a presentation to a business audience, I spoke about how A Players do not push back on initiatives without providing better solutions. I've long been fond of Paul Martinelli's (CEO of The John Maxwell Team) saying about "Not letting the Devil in the room" in reference to people who think they are being helpful by being "the Devil's advocate." A gentleman approached me after my presentation and contended that he thought we should have people on the team who disagree with our thinking, even if they don't offer solutions.

While I happen to disagree with that point, what I do know for certain is that people who bring solutions to problems are far more valuable than those who don't. I'm a fan of what U.S. President Theodore Roosevelt said: "Complaining about a problem without proposing a solution is called whining." Don't get me wrong, diversity of thinking is excellent and we don't want a situation where the employees are just "yes men." The truth is that the best employees bring diversity of thinking and a diversity of *solutions*.

Therefore, an axiom for being an A Player is not bringing problems to leadership, but instead bringing several solutions, and of those solutions a concrete recommendation with the ramifications calculated and measured out. When you think about it, the highest paid people are paid to solve the toughest problems. I still vividly remember when I became the newly minted Taurus brand manager at Ford Motor Company, and I approached the car group brand manager to get his thoughts on some market challenges I faced. He looked me dead in the eye and said "you look like the new Taurus brand manager, but the Taurus brand manager I hired always comes with a recommended solution to his problems. Therefore, go and find that guy and ask him what he thinks. When you find out, come back with a recommendation."

Does that sound like tough medicine to you? Well it may have been, but it also taught me a valuable lesson I use every day in my business life. That lesson is to bring solutions, not problems, to the table. In fact, I do not think that I ever repeated that mistake all of these years later!

That direct form of communication can be extremely valuable in managing employees and obtaining the preferred outcome. It is of obvious importance to demonstrate respect and tact in the process, but again insist that people bring solutions and not problems to the table.

So how then should the A Player employee help the critical thinking of the organization without either being "the Devil's advocate" or simply a "Yes Man?"

Consider the following Critical Thinking Model as a very useful tool to improve decision making and problem-solving skills:

CRITICAL THINKING MODEL

| | Options | | |
Strategic Questions	A	B	C
What benefits are derived from this option?			
What do we really get by pursuing this option? (digging deeper)			
What assumptions are we assuming to be true that if are incorrect will cause the option to be invalid?			
How can we validate the assumptions we are making?			
What risks are inherent?			
What other options can we think of that will give us a better result?			

The Critical Thinking Model is an excellent tool to evaluate decisions because it challenges us to evaluate assumptions. Instead of the annoying and unproductive "Devil's advocate" or "wet blanket" approaches that plague many organizations, the Critical Thinking Model provides a structured approach with strategic questions that allow the uncovering of crucial critical thinking to drive better decisions. As you can see from the model, each question uncovers a deeper level of thinking, and uncovers weak assumptions that are inevitably present in every decision-making process.

As an A Player, you should adopt this decision-making process, or refine your current process to include these strategic questions and the evaluation of several solutions to further enhance your decision-making value to your organization. Remember, A Players work on making things work, and B and C Players spend time on explaining why things won't work. Both your bosses and peers will appreciate this approach for its professionalism, collegiality and, most importantly, its rigor in supporting a great decision-making process. You will find your colleagues to be much more open to your input than the hip-shooting devil's advocates that run rampant in many organizations. Even more importantly, your organization will benefit from enhanced decision making that will fortify both the bottom line and your everyday interactions.

Let me be crystal clear: We are not looking for "Yes Men" and "Yes Women" in the organization. Nothing could be further from the truth. I had the pleasure of attending a summit on transformational leadership where George S. Barrett, chairman of the board and CEO of Cardinal Health, shared a very interesting perspective on the magnetic pull of the employees who surround the top leaders in an organization. For those not familiar with Cardinal Health, at the time of this writing, it is ranked 21st on the Fortune 500 list, with revenues of over $102.5 billion in 2015.

Mr. Barrett shared that in any organization there are a group of glad handers surrounding leaders on the ascent who feel their best interest is in carte blanche alignment with the leaders' opinions. By the way, Mr. Barrett did in no way indicate that these surrounding employees had less than pure motives. He simply stated the magnetic force naturally occurs and the leader should purposefully seek out dissenting opinions as well.

True diversity is actually diversity of thinking. Mr. Barrett actually has processes to seek out dissenting viewpoints before decisions are made. My point is that an A Player does better than just provide the dissenting view; they come with facts, data, and solutions presented in a collegial way. They also are brave enough to come to the table with these facts and data before it is too late and a bad decision is made. They also seek out dissenting views from their peers, direct reports, and superiors, and reconcile these views into truths and plans of action.

In fact, a very powerful decision-making process used by A Players is to actually split the decision team and have both sides of the team make the supporting argument from multiple sides of a decision. I have participated in this process on many occasions and it is amazing how the other side of an issue looks from another's perspective. After making the argument from multiple perspectives, come back together and coalesce what the team learned and, based on these learnings, come to a final, aligned decision. You will find that your decision making improves, and you are able to meaningfully incorporate dissenting viewpoints to create effective conclusions. This process also has the substantive advantage of driving better alignment with the team, as team members become more empathetic with others' point of view.

True leaders want to make the best, not the most popular decisions. Too often decision-making processes are fueled by beliefs and opinions and not facts and data. In fact, I get really suspicious when I hear an argument or justification that begins with either: "I think" or "I believe." One painful example of this came from my time at Ford. Ford used to compete profitably in minivans. We had very good market intelligence that the segment leader, Chrysler, planned to add a left hand sliding door, which was revolutionary at the time. Conventional wisdom was that the left hand door added a ton of weight and cost just to allow access to essentially one seat. Ford researched the concept with hundreds of customers using real vehicles modified with left hand sliding doors and found out decisively that customers were willing to pay for this feature and that it was their desired configuration. In fact, the deeper insight was that mothers of infants wanted a left hand powered sliding door so they could put in their child seat hands-free. Despite this overwhelming factual data, the decision was made not to engineer the left hand sliding door. I remember being at the meeting where decision makers offered a myriad of beliefs and options as an excuse for not engineering the door. Not only that, the bearers of the market research data were belittled. The senior executive leading the meeting at a special Saturday session berated us saying, "we were going to win the Holy War without a left hand sliding door." As a result, we were outgunned and the new Chrysler minivan with the left hand sliding door embarrassed the Ford products, relegating us to C Players in this segment and eventually forcing our exit completely. I know in retrospect this decision sounds silly, but you can't make this stuff up! It cost Ford billions[14]! All from one bad decision.

As an A Player, provide value to your ownership and leadership team by bringing these facts and data to the decision-making process. Facts and data are very hard to argue with (though some may try). Besides having the advantage of being true, they are far less emotionally charged than beliefs and opinions. Taking the time to dig into the facts and data, and taking dissenting viewpoints

---

14   Ford dominates essentially all other truck segments, which makes this fateful decision even more painful.

into account not only distinguishes you as an A Player, but also as an A Player leader. Taking this approach will help to create appreciation by both your peers and your leadership team. People will seek you out for positions of increasing authority and want you to be on key teams. Great things happen to people who do the right things!

A Player Tip: Be Flexible in the Give and Take of Decision Making

As you are bringing solutions to the table, be cognizant to let your boss and peers participate in the ideas, so they can take ownership in both the process and the ultimate solution. As Donald Asher points out in his useful book, *Who Gets Promoted Who Doesn't and Why*: "Don't love any one idea more than you love solving the problem!" This is excellent advice. In fact, when I became more skillful at collaborating with others, and making them think the ideas and solutions I had developed were theirs, my career literally skyrocketed. This is a fun skill to develop and makes for a highly effective, rewarding, and collaborative work environment. When others take ownership for an idea, it gets done!

Going Further—Putting the Business Case in Writing

"You can make anything by writing"
—**C.S. Lewis**, British author

As A Players, we are not only evaluating decisions, but we are driving the organization with new ideas and initiatives that will make our companies more efficient and profitable.

Too often in organizations, we see employees hip shooting ideas all the time. Hip shooting is defined as an action or idea that is quick and often reckless. Unfortunately, these ideas are not only random, but are proposed in an unstructured and haphazard way that does not drive formal evaluation and execution. Unstructured musings of "I wish we did it this way," "management ought to" or "this would be a great idea" often go nowhere and waste a lot of valuable time because of their lack of scrutiny and follow-up with no formal decision process.

For A Players, the gold standard is to put a solution in writing in the form of a business case. What exactly is a business case and what should be in it? A business case is an articulation of a solution to a business need. It is the combination of a situational and financial analysis of an issue, problem, or opportunity. It shows your management how they will be better off both operationally and financially by approving your initiative through a business case.

The business case starts with what is the background of the issue, opportunity, need or problem. It then shares supporting data on the scope of the issue and alternatives. Next, it addresses the potential solutions to solving the problem and alternatives considered in solving the need. Then is the actual business case portion. This section details the return on investment or ROI associated with executing the solution. The final portion is called Action Requested. This is the part where you make a request of leadership for the support and funding required for your initiative. This section also details next steps in the process.

Below is the outline that I recommend to A Player employees:

Business Case Outline

Background:
Provides the pertinent context on why this is an important issue or opportunity.

Supporting Data:
Provides facts and data (not opinions) surrounding the issue or opportunity.

Alternatives Studied and Potential Solutions:
Shows the scope of altenatives considered and potential solutions.

Recommended Solution:
Narrows down to the recommended solution with strong rationale and facts.

Business Case/Return on Investment:
This details the financial return of the action.

Action Requested/Next Steps:
This makes the request of management and details the Action Plan.

The above outline has proven to be a very powerful tool for A Players to drive business and organizational results. I have used it during my almost 30-year business career to get some key initiatives approved, and likewise, my clients have used it to drive approvals of important projects in their businesses. Part of its power is its simplicity, which requires the employee to sharpen both their thinking and the resultant business case.

Typically, a great business case can be summarized in 2 to 3 pages. While a longer and more detailed business case may be required for more elaborate corporate-level initiatives, I have found that a short and well-thought-out 2 to 3 page business case using the outline above is an excellent tool for A Players to propose and fund meaningful initiatives that drive results in an organization. Create a 2 to 3 page business case to get your thoughts, benefits, and return on investment organized and you will find that you will see many of your great ideas take off and help your organization.

Keep in mind that you won't get 100% of your ideas and initiatives approved. But that doesn't mean you aren't doing a great job. Opening the doors to meaningful conversations is just as important as finding the actual solution. Your ownership and leadership team will always appreciate your well-thought-out and structured approach. As mentioned before, everything in your organization should have a business case. With that said, let's take a look at some areas where your business will benefit from a 2 to 3 page business case approach:

1. New equipment expenditures
2. Hiring of new personnel
3. Labor plans and overtime approval
4. Pricing, feature, and margin decisions on product lines
5. Conference travel and training
6. Approval of marketing programs
7. Approval of sales contests and incentive plans
8. Brand development initiatives
9. Decisions to outsource or keep in-house
10. Process changes

While this is not intended to be an exhaustive list, it should help to stimulate your thoughts and support the notion that everything should have a business case, whether it be something relatively small like purchasing a piece of office equipment to help your productivity, or larger and more strategic decisions like investments to support brand development initiatives.

For example, one of my fondest memories of my 13 great years at Ford Motor Company was writing the business case for the series naming strategy for all Ford Division car lines. I wrote the business case because I saw an opportunity to have a more consistent and powerful brand presence on our car lines that would also help to support the selling of a greater mix of better looking, higher satisfaction, and more profitable high series vehicles. I literally wrote the business case on a Friday and put it in the Ford Division President's weekend mail. It was approved to advance to the Ford Division operating committee by Monday morning due to his enthusiastic response to both the strategy and the business case.

I can happily report that, over 15 years later, this car-line series naming strategy is still intact and being well executed! I like to think this is no small part to the success Ford has had selling better equipped, better looking, higher quality vehicles that are leading the industry today. Of course it took a lot of hard focused work by literally thousands of Ford employees to achieve this great outcome, but a two-page business case on the merits of an outlined car-line series naming strategy, detailing the type of content on each series served as an important catalyst to gain alignment and momentum.

I share this story to highlight the enormous power a well-thought-out business case can have on a company or organization. It is incumbent on A Player employees to drive positive return on investment (ROI) level strategies, thinking, and execution in our businesses. Please don't tell your boss that you want something, or that you wished the company or organization did business another way without writing down a plan. As an A Player, take the further step in improving the value of your idea to the organization with a solid and strategic business case.

Chapter 10

WHY *A* PLAYERS DON'T
REALLY WORK FOR MONEY

"Don't aim for success if you want it; just do what you love and believe in, and it will come naturally."

—**David Frost**, Journalist

One of the most powerful realizations that came out of the interviews with CEOs, senior leaders and internationally recognized thought leaders is: *A Players don't work for money.*

Do A Players need money? Yes. Do A Players enjoy the fruits of their labor? Of course. Do A Players know their market value and expect fair compensation? You bet. Will an A Player make a career move for more money? Possibly. Regardless of these affirmative responses, A Players absolutely, positively DO NOT work for money.

So, wait a second you think! In *Chapter 7* we covered how employees must be profit and prosperity centers for their organizations. If that is the case, then how can it possibly be that companies and organizations demand quantifiable value from their employees, yet the A Player employees themselves actually do not work for money?

This is the paradox that eludes the B and C Players who work for nothing more than money. So that being said, the answer to this somewhat complicated question revolves around three key principles that drive the A Player:

1. Love
2. Purpose
3. Value

Let's take a few moments to look at each one of these core values.

Love: A Players love what they do. On the eve of the 2014 Wimbledon final, tennis great Roger Federer remarked: "you have to love what you do, otherwise you would not endure the hardships." A Players are very self-aware about what they love, and they align themselves with careers and organizations where they can practice what they love doing most. As mentioned in the Bible, "Work is ordained."[15] Your life has more meaning and you brighten up those around you when you love what you do. Remember, it takes passion to win and it takes love to create passion.

The French writer François-René de Chateaubriand vividly described A Players in action in his late18[th] century, early 19th century writing:

A master in the art of living draws no sharp distinction between his work and his play; his labor and his leisure; his mind and his body; his education and his recreation. He hardly knows which is which. He simply pursues his vision of excellence through whatever he is doing, and leaves others to determine whether he is working or playing. To himself, he always appears to be doing both.

Visually speaking, take a moment to review this quick diagram to demonstrate the fundamental difference in A Players, B Players, and C Players:

Instant A Player Assessment: Loving What You Do

A Player	B Player	C Player
Love and Passion	Make a Living	Could Care Less

---

15 Colossians 3:23

The second core value of A Players is purpose.

Purpose: A Players align their core purpose with the core purpose of the organization in which they believe. Again, the core purpose does not need to be some super lofty goal like solving world hunger. In fact, noble purposes usually center on helping others or providing a useful good or service.

I like what Nobel purpose expert and author Lisa McLeod says about the idea of a greater purpose:

Average people approach their interactions focused on their own goals. Superstars go into situations focused on their goals AND the goals of the other person.

This seemly nuanced difference in thinking is why superstars create better relationships and garner more support for just about everything they do. Customers and Colleagues can feel the difference.

You can create success alone, but the only way to be super successful is to help other people.

Remember, like love, it is up to the employees to reflect on their purpose and to do their homework to find an organization that aligns with their belief system. It is not up to the organization to help people "find themselves." It is up to the employees to accurately portray their purpose and interests to the potential employer and not simply apply for a job to opportunistically pursue nothing more than a paycheck. That would be how B and C Players operate.

The final core philosophy of A Players is value.

Value: The concept of value explains how A Players don't work for money, but actually work to make an organization better by applying their talents. A Player employees realize that they must provide greater value to the organization than they are being paid. They actually embrace the notion that if they want or need more money, they in turn need to first provide more value. By the way, it's perfectly fine for A Players to have income and earnings goals. Their mental mindset is as follows: They set the income and earnings goals for the long, middle, and short term and then ascertain the value that they must create for the organization to achieve those same goals. Philosopher Buckminster Fuller's

Law of Precession is at work here.[16] It states that for every action we take there will be a side effect arising at 90 degrees to the line of that action. For example, bees are attracted to flowers for the nectar they contain. With that nectar they make honey, which is their goal. In fact, the 90 degree side effect to this activity is that the bees actually cross-pollinate the flowers, which is actually a bigger benefit to the ecosystem than the production of honey itself. Money behaves exactly the same way. In and of it itself, money has no value. It is what we do with that money that creates value. If money becomes the cause of what we do, we compromise ourselves. This is the domain of B and C Players. When money becomes the side effect of what we love to do, we become excellent in what we do. This is what A Players do. A Players look to add value; and in the process they make money. Because they are so intent on adding value to their organizations and other people, they almost always end up making far more money than if they were focused only on making money! This is the paradox that B and C Players don't understand. By the way, if you are an A Player leader who influences or decides compensation, you should be looking for ways to put as much money as possible into your A Players.

Instant A Player Assessment: Beliefs about Money

A Player	B Player	C Player
"*Add* More Value"	"I *Believe* I'm Worth More"	"*Complains* about Not Having Enough"

Growing in your Company:

One of the greatest benefits A Players receive from well-run and profitable organizations is they often grow and prosper along with the company. This really happens in two ways:

1. Your job gets bigger: The first opportunity for success is that the role you are currently in grows in scope, magnitude, and importance. For

---

16 Usually the side effect of the Law of Precession is more powerful and enduring than the directed action. Thus, our objective is not to make money, but to provide value to others. As we add value to others, making money is a natural and abundant by-product.

instance, perhaps you are the financial controller of a $300 million dollar company. Thanks to you and the efforts of other A Players on the team, the business grows at a little over 20% per year. In three years' time, the business may now be valued at a $500 million dollar revenue level. In most cases, the bigger a company gets the more scope and responsibility the existing jobs have. Most likely you will have more people reporting to you in order to manage the additional workload. Your job is now bigger and the leaders will most likely reward you for this with commensurate compensation.

2. You are worthy of a promotion: This can actually happen two ways. The first is similar to the scenario above. In this case the growth of your role is so significant that the position and title are elevated, and you are formally promoted. The second is that you are ready to be promoted to another higher-level position within the company. In this situation, your leaders can already envision you performing the duties of this elevated position because of the value and leadership you are providing to the organization. In all of these cases the roles come with increasing responsibilities, and thus you are growing not only your capabilities, but your compensation as well.

Often, I find that employees and executives are itching to get a promotion. To prove your value to the organization, you will need to behave and act like you are in that position before it is bestowed on you. As stated above, your leaders need to be able to envision you doing the job. Also, usually your biggest fan for your promotion should be the incumbent for the position. Be careful not to step on his or her toes in your eagerness to get the position. Additionally, make sure you are meeting all the requirements of your current role. Sometimes people start acting funny and begin to take things for granted when they are so close to getting promoted. Through these actions, they end up screwing up their chances as management chooses someone else. Don't rescue defeat from the jaws of victory! Instead, I always tried to get my bosses promoted so I would be the clear successor. Likewise, it was always a thrill when an A Player on my team was promoted to my former position after I was promoted. It's a great feeling to develop someone!

Act Like You Belong in the Role Before You Get the Role:

Often when working with executives, the notion of promotions comes up frequently. Too often, the conversation goes like this:

Executive:	"You know I am overdue for that promotion to divisional president"
Rick:	"Why's that?"
Executive:	"Well, Rachel from my training class ten years ago just got promoted to divisional president. I need to catch up to her."
Rick:	"What has your boss said about your readiness to be a divisional president?"
Executive:	"I told him that was my goal."
Rick:	"Yes, and what specifically did *he* say you need to accomplish or master before assuming that position."
Executive:	"He told me he wanted me to perform like I was in the position, before I got the job. He also said he wanted me to take more ownership of handling emerging situations in the market. But I'd need to be the president before doing all that."
Rick:	"How are you performing in your current role and what is stopping you from acting like the president right now?"
Executive:	"Really good. I was 90% of budget for the 1st half, and even though we did not meet our profit target, I worked really hard. And we had 80% of our shipments on time, which was better than last year. Of course a portion of the team does not report to me, so I have no influence over them."
Rick:	"90% and 80% do not sound like very strong results. How did those results compare to your SMART goals?"

Executive: "I don't know why the company set the budget so high, and the 95% on-time shipment goal was unrealistic. Had the goals been just a little over last year I could have hit them."

Rick: "What is your plan to show more ownership so you act, behave and produce the results of the president before you become the president?"

Executive: (silence)

Sadly, conversations like the one above are all too common at businesses all across the world. Employees focus far too much on an entitlement mentality of what's in it for them, rather than considering exactly how they are performing on their current assignment and whether or not they have the right ownership to perform their future assignment and responsibilities. These are classic B and C Player mindsets. Make sure you are performing in your current role and hitting your goals before you aspire to the next level. Otherwise, you will end up very frustrated.

If we are 100% honest with ourselves, it is painful to admit that many of us have this same entitlement mentality relative to promotions and money. I have been there myself. Early in my career, when I was at Ford Motor, my MBA classmate from Duke, Torrey Galida, received an early promotion. My first reaction was to ask my manager why Torrey was promoted when I hadn't been. I now cringe at my immaturity in handling this situation! The fact was Torrey was more mature and polished, and delivered a more compelling presentation than I had to our EVP of Sales and Marketing. Torrey's presentation better captured the EVP's attention and led to his recommendation for a prime opportunity in Ford's motorsport's division. To this day, I wish I knew what I know now and instead had asked, "What can I do to be better? What value, skills, results, and behaviors do I need to exhibit to become valuable enough to be promoted?" Man, was I a C Player at that moment!

The moral of this story is that A Players assume the ownership, accountability, responsibility, results, actions, behaviors and leadership of the next position before the position is given to them. And be careful in what you ask for! The higher positions come with significantly higher accountabilities and responsibilities. If you can't handle them and end up performing as a B or C Player, you will be asked to move on. However, when you are acting and producing the results of the next level, you'll almost inevitably create a situation where it is a foregone conclusion that you are the right person for the promotion.

How to Talk to Your Boss about Your Value

Notice that this section is not titled: "How to Ask Your Boss for a Raise." That's because A Players never ask their boss for a raise. A Players start by showing their tangible value to the company. They understand the relationship between profitability or savings generated for the organization and the compensation paid to them. Compensation is defined as salary, bonuses, and benefits.

Key questions to ask yourself:

1. *How was my performance in the past period?*
2. *How was the company performance in the last period?*
3. *How did I increase my value in tangible ways in the last period?*
4. *What is the market rate for the value I provide?*

Usually, the best companies and managers consider these questions relative to the A Player. After all, no organization wants to lose their top performers. If for some reason your value has far outgained your compensation, then in a nonthreatening way, show this to your leader. If you are being courted by another organization, but would rather stay, then share the competitive offer with your manager and develop a mutual plan to be compensated for your market value at your current company. They will either be able to match the compensation and responsibilities, or they will tell you that the external offer is worth taking.

A Players are very open with their employers, and broker ways to meet career and earnings goals. In turn, organizations process this information and set targets for the employees on what value they must produce to accomplish those goals. B and C Players go to employers with demands to make certain salaries and offer no performance commitments in return. They usually throw out a number and when asked for the reasoning behind that amount, come back with external nonbusiness related factors like they are buying a bigger house, getting married, or their peers are making that kind of money. Asking your employer for more money like a B or C Player would do shows that you only work for money. It just wears your leader out and accelerates his or her need to replace you with a real A Player.

Don't get me wrong. There is nothing wrong with wanting to make more income. Just like profit in a business, money is like oxygen. A Players may want to make more as well. Nothing is wrong with this. However, the way in which an A Player asks for more compensation is vastly different. A $95,000 per year A Player who wants to make $100,000 asks their manager "What value do I need to contribute to be worth more?" This is a totally different mindset than the B and C Players have. If you want to make a certain higher income and/or get promoted, a good manager should be willing to help you map out this plan. It's a great way to align with your manager, help the company, and meet your personal income and career goals.

In his excellent book, *No Excuses! The Power of Self-Discipline*, business expert Brian Tracy makes an excellent point regarding making more money. When an employee indicates the company is not willing to pay him or her more money, Brian asked him or her if other people in the company make that higher amount? The answer is inevitably yes. The light bulb should be going on for that person that the present situation is not a result of the company's unwillingness to pay that amount of money, it is that the individual is not contributing enough value to be worth that amount of money. The responsibility to create the value to be worth the money is the employee's, not the company's. A Players understand this, while B and C Players don't.

So give yourself a raise by adding more tangible value to the company!

Instant A Player Assessment: Having Conversations about More Compensation

A Player	B Player	C Player
Shows Results and Increased Value	Asks for a Raise	Complains about Not Getting Paid Enough

A Player Tip: How Not to Think About Compensation

As I mentioned earlier, if the CEO or business owner is traveling or otherwise unavailable, I often hold "skip level" sessions with the CEO's or owner's direct reports, or other executives in the organization. The topic of compensation sometimes comes up in these conversations, and I'm OK with that. My first question always is: how have you as the employee added more value to the organization? What tangible results have you *personally* produced that have directly improved the bottom line? If there are not big results to discuss, the employee usually gets the cue and moves on to plans he or she needs to make to produce results!

If for some reason I find myself stuck in a coaching session with B or C Players, they usually want to talk about entitlement mentality stuff like cost-of-living adjustments. I'll say right now that I am not a big fan of cost-of-living adjustments. Why? If you have not shown enough value in the organization and have not qualified for bonuses that drive your annual compensation more than a measly 3%, you are really missing the boat on the responsibility needed to be successful and control your own earning destiny. Building on what self-improvement expert Brian Tracy shares in *No Excuses! The Power of Self-Discipline*: "People whose income is increasing at 3 percent a year seldom get ahead." Do not rely on cost-of-living adjustments to get ahead! I'd recommend you purge that notion from your mindset and focus on creating value that creates the need for employers to promote you.

As we wrap up this chapter, remember that A Players don't really work for money, but instead work because they love what they do and are very good at it. Great compensation is the result of providing excellent value to your organization. In the next chapter we will challenge conventional thinking on what responsibilities and rights an organization has versus an employee. I cover this in detail as A Players have a far different relationship with their employer than a B or C Player, and it is important for you to see the differences.

Chapter 11

THE EMPLOYER AND EMPLOYEE BILL OF RIGHTS

"The old adage about giving a man a fish versus teaching him how to fish has been updated by a reader: Give a man a fish and he will ask for tartar sauce and french fries! Moreover, some politician who wants his vote will declare all these things to be among his 'basic rights.'"

—**Thomas Sowel**, American Economist,
Social Theorist, Political Philosopher, and Author

Have you ever noticed that A Players have a far more synergistic and harmonious relationship with their company than B or C Players do? One thing that I noticed years ago was that B and C Players always felt the company was trying to take advantage of them. In fact, to be blunt, they felt like they were being screwed. One day, I saw the correlation between underperformers and their high levels of complaints, and the A Players who almost never complained and got the best results.

The root cause here has to do with the entitlement mentality on the part of B and C Players and ignorance on how businesses really operate and their purpose for being. Much is said about employees' rights. However, not enough is said about employers' rights. Employers have rights too. An employee's alignment with the employer's rights will impact their success and career trajectory.

It is always popular for politicians to say that businesses need to create jobs. As we covered in earlier chapters, job creation is the by-product of a prosperous, thriving businesses. To build on this idea, I would contend that relative to employees, the need for businesses is not to create jobs, but instead to grow people. In this context, let's take a look at both the Employer and Employee Bill of Rights.

The Employer Bill of Rights:

Amendment # 1: The Right to Make a Profit: The business not only has a right, but has a natural need to make a profit. A business requires profit to fuel growth and prosperity. These profits allow the business to become more valuable and create a return on investment for the owner. Profits also allow for exciting new products and services to be developed that society needs and wants. The accompanying business growth and profit also allows for employees to grow with the company in terms of income, personal development, and more fulfilling, challenging roles.

Amendment # 2: The Right to Run Their Business the Way They Choose: Within the boundaries of moral and ethical principles, the organization has the right to choose both its culture and its business operational doctrines. For example, that means if a business or organization's ethos is to work 60-hour workweeks, then weekend work is likely expected. The truth is that it is their right to operate that way. Too often I hear employees complain about a culture *after* they join it. The example I give is if a company mandated their employees to wear pink uniforms as part of their culture and brand, you have no right to complain about the pink uniforms after you join.

The beautiful thing is that in every first world country, you can choose whether you want to work at a specific company or not. Remember, you should research the company before you join, and make the active choice to work there. If you are joining a public company, be sure to also research and study the company's financial statements to understand their financial health and growth prospects. If a private company, ask these exact questions in a tactful way as you interview. Stay away from companies with stagnant growth, lots of debt, low cash flow, and weak balance sheets. Ask about the culture and ethos before you join. If you do not like the ethos, then either improve it within your power, or leave. Whatever you do, don't just complain about it.

Amendment # 3: The Right to Have the Job Function Fulfilled: When the employee accepts the terms of the job function, the employer has the right to expect that the employee will fulfill the roles, responsibilities, and results of the job. Remember, you accepted the terms of the job when you accepted employment. You knew the expectations. If you do not really intend to fulfill the job responsibilities, you are not being 100% honest with your employer. By the way, employers who keep good records on employee performance may not need to pay unemployment benefits if an employee did not acceptably fulfill the job function.

Amendment # 4: The Right to Change the Job Role to Meet Market Demands: Market conditions frequently change. An employee's job role may need to change to be relevant to these market changes. One current example is the switch in the marketing industry from traditional media to digital media. At a minimum, traditional marketers need to add digital marketing skills to their repertoire to remain relevant. The role you were hired for most likely will change to meet changing market demands. Remember to stay flexible. It is your employer's right to change the job role to meet the demands of the market. It is your responsibility to stay relevant to these changes.

Amendment # 5: The Right That the People They Employ Are Who They Say They Are: Here, the employer has the right to fill the job function. We often see a lot of job-hopping on the resumes, Topgrading career history forms, and applications of B and C Players. The root cause of this is the opportunistic nature of most people. Shame on the employer for getting fooled in hiring them, but the bigger issue is usually that the prospective candidates were not 100% honest with the employer about their long-term interest in the role. The employer has the right to interview upfront and honest employees, and not folks looking for a temporary paycheck until something more appealing comes along.

Related to this issue are employees who try to immediately negotiate their salaries upwards as soon as they join. This is simply an opportunistic and selfish move, and I recommend to my clients that they terminate these employees immediately.

Remember, you knew the terms of the job when you signed up. To accept it under the false pretenses of being happy with the offer until something better comes along is fraudulent and unethical as an employee.

Amendment # 6: The Right to Have Employees Who Are 100% Engaged at Work: It's ironic how often employees waste time around the water cooler, lamenting about how their favorite sports star did not give 100% during a game. According to a recent and ongoing Gallup study, *State of the Global Workplace,* only 13% of employees are engaged, 63% are not engaged, and 24% are actively disengaged, meaning that they are unhappy and counterproductive at work. This means that only 1 in 8 employees worldwide are psychologically committed and actively contributing towards their jobs. Too often we overhear employees talk about how they are just getting through the day and biding their time until they can clock out. They often even overtly brag about how little contribution they are making as a percentage of their capability. As an A Player, it is not only our responsibility to be one of the engaged employees, but also to help coach up or coach out B and C Players who are not fully engaged. Remember, we all signed on to our job descriptions.

Amendment # 7: The Right for Employees to Respect the Organization: When an employer extends an offer for an employee to join an organization, one of the collateral responsibilities as employees is to become an ambassador for that brand. It is an employee's responsibility to speak positively about the organization, both publicly and within the walls. Anything else is to wrongly disparage the organization. Remember, if you don't like the way something is run, then address it in a collegial manner with your management team. Keep in mind that this respect extends to management team and coworkers as well. If the issue cannot be mutually resolved, then it is time for the employee to leave and select a new organization that is aligned with his values. Move on, don't disparage.

A Player Tip: Adopt an Internal Customer Mindset to Stay Relevant

As mentioned above, market and business conditions are always changing. As such, the employer has the right to change the job role to meet these conditions. Much is said about an internal customer mindset and for good reason. Imagine for a second that you are an external consultant and your client's needs are changing. You would need to adapt your service offerings or become obsolete and get fired, right? Apply this thinking to your internal customer, and apply continual learning to your skills to stay relevant as an A Player. Nobody owes us a job.

The Employee Bill of Rights:

Of course, business is a two-way street, and employees have rights as well. Here is a summary of the core rights employees have. This list of core rights may be smaller than the catalog of entitlements many employees think they have. This list is not meant to serve as a legal document, but rather as a guideline to A Player employees on what really counts.

Amendment # 1: The Right to Be Treated with Respect: Employees have the right to work in an environment where they are treated with respect as human beings. This means conversations in a collegial tone and not attacking people personally. Please remember to also extend this courtesy to your managers and coworkers.

Amendment # 2: The Right to Be Treated with Empathy: As human beings, there are times when tragedy or the maladies of life hit us. It could be something temporary like a bout of bronchitis or pneumonia, or something far more serious like a cancer diagnosis or a dying family member. During these periods of disease or suffering, we are simply not physically, physiologically, or psychologically 100%. In fact, during these times the human mind produces biological changes that lower our energy level and enthusiasm. Psychological studies show these physiological changes help us to become introspective and allow us to mourn and contemplate our next steps as our energy gradually returns. Employees have a right to be treated with empathy during these times.

Amendment # 3: The Right to Be Paid on Time: Notice here I intentionally cover the promptness of payment, and not the notion of fairness of payment. Remember, as an employee, you knew the terms of the job when you accepted it. Therefore, your right is being honored so long as your employer is paying you according to the terms set out in your employment agreement.

Amendment # 4: The Right Not to Be Harassed or Discriminated Against: In every part of the free world (and in particular the United States), the laws on harassment and discrimination are quite clear, so we will not dwell on them in detail here. Every employee has the right to work in an environment without harassment of any kind. In addition it is wrong to discriminate based on race, color, religion, sex, sexual orientation, military status, national origin, disability, age, or ancestry. There is zero tolerance on these areas and federal and state laws provide excellent protection for employees.

A Player Tip: Why A Players Don't Need to File Government Complaints

In my profession I have come to know a number of excellent employment attorneys. Several have stated to me that A Players are essentially never the ones filing the Equal Employment Opportunity Commission, National Labor Relations Board, or similar complaints to state labor agencies against their employers. It got me thinking, given the importance of great employees to organizations, could it be that many of the Department of Labor laws are outdated and serve as only bureaucratic drag to protect underperforming B and C Players? My reason for this thinking is simple: Employees at companies who have 100% A Players do not need these man-made laws, as the natural law of supply and demand dictates that an A Player employee who is not being treated fairly would simply go to a better opportunity, due to their great marketability. Also, to treat great employees with anything short of an excellent experience would simply not be in their best interest, as A Player talent will simply leave for a better opportunity and treatment. Remember, A Players are the most productive employees, who are driving all of the profitability of the company. The attorneys' views were rather that these laws largely exist to serve the underperformers who are not contributing on their own, and therefore choose to sue rather than contribute. Of course, there are exceptions when employee rights do need state and federal oversight, but one thing is for certain, we could radically reduce the size of these huge government agencies and subsequently improve productivity if the world was filled with only A Players. A Players perform, not sue!

This section was written to point out the environment in which the A Player plays. We realize that our relationship with our employer is a symbiotic one and we win when the organization wins. Too often, B and C Player employees are preoccupied with perceptions of getting screwed by the organization and lose sight that the employer has significant and essential rights as well. More often than not, the average employee is not living up to his or her end of the bargain. This is an opportunity for the A Player employee to shine. Remember, A Players have great attitudes and have positive relationships with their employers. We will continue this theme into the next chapter as we explore A Player acumen.

Chapter 12

A PLAYER ACUMEN

"The price of success is hard work, dedication to the job at hand, and the determination that whether we win or lose, we have applied the best of ourselves to the task at hand."
—**Vince Lombardi**, Hall of Fame NFL Coach

To this point, we have outlined actions that differentiate A Players from the Bs and the Cs. In this chapter we will dive head-on into some very specific behaviors that define the A Player. I call these success principles A Player Acumen. You will immediately recognize and value these traits when you see A Players in action. Let's make sure you possess them too. These success principles are universally proven and valued in virtually any organizational environment. Thus, let's take some time to review this valuable acumen so you can better understand what it takes to have "the right stuff."

1. A Players produce a customer experience that is WOW!

The only sustainable competitive advantage in business is to consistently WOW! your customers. Simply stated, WOW! is being so good that your customers say WOW! every time they interact with you. WOW! is measurable: One great way to do so is through using the Net Promoter Score (NPS) methodology.[17] NPS has a special question they call *The Ultimate Question*, which is extremely predictable of customer loyalty. *The Ultimate Question* to ask your customer is this:

On a scale of 1-10 (with 10 being the highest): How likely is it that you would recommend our company/product/service to a friend or colleague?

In NPS standards, the 10s and 9s are Promoters. Detractors are those who respond with a score of 0 to 6, also known as unhappy customers. Scores of 7 and 8 are passives. NPS is calculated by subtracting the percentage of customers who are Detractors from the percentage of customers who are Promoters. Passives are neutral and count towards the overall number of respondents, but are omitted from the direct calculation. To provide a sense of the score, an NPS score that is positive (e.g., higher than zero) is considered good, and an NPS of +50 is excellent. One of my clients, ShelfGenie, a maker of premium glide-out shelves, has an NPS of 68!

Speaking of ShelfGenie, they are an excellent example of how A Players drive a WOW! customer experience. ShelfGenie is stacked with A Players. Only a team of A Players can drive an A Player customer experience. In turn, A customers are willing to pay a premium for this great service, which produces an A business. An A business needs to be led by an A leader. An A leader is required to lead a team of A Players. The model below illustrates this virtuous cycle.

---

17 Developed and popularized by loyalty expert and author Fred Reichheld in his book: *The Ultimate Question: Driving Good Profits and True Growth*

2. Being early is on time for A Players:

Legendary Green Bay Packers coach Vince Lombardi was fastidious about being on time. He considered his players and coaches not being 15 minutes early to a meeting or practice as being late. Because of Lombardi's leadership, and hence his sustained success, this practice of "pre-timeliness" has come to be known as Lombardi Time.

A Players practice Lombardi Time. It's amazing the opportunities afforded to you when you are prepared and at meetings and events early. At one point early in my career, I arrived at a Ford Motor Company dealer reception 20 minutes ahead of the start. One of Ford's outstanding, but smaller dealers was there as well, hoping to spend some time with Jim O'Connor, the Ford Division president. Since I was there early, I naturally and immediately engaged the dealer, and when he mentioned his hope of meeting Jim, it was easy for me to make an introduction when Jim arrived a few minutes later. That dealer had an excellent track record of both sales and customer service performance and both the dealer and Jim thanked me afterwards for facilitating the meeting.

On the reverse side, tardiness will stunt your career. Your managers won't trust your commitment and you will become very unpopular with your coworkers as they spend their time waiting and covering for you. As author Glenn Shepard points out, being late is not only a problem in itself, but is a symptom of a bigger problem. This bigger problem is disrespect for the organization, managers, and teammates, and the value of their time.

3. The world of business rewards early risers and late closers

The world of business rewards people who are early into the office as well as those that stay later at night. There are two reasons for this:

1. While quality always trumps quantity of hours, for a lot of projects and organizational roles it simply takes dedicated critical thinking time away from meetings and distractions to get our best work done.
2. Executive teams often make critical decisions early in the morning or at the conclusion of the day. You need to be there and be available to be part of the action.

A Players recognize that longer hours are a reality of business. That's a key reason why we need to be passionate about the work we do. I'm not an advocate by any means of simply putting in "face time," but I do recommend to those aspiring A Players to be cognizant when key decisions in their organization are made and to be available during these key times. Our typical workday started around 6:45 a.m. when I was at Ford Division. We began by analyzing the prior day's sales results so we could formulate our marketing and sales plans. Executives who were not available to participate in these discussions did not last long in the division. They were relegated to less mission critical areas. After the key meetings of the day were finished, executives would typically use the early evening to then develop longer-range strategic plans.

As a quick side note on how to make your day more productive, best-selling author and personal effectiveness guru Brian Tracy also advises that you work through lunch to take advantage of an hour most B and C Players waste on frivolity and idle chitchat. It is far better to eat a quick meal at the desk and use your valuable lunchtime on planning or peer coaching with a coworker, or taking a valuable client out to lunch.

4. Remember: the customer writes your paycheck

The customer is not always right, but a good customer always does write your paycheck. A Players realize this fact better than most. Connect yourself in the most direct manner possible to the customer or client. This will ensure unfiltered "Voice of the Customer" feedback that is invaluable for solid decision making. Never guess or make conjectures as to what the customer wants. Simply provide direct and unfiltered voice of the customer feedback to your management team to ensure the best decision making and results. I always advise clients not to use the words "believe" or "think" when describing the voice of the customer, but instead put the customer's actual statement in quotes. "Believe" and "think" are actually qualifiers that decrease your credibility. You will find that you will get the attention of management when you use the customer's actual words and not your own version of the truth.

For those of you in the important field of project management, you know well the project management disciplines of Scrum and Agile are all the rage.

Often these two processes are intertwined. Scrum received its name because the face-to-face nature of the process is reminiscent of a rugby scrum as the players face off. Often, using the Scrum/Agile methodology, direct customer interaction is inserted in the product design process. Saab's successful Griffin fighter jet was developed with direct customer input using this methodology, and the resultant cost is one twentieth of the cost of the vaunted F-35 Lightning II fighter jet, which as of 2014 was $163 billion over budget and seven years behind schedule.

5. Sales is the lifeblood of the enterprise

Your paycheck (and also your organization's operating budget) is the result of revenue that was derived from a sale to a customer or client. For an ongoing enterprise, sales revenue is the lifeblood of the organization. Unfortunately, in many organizations, people think that sales are beneath them.

The fact remains that salespeople are the only people in the organization whose ability to perform is *directly* influenced by outside competition. Think about this: most employees are working on internal projects. In contrast, each day salespeople are at the whim of the customer and competitors' pricing and product actions in order to meet their goals.[18] A Players recognize these facts and do everything possible to support and/or participate in the selling effort.

In my session with Mark Cuban, his first point was a National Basketball Association concept known as KYP. KYP stands for Know Your Personnel. Mark talked about the need to know the talents and idiosyncrasies of your internal team. He immediately transitioned into talking about everybody in an organization needing to know customers intimately. "Everybody needs to be selling," he said.

Funny enough, if you have ever gone on a date, you have been in sales! A Players develop their selling skills and use them to sell ideas, influence decision makers, obtain budget approval, and inspire teammates. Getting as much sales experience as possible (including direct customer contact) will further your business acumen. As former Ford Division general sales manager Phil Novell advised me: "Rick, I never want to have a dealer or regional personnel say to you:

---

18   It could be argued that functions such as purchasing and legal are also subjected to external forces such as material costs and legislation. In these cases, selling sells are also directly needed to be successful in influencing these external forces.

'You have never done this job!'" As an A Player, embrace sales and get as close to the customer as you can.

Sales is not really about sales. It is really about helping customers solve a need. One of The Container Store's key principles is Man in the Desert Selling^{SM}. This philosophy is that a man in the desert does not just need water, as a deeper insight will also reveal he needs a hat for his head, sandals for his feet, and sunscreen for his skin.

6. Don't worry about being screwed

In his book *Who Gets Promoted, Who Doesn't, and Why*, Author Donald Asher tells a story of a smart but bitter MBA. Despite a great educational pedigree, this MBA spent most of her time discussing how she'd been screwed, how she might be currently getting screwed, and how she was going to get screwed in the future.

This graphic shows what employees with this mindset look like.[19]

Almost nothing is more of a turn off to management than a bitter employee who expects entitlements. If leadership knows that you will not appreciate rewards and opportunities, they are not likely to give you more of them.

---

19 Graphic developed by Andra Loiuse

Instead, A Player employees are grateful for the opportunities they have. Even on the roughest days, they take solace in the fact that they are gainfully employed and have an opportunity and lifestyle few in the world have. Practicing this productive mindset is called an attitude of gratitude. We will cover this important mindset in more detail later on in the book.

7. Understand periods of peak demand

Every business and organization has times during the year that call for higher demand or work requirements. This is particularly evident in organizations with acute seasonality.

Not only should A Players forecast these periods, but they should also plan their scheduling accordingly to account for the higher level of workload necessary to complete critical tasks. As an A Player employee, you know this is not the time to schedule vacations or book doctor appointments. Instead, think of this as "Game Time," with the opportunity to make your biggest contributions to the organization. Leave the complaining about longer hours and a more intense workload to the B and C Players!

This is a great place for teams to come in. I really like the concept of Self Directed Work Teams (SDWT). In SDWTs the team is empowered to hit goals with very little direct management intervention. In the case of periods of peak demand, the team knows the amount of workload needed by each member, and self-polices to ensure everyone is pulling his weight. This is a highly effective and empowering strategy that my clients employ.

8. Love what you do or do something else

Ford Division president Jim O'Connor was fond of saying, "Love what you do, and you'll never work another day in your life." What Jim was really saying is: Life is too short to do anything you are not truly passionate about. This is exactly the same sentiment author Marshall Goldsmith immediately shared with me when I asked him what separated A Players from the rest.

Regrettably, there are too many passionless people in the workforce. This is unfortunate because these types of employees are not honest to their employers. How so? Well, think of it this way: the employees knew all of the terms of employment, including the performance expectations, salary, and benefits when they took the job. When they accepted the offer they made an implied contract that they would perform up to these standards. Then they haphazardly go about their day, punching the clock and doing the bare minimum to maintain employment.

A Players truly love what they do based on two factors:

1. They tend to enjoy things that they are naturally good at. These things just come easier to them, and therefore are very enjoyable to perform.
2. A Players understand their own personal mission and how it aligns with the mission of the organization. This second factor contributes deeply to the A Player employee's understanding how their own personal contribution and the contribution of their organization helps others. Helping others is a deep-seated motivational need that drives significance.

9. Life is too short, be happy

Perhaps the *"Je ne sais quoi"*[20] of A Players is their happiness. Related directly to the above point of loving what you do, A Players bring joy, fun, and happiness to the workplace. This is no trivial point. In today's ultra-competitive workplace, happy and successful people bring energy to us all. In fact, the opportunity to work with other happy, motivated A Players is one of the biggest benefits a company can provide to its employees. These inspirational people are a big reason we are excited to get to work in the morning.

If your teammates are not happy people, it is a telltale sign they are not A Players. A Players are confident and friendly, and most of them want to share the good vibes that are going on in their lives to brighten your life too. As world-renowned performance psychologist and author Dr. Jim Loehr shares in his book *The Only Way to Win*:

> *Happier, more fulfilled people constantly outperform those who are unhappy and dissatisfied. You will be happier than you were, and happiness, as*

---

20 French for denoting an essential but hard to name characteristic

discussed earlier, breeds success. We've seen how the reverse statement—success
breeds happiness—is simply not true.

A Players find out what they truly love to do and then share happiness with others. Fortunately, there are A Players everywhere we look. They can be the CEO, the account executive, the production worker, etc. As I write this, I am staying at the Embassy Suites in Charleston, South Carolina, where each morning Pealy, the A Player breakfast chef, brightens my morning and that of the other guests as he masterfully whips up delicious custom made omelet creations. Pealy lights up the restaurant with not only his great food, but also his engaging demeanor and good cheer. God ordains work to be good[21]. Put a smile on someone else's face by sharing joy in the work you do.

10. A Players are the energy of the organization

Over the years, one of the insights I have gleaned from A Players is that they add energy to the work environment as opposed to drawing from it. Not long ago I was speaking to a large group of business owners about A Players and accountability, and shared this instant test to ascertain who was an A, B or C Player based on energy flow:

Instant A Player Assessment: Energy Flow

A Player	B Player	C Player
A little bit of energy invested in the A Player returns a multiple of energy. They feel like a joy to manage.	Variable: A great investment of energy can return a short term yield (e.g. a "sugar high"). However, the effects are not long lasting. They are like pumping up a tire with slow leak (e.g. "The Inflatable A"). You put more energy in than they return.	More energy is pumped into the person than they produce. The energy you expend wears you out.

---

21 Colossians 3:22-24

11. A Players focus

A Players focus on activities that contribute to the achievement of organizational goals. They are not sidetracked by superfluous things that look like work, but do not produce meaningful results. As mentioned in *Chapter 10*, a unique attribute of A Players is that they go into situations focused on their goals and the goals of others simultaneously.

To achieve A Player focus, always ask what action will provide the greatest return/yield? Always evaluate what action you can take to provide the greatest value/benefit to the company. One key aspect of focus is that it produces an exponential effect. Typically only 10 to 20% more effort and focus produces 2 to 3 times the results. Do you have A Player focus?

12. High self-awareness and no fixed mindset

One of the hallmarks of the A Player's acumen is high self-awareness. Just like the elite athlete who comes off a convincing win and then proceeds to tell the interviewer exactly what parts of his or her game he or she needs to work on to be successful for future matches, A Players are extremely aware of both their strengths, and more importantly their opportunities to get even better. In short, they are consciously incompetent on the skill they are developing and seek to refine their mastery of it. What I find fascinating is the correlation between a person's level of self-awareness and his or her success in life. If you look at their results in almost any area of their life, the most successful people are always improving through a defined plan. This takes self-awareness, discipline, and hard work. These are the A Players. In stark contrast, the B and C Players have what Stanford University psychologist Carol S. Dweck calls a "Fixed Mindset." Just ask them, and these people will tell you "they know all there is to know!"

To get a sense of this phenomena, think of a friend who beats you at a game and then never wants to play you again for fear of losing. Likewise, these people are content to perform at a certain level in your organization. They are resistant to change, as it will require them to do or learn something new. Even if their results fall short, they will tell you their plans are working. An interesting and dangerous trait these fixed mindset individuals have is that they avoid practice so they can attribute failure to lack of practice, not lack of ability[22]. One quick way to spot these people is in how they constantly say, "I Know." The antidote for this is to constantly search for application and new understanding. Replace "I know" with "How can I apply?" or "What can I learn?"

On the other hand, A Players have what Dweck terms a "Growth Mindset." This is by far the preferable mindset. They are insatiable learners. They love what they do, and will put countless hours into improving their craft. One of my favorite examples of someone with a growth mindset is arguably the greatest tennis player of all time, Roger Federer. Federer holds a record 17 men's singles Grand Slam titles and is well-known for his growth mindset that he still hasn't mastered the game of tennis.

13. Become a student of the business

When I assist my clients in selecting A Player talent for their organizations, two of the questions we always ask candidates are:

1. "How are they staying current in their profession?"
2. "What business or personal growth book they are currently reading?"

Inevitably, the best candidates are those that are investing in their own personal development. As Super Bowl championship coach Jon Gruden is fond of saying: "You never stay the same. You either get better or you get worse." Becoming a student of the business through reading business, management, leadership, trade, specialty, or personal development books and technical articles is the most powerful way to grow and increase your skill set and value.

According to an often-quoted study by the Jenkins Group, 42 percent of college graduates never read another book after college. Although this may be a hard statistic to accept, I believe it to be directionally true based on the many candidates I've seen.

---

22   Researchers Crocker, Brook, Niya, and Villacorta, as reported in Dr. Jim Loehr's *The Only Way to Win.*

Average employees simply do not invest in their own professional development by reading professional books. This is a shame, as all reading leads to your cumulative knowledge. If you are not improving your skills, your competition is!

A Players are always reading a business or personal development book. Want to know who reads business books? Your CEO! They tend to be voracious readers, finishing two or more business or self-development books a month. If you want to keep up with him or her, you better be reading what they are. Most CEOs I work with and interviewed attribute more of their learning to business, leadership, personal development, and technical books than they do their MBA or other advanced degrees.

For the A Players looking to improve their leadership skills, leadership expert and best-selling author Jim Kouzes' colleagues, Lillas Brown and Barry Posner, statistically found through research studies that learners are better leaders. This is an enormous finding that validates what the top executive business coaches have long intrinsically known. It is also exciting news for those of us engaged in increasing our leadership acumen that the simple act of formal learning is a key determinant of our success in this area.

Often I hear employees complaining about the lack of training provided to them. They whine because the company won't send them to a $2,000 seminar on a job-related topic. I have a simple rule with the companies I work with: No off-site training for an employee until they demonstrate the initiative first by reading a book, taking an online course, reading the technical manual, or at least reading an article. Books are to seminars as books are to movies: Even if the movie is great, the book is always better! That's because books always provide more detail, are a $10-$25 investment versus hundreds or thousands of dollars, and are a handy reference guide readily located on your shelf when you need to refresh on a topic.

Want to make an immediate impact on your company's training program? Then institute a learning program in your department. Develop an approved list of books that are aligned with the needs of your organization. Have an employee purchase a book from that list. Have a short one-page write-up with two critical questions:

1. *What am I personally going to do as a result of the learning?*
2. *How can the content of the book help the organization?*

After this short one-page write-up has been shared with your department, then the employee is reimbursed for the price of the book and receives a $50 to $100 learning bonus, depending on the organization. Most of my clients have instituted this program, and they are thrilled with what it has done for both the skill level and culture of their organization. It is pennies on the dollar cheaper than your existing training budget, yet yields an amazing return on your investment.

Don't get me wrong; there is a tremendous place in your organization's training program for workshops and on-site classroom training. In fact, every year I invest thousands of dollars attending workshops and conferences. (Those are my rewards for reading the books!) I typically find this interactive training with other professionals is most valuable after the employee has gained a working knowledge of the topic through books and other printed resources. We can then network and go deeper on the application.

One issue that I frequently run into with employees of new clients is the excessive length of time it takes to get them up to speed on the job. In my experience, the employees need to take more ownership for their own job training and expect less handholding from their boss and organization. After all, we are professionals. When we accepted the job, we essentially made a covenant with our employer that we can do the job. Professionals are expected to be prepared for the job. Most of the training materials are documented and already exist. A Player employees do whatever it takes to be fully productive on the job in as short a time as possible. If this takes some nights and weekends of study in preparation, then it is their obligation to do that to be the A Player they are hired to be. New employees should be producing and contributing within days and weeks of being hired. Taking months to contribute is a telltale sign of a B or C Player.

One of my clients recently fired a C Player who had bluffed his way through the interview process. The C Player complained about not being trained in a production operating system known as JobBOSS. In front of the whole team we pulled up over 200 detailed videos within seconds on YouTube that had great JobBOSS training modules. We advised him that A Players keep their training current, as the "wisdom of the world[23]" is available on books and videos and it was his responsibility to keep his own skills sharp to be an A Player. He used the same excuse with the CEO two weeks later and was fired.

As professionals, we cannot rest on our laurels. If our work is based on what we already know how to do, we will eventually be overtaken by somebody else who can do it better, cheaper, and faster. More than likely this person will also be younger. Don't let your skills atrophy. Instead, become a student of the business and a continual learner.

14. Speak up and write well

I am often surprised that employees often do not take advantage of the opportunities for either public speaking or writing an article, business case, or process improvement. All of these activities are not only highly valuable to your company or organization, but also to your own personal professional development and career advancement.

The reason is as follows: both public speaking and quality business writing position you as an expert. Great things happen when you are positioned as an expert. If you are speaking on behalf of your company or nonprofit organization in a public forum, a number of positive outcomes can arise. For example, if you are speaking to an industry audience, you may generate new business for your company. If you are speaking to your customer base, you can add value by alerting them to new processes and innovations. If you are speaking internally, you can share best practices with your teammates. If you are speaking on behalf of your nonprofit organization, you may very well garner support and donations for your cause.

The same applies for great business writing. With the magnet that the Internet and social media create, producing intellectual property in the form of articles becomes very valuable to your organization. The more valuable content your organization has on its website, the more relevant it will be to your constituents by drawing them to your site for important information.

---

23   Jim Rohn

Businesses and organizations run on processes and systems, so creating process and system documents becomes extremely valuable to your organization. Talk is cheap, so thoughtful consideration on how to improve a system and committing it to a written document becomes a significant benefit to your organization. As mentioned earlier, best-selling author Brian Tracy informs us that writing is a "psycho-neuro-motor activity." This means that writing forces you to think and concentrate. In turn, your thoughts will be better and more refined as you commit them to written word.

Your leadership will love you for investing the time to create written documents. My advice is not only to write it, but also to take the additional initiative to present it to your team. That way you take advantage of these two key skills that the A Player possesses. In fact, in the businesses that I coach, we institute process improvement programs where we utilize a common format for all process improvements. Employees document their process improvements in this common format and then present them to their team to get buy-in and implementation. In fact, in each case, the company provides a financial incentive to employees as they create, present, and implement their process improvement and cost-saving recommendations.

If you are not as comfortable with public speaking as you would like, I highly recommend joining Toastmasters or a similar organization where you can develop and hone your public speaking skills. Many CEOs, executives and managers I work with have joined Toastmasters and made significant improvements to their public speaking, influence, and leadership skills.

From time to time, one common pushback I hear is that developing presentations, and writing articles and system improvements take extra time. They do, but they actually take surprisingly little extra time. The bigger factor is dedicating a little bit of focus and setting deadlines to get them done. The A Player use their discretionary time and sometimes their own personal time to take the extra effort to get these done. These projects are a great use of an early morning or the close to the day, as discussed above. Focus in this area will pay big dividends in your value to the organization. The CEOs and senior leaders I interviewed for this book unanimously agree they place high worth on these incremental initiatives. In fact, these leaders basically point to incremental initiatives as the truth serum to identifying A Players. Givers gain, and you will reap the long-term rewards.

15. Become a problem solver

Believe it or not, as leaders we don't want to hear your problems! Problem solvers are the most valued people in organizations. If there is a problem or a shortfall in an area of the organization, we don't need to hear, "We're busy trying to figure it out; please leave us alone, we are *trying.*" Sorry, leaders need a little bit better than that. A Players are *problem solvers.* They deliver the results that no one else can.

When work is off its pace, the superstar A Player employee has contingency plans that allow him or her to live up to his or her commitments. We are constantly testing viable solutions and have the resiliency to hit our original goals. Being a problem solver and having resiliency are key pieces of the A Player employee's acumen.

Traction author Gino Wickman has excellent advice for problem solving: "Live with It, End It, or Change It." In other words, you only have three options. The best is to change it, or as I prefer to say, fix it. If you can't fix it or end it, then agree to live with it and don't complain.

16. Partner with your boss instead of pushing back

Inevitably, there are times when you will disagree with your boss, or point out that his or her plan won't work as well as they thought. But the manner in which you handle these situations defines the A Player.

Leaders don't want those around them to have an "Emperor's New Clothes" Pollyanna about them; the proverbial "Yes Man" if you will, but they also don't want those that suck the energy and enthusiasm out of every idea. An employee with a proven track record and credibility will replace those that simply push-back any day of the week.

The best way I have found to remedy this is through what I call "Possibility Thinking." When your boss makes a request, I advise A Player employees to think of the possibilities instead of the negatives. For instance let's go through an example of how A, B and C employees respond to exactly the same request:

Boss:	"We need to have the materials to the client by Friday."
A Player:	"That's tight timing; are you open to ways of letting me prioritize my workload to get that done?"
B Player:	"I'll try; I can't make any promises"
C Player:	"There's no way! I can't believe you asked me given my existing workload! Why does the client need this anyway?"

Sound familiar? Sadly, those scenarios are all too common in organizations. Unfortunately, the passiveness of the B Player's lack of commitment and subtle pushback is really the silent killer of executional excellence in organizations. The surly C Player should not be allowed to survive in any organization worth its salt.

As we also know, the boss is seldom always right; or sometimes is making a decision without all the facts. I've observed that C and B Players love to try to zing their boss in these cases, by trying to appear smarter with their snideness. They take the energy out of the organization with a variation of "That won't work." A Players take the high road and use both a partnership model and *Possibility Thinking* to improve, not shoot down the idea. They ask good, clarifying questions that add to the solution and the possibilities of success, rather than deflate. In a way, it is how to say "no" without saying "no." Understand what it will take. What are the impacts? These are legitimate concerns that need to be vetted out before decisions are made and actions are taken. Bad ideas will fall under their own weight. For clarity, let's look at A, B and C Player responses to a challenging request:

Boss:	"We need to get the cost reduction on that component to $5.00 per unit."
A Player:	"Before we proceed, would it be OK if I pointed out a few things based on my research? Are you aware the quality of the $5.00 part does not meet our quality standards? Our $5.50 part exceeds them. Are you open to other solutions? If the total system it resides in comes under budget, can we use the $5.50 part, or is there another reason driving the $5.00 cost structure I need to be aware of?"

B Player: "These requests are pretty impossible. I'll see what I can do."

C Player: "Good luck with that one! I wish management would make up their minds!"

These examples would be funny if we did not hear excuses like these every day! At the root of the A Player responses is a foundational respect for others' jobs and motivations. As A Players, we trust our bosses' and coworkers' professionalism, skills and judgment. We practice an abundant mindset versus one of scarcity, and are not trying to compete with either our boss or coworker. Leadership expert Jim Kouzes advises not to pushback, but instead to respectfully *challenge the process,* to use his parlance from his seminal book, *The Leadership Challenge.* Remember to *Partner* with your bosses by using *Possibility Thinking* to develop solutions to issues. Taking the ownership and accountability to come up with solutions increases your value as an A Player. Be a Partner, not a PITA (Pain in the Ass)!

17. Knowing when to edit

One of my favorite areas of the executive recruiting part of my practice is assisting clients with the identification, recruitment, and selection of A Players. We use Dr. Brad Smart's Topgrading® interview process as part of this procedure. A key element of the Topgrading process is a four-hour-long in-depth interview. My clients and I referred to this as the truth serum process, as it is amazing how many candidates do not know how to press the edit button on themselves as they ramble on with spurious information. They seem to have absolutely no clue that they are talking themselves out of the interview!

As this is a section on knowing how to edit, I'll keep this short.

A Players know when to edit. In other words, they have a built-in filter and time clock and they know innately when they have said enough and when to shut their mouths. We've all seen plenty of B and C Players who try to showboat, and in the process crash as the house of cards their arguments were based on crumbles under its own weight.

Another item to watch for is making superfluous comments. If you have to modify all of your comments with "just kidding" you are probably both talking too much and talking about the wrong things. Another related area is being defensive or covering up an error with language like, "I'm really an expert," or "I'm real good." Really? Just fix it, as actions speak louder than words! Leaders can do without the compensating color commentary. B and C Players are always trying to lobby and promote their accomplishments. They are not confident enough to let their actions do the talking. This is the realm of B and C Players, as the A Player knows to edit here.

Executives and leaders are impressed by results more than words. Show them don't tell them[24]. Once they are sold on your idea, thank them and move on. Many times, they are very interested in what additional thoughts and ideas you may have, and you can tell this by their thoughtful questions of you. Again, less is usually more. Thank them for their questions, provide some thoughtful insights, and as the old business adage goes, use your two ears and one mouth in the proportion that God provided them to you. Nobody likes a know-it-all! Remember, you are paid for results, not opinions. A Players don't need to tell anyone how smart they are or how great they are doing at something. B and C Players do in a fruitless attempt to compensate. Remember it's more important to be interested than interesting!

18. 𝐴 Players are specific

When making commitments and describing results, A Players use very specific language. They will specify exactly when they will deliver on a commitment and exactly the progress they are making on an objective. An A Player's specifics will include concrete quantitative progress expressed in numbers, next steps, and commitment dates and times. In contrast, B and C Players speak in generalities because they are poor at delivering on commitments. To illustrate this, think about how average students will describe their progress on homework as "pretty good," when A Player students will tell you exactly how many chapters they read

---

24 Ohio State head football coach Urban Meyer has a great saying about results: "I see better than I hear."

and what grade they achieved on the quizzes. Exactly the same principle applies in business!

Traction author Gino Wickman makes an excellent point about an additional benefit of being specific: With vague goals, it's difficult to assess if you were successful or not. Wickman contends you tend to rationalize you were better than you were. Furthermore, without specifics, there is no way to focus your improvement actions, thereby impeding progress to get better. This is why golfers who tend to measure the specific elements of their golf game by measuring fairways in regulation, greens in regulation and putts per round, tend to improve faster than those who do not.

19. Write your own performance review

Performance review time for the A Player employee should be like Christmas Day, except without surprises. The reason for this is your performance review should literally be a highlight reel of your contributions over the past period.

I recommend the following two-step process to ensure a successful performance review:

Step # 1: The first step is to expand well beyond the typical annual performance process and goal-setting process, and instead translate the annual goal-setting process into a robust quarterly plan. Breaking your annual goals into quarterly goals is a powerful step to get much more specific and immediate in your performance achievement.

Step # 2: The second step is to make sure that your contributions are aligned to the overall organizational goals and strategies. It is helpful to keep running documentation of your accomplishments with a very specific focus on driving profitability or organizational efficiencies. Key areas to focus on include project milestones met, cost reduction secured, growth rates achieved, effectiveness and return on investment of marketing actions, and profitability improvements.

As these achievements are met, take time to summarize them on paper. This will serve to sharpen your focus on achieving results. A sample summary for an A Player should appear as follows:

Led our 8 person marketing team in the strategic conception and execution of 21 marketing campaigns in the second quarter. These campaigns were executed for $8 million that was a 27% improvement versus the $11 million budget. Incremental profitability of these campaigns was $20 million which generated a 250% ROI on the 2nd quarter marketing budget. These actions also cleared out $3 million in aged inventory freeing up that working capital to be reallocated for the new Omega project. Not only is that capital critical to the company's R&D efforts, but the actions save the company approximately $210,000 in annual inventory interest savings.

Documenting strong results in a similar fashion to the example above is excellent business acumen for the A Player. Your management will appreciate the updates as these recaps provide him or her with the quantifiable results needed to assure the top leadership that the strategies and execution are working. I have found that almost nothing gratifies top leadership like knowing that the company strategy is being properly executed to achieve results. Not only will this create stellar performance reviews and career advancement opportunities for you, it will also almost guarantee an unlimited operating budget for your department to execute against, as you predictably show your actions produce a quantifiable return on investment.

20. Be clear on your expectations and give people a chance

A Players have a real gift at giving others clear expectations on the performance expected of them and the timing needed to achieve those ends. I advise clients to use a 4-step leadership model when setting goals with others:

1. **What:** As mentioned above, be very specific on what you want. Employees cannot stand indecisive leaders. It's better to be a little too demanding and negotiate down than to not know what you really want and expect. Even in this age of teams and collaboration, everyone expects leaders to be clear on the goals.

2. **When:** When do you need it? Be very clear. Use a date and time like "before noon on Thursday" instead of a vague request like "sometime next week."

3. **Why:** This is by far the most important. Unfortunately, it is also the least practiced. You should offer people the context of the request to inspire them. You will be amazed by how much better they will be at meeting your request when they know how the goal plugs into the larger picture.

4. **How:** This is actually the least important. With the *What, When and Why* defined, the A Player should fill in the *How* based on their know-how. Only jump in when assistance is needed, or you will be micro-managing.

What sets A Players apart from others is their ability to turn underperformers into over-performers. They do this by elevating and empowering them with their leadership. Let me give you an example: If you receive a project late and the sender justifies it with an excuse, don't say it's OK they are late. Let them know the impact to you and the organization. However, here's the real key: Give them a chance! Let them know you believe in them, let them know that you know they can do it next time; let them know they can become the person they want to be. Ask them what it will take to get it done? Follow up by having *them* articulate their commitment to the next event. When you believe in someone and inspire them to be the person they want to be, amazing things happen!

We just covered twenty key aspects of A Player Acumen. Of course this list can go on, and I'd encourage you to add your own specific A Player success principles for your industry to this foundational list of acumen. Customizing these A Player traits for your organization is a very powerful take-away from this chapter. The best performers calibrate their performance against this acumen all the time.

Next we'll journey into the very powerful topic of character, and how A Players distinguish themselves when integrity is on the line.

Chapter 13

CHARACTER COUNTS

"Watch your thoughts for they become words.
Watch your words for they become actions.
Watch your actions for they become habits.
Watch your habits for they become your character.
And watch your character for it becomes your destiny.
What we think, we become."

—**Margaret Thatcher**, British Prime Minister

Several years ago, I was deeply influenced by a presentation I attended by Dr. Jim Loehr, author of the book *The Only Way to Win*. Conventional wisdom holds that having great achievements and success contribute to self-esteem and strong character. This is consistent with the "I'll be happy when philosophy." Based on over two decades of work with high performance athletes and Fortune 500 executives, Dr. Loehr contends that the blind pursuit of external achievement often results in emptiness, addiction, and, ironically, poor performance. In fact, Loehr champions that the only way for a person to win and have lasting success, happiness, and fulfillment is by building up the elements of their character traits such as integrity, honesty, gratefulness, humility, optimism, and compassion.

A Players constantly exhibit strong character, even in a society where people with high character are often few and far between. We live in a society where winning at all costs is usually the mantra. As a result of this, our Western culture lets people off the hook for moral improprieties all the time. Basically, our senses for high ethics are dulled. We value self-esteem in the United States, and other Western cultures, over character ethics. Think about it: all the talk in the media is about individual freedoms over all else. The mantra is, "if it feels good then do it." We are taught that self-esteem is paramount and it is all about us. From an early age, we are conditioned to be preoccupied with ourselves. We have basically built a culture of self-serving narcissists that believe they are entitled to everything. However, we are going about building self-esteem the wrong way. We lie to ourselves by rationalizing that "everybody is doing it" and therefore think a white lie here, a bit of deception there, a little steal here, and a half-truth there are all ok. We must win at all costs. We also try to justify if we are not doing these things, someone else will, so we might as well be the one winning. A culture of unreality is created.

How often do we hear individuals tout their high character traits and in the same instance negate their statement within the same sentence with a lie, stretching of the truth, not intending to meet their commitment, or some other transgression? It occurs every day! Be on the lookout for it in your interactions in the upcoming week. The fact is, talk is cheap, and people of high moral[25] character are rare. A Players are people of exceptional character integrity. To examine character, let us first take a look at the components that comprise character. After all, sadly, many of the people espousing to have good character may likely have trouble really practicing its elements or really walking the talk.[26]

---

25 Moral and ethical character are used interchangeably
26 I am referring to the countless incidents when people espouse to have the character trait of integrity and then in the same breath make a commitment they have no intention of honoring. The same is true of people who claim to be honest, but in short order tell a white lie or a half-truth. I often observe commitments being broken within seconds of being made.

Just to calibrate how rare strong character traits are, the Josephson Institute for Ethics 2012 study *The Ethics of American Youth* reports that 76 percent of teens lied to their parents about something significant in their lives. When those youngsters grow into adults, do you think this behavior miraculously changes? Just think about how often your coworkers who claim to be of high character break their commitments on a deliverable or deadline. They may even do it on a regular basis. Yes, character counts, and real character is very rare!

In *The Only Way to Win,* Dr. Loehr distinguishes between performance character strengths and moral character strengths.[27] He defines performance character strengths as those values that govern our relationship with ourselves. Are we smart, decisive, determined, punctual, etc.? The list goes on. Great attributes to be sure, and the A Player has these in spades. These character strengths define our inner-relationship because it is easy to feel great about ourselves when we perform highly in these areas. And there is nothing at all wrong with this in itself. They are necessary factors in becoming an A Player. Interestingly enough, performance character strengths also define us on society's scorecard of external performance. This is how others typically judge our value as well. We tell not only our celebrities, but also our children, how great they are and how talented they are at every opportunity. Is it no wonder we have created a culture of entitled narcissists who crumple at the first signs of challenge or struggle. The other problem with achievements based on performance character strengths that lack moral character strengths is that these can be obtained in ruthless or cold-hearted ways at the expense of others. As you well know, this happens often.

In contrast, moral character strengths are those values that govern our relationships with others. These are the character attributes like truthfulness, justice, compassion, respect and honor that define who we are as human beings. Moral character strengths define the intrinsic growth and genuineness of a person. These are the humanistic character elements that not only help you fundamentally grow as a person, but also as someone who helps and adds value to other people. This is the true measure of character: The "real you," so to speak.

---

27   Both performance character and moral character strengths are derived from Dr. Jim Loehr, *The Only Way to Win.*

People are drawn to you in this regard because of who you truly are in terms of your personhood.

Think of performance character strengths as external measurements and moral character strengths as internal measurements. Both are essential to being an A Player. Think of that small group of great people such as investor Warren Buffet, former Yankee captain Derek Jeter, Marine General Joe Dunford, AMEX CEO Ken Chenault, The Container Store CEO Kip Tindell, FedEx founder and CEO Fred Smith, and Duke men's basketball coach Mike Krzyzewski. What do they all have in common? In short, they possess both high performance and high moral character strengths. These individuals lead with results and compassion. They play to win, but they play the right way. They stay out of scandals and have respect for other people. A great testament to these individuals is the great respect and admiration their rivals have for them. A Players have these deeper moral character strengths in addition to performance character, which makes them transformational individuals. These are the people who are truly worthy of our trust.

Summary of the Relationships and Measurement of Performance and Moral Character Strengths

	Performance Character Strengths	Moral Character Strengths
Relationship:	With Ourselves	With Others
Measurement:	External	Internal

Let's take a look at comprehensive lists of both performance character strengths and moral characters strengths, and then we'll look at some examples of what these look like in the real world.

Performance Character Strengths:

- Commitment
- Seeking Challenges
- Resiliency
- Self-Control
- Ambition
- Adaptability
- Resourcefulness
- Reliability

- Courage
- Positivity
- Competitiveness
- Ownership*
- Accountability*
- Responsibility
- Punctuality
- Decisiveness
- Mental Toughness
- Bravery
- Self-Compassion
- Patience with Self
- Diligence
- Effort Investment
- Perseverance

- Self-Discipline
- Constructiveness
- Capacity for Hard Work
- Optimism
- Determination
- Concentration
- Wisdom
- Hope
- Love of Learning
- Creativity
- Critical Thinking
- Humor
- Confidence
- Focus
- Best Energy Investment

* Character strength added by author to Dr. Loehr's list for completeness and consistency with the Above-the-Line model described in Chapter 16.

Just to be clear, these performance character traits are excellent qualities worth possessing and developing. Good employees aspire to have these qualities and employers covet them. In fact, they are integral parts of becoming an A Player. You will see many of these traits reiterated in the Appendix on competencies of A Players. As we stated, they govern our relationship with others and the value we provide to them. However, as good as they are, they are not enough by themselves. With that preamble, now let's turn to the moral character strengths.

Moral Character Strengths:

- Love for Others
- Justice
- Fairness
- Generosity
- Compassion
- Loyalty to Others

- Patience with Others
- Respect for Others
- Honor
- Care for Others
- Kindness
- Honesty

- Truthfulness
- Integrity
- Humility
- Gratefulness

As mentioned above, these moral character strengths govern our relationships with others. What differentiates these elements is that they are intrinsically good and serve as the bedrock and benchmark for a truly successful life. Said another way, moral character strengths are the table stakes for being a good human being. Even if we have all of the performance character in the world, without moral character our wins are vacant and meaningless. Here is the test: Would you continue to follow your leader if the economic benefit of following that leader went away? How many leaders in today's world possess both excellent performance and moral character strengths? As we saw above, the list is shockingly small. What other names do you think deserve to be on that list?

One of the best examples of excellent performance character strengths with some deficiencies in moral character strengths is American cyclist Lance Armstrong. Armstrong had tremendous performance character strengths. His self-discipline, leadership, toughness, and determination were legendary. On the surface, Armstrong had it all; he had seven consecutive Tour de France wins from 1999-2005, blue-chip sponsorships galore, adoring fans, and a successful charity called Livestrong (remember how we all used to wear the yellow rubber wristbands?). To top that off, just as his career began to skyrocket, he had the resilience to overcome life threatening testicular cancer, which his doctors diagnosed with only a 0-20% survival rate.

Amazing stuff! But Armstrong lacked bulletproof moral character. Propping up those apparent Tour de France victories was Armstrong's act of knowingly and tacitly using illegal performance enhancing drugs to achieve these victories. In 2012, a United States Anti-Doping Agency investigation concluded that Armstrong had used these drugs throughout his career. To make matters worse, he has refused to testify about the full extent of his use of performance enhancing drugs. As a sad post note to his era, CNN proclaimed: "The epic downfall of cycling's star, once an idolized icon of millions around the globe, stands out in the history of professional sports."

My point here is not to villainize Armstrong. Like many of you, I was a huge fan when he was representing the United States atop the world podium. But the tragedy is this: we all collectively lost our own innocence when the truth was revealed. But even more indicting is that you have to wonder how many of us would have done the same thing to win.

The list of our flawed heroes goes on and on: Ken Lay, Tiger Woods, Bill Cosby, Richard Nixon, Bill Clinton, Joe Paterno, David Petraeus. All had tremendous contributions, but because of transgressions in the strength of their moral character, their accomplishments, if not erased, will always be accompanied by an asterisk in the history books.

Entire corporations are not exempt from this scrutiny either. Companies such as Enron, Arthur Andersen, WorldCom, and Tyco perpetuated cultures of corporate wrongdoing and hurt lots of people in the process. Due to their lack of ethics, tens of billions of dollars were lost, and many shareholders lost their life savings on the stock market when it was found out that their earnings had been falsified. To add to this list, the environmental darling carmaker Volkswagen was caught in the fall of 2015 for falsifying fuel economy data. The prior several years Volkswagen had been a leader in the Corporate Social Responsibility index. Once again we were duped and our trust was shattered.

Sometimes these ethical lapses happen a little under the radar as well. A consulting firm in my line of work is shamelessly ripping off Jack Canfield's work as their own. It is one thing to share a great concept and give the source credit, quite another to claim it was your invention.

Just because we may not be celebrities or CEOs does not exempt us from these ethical standards. As human beings, we are by definition imperfect and have massive room for improvement in our moral character. Want proof? In the last month or so, how often have you exaggerated a little, cheated on a test, lied to a friend, stolen a pencil, taken office supplies, pretended not to know something, helped your kid too much on their school paper, not been upfront with a job candidate, told a white lie, covered something up, deceived someone, stretched the truth, embellished a resume, rounded up a GPA, stolen intellectual property, downloaded music, used unlicensed software, photocopied a book, borrowed an ID, told a half-truth, been frustrated with a loved one, missed a deadline, let down a colleague on a commitment, skipped an offering at church, fibbed about the status of a project to your boss when you were put on the spot, taken a shortcut on a project, skipped out of work early, rounded up your hours, broken the speed limit, texted while driving, not properly cited work, plagiarized, downloaded clipart you did not buy, taken advantage of a tax loophole, driven with an extra drink, lost your patience, bullied, or been mean to someone? Probably a little more than you'd like to admit.

Think I am being a little too picky? That these improprieties are trivial compared to the above? Think again. True, some are more egregious than others, but they all cause damage. The real losers are each of us. Low moral character strength is actually what causes damage to our self-esteem and psyche, not outside forces. We lose a bit of ourselves every time we compromise our ethics. We are lying to ourselves or not being the person we know we can be. We all know people who are so fragile because their whole lives are built upon lies, bullying, and lack of compassion that they essentially collapse under the weight of it all. They tend to be extremely lonely people because few are attracted to their low moral character. Again, when we fall short in these areas it hurts inside because we know we are not living up to who we know we should be. Think about how good our souls would feel if we cleaned up this personal rubbish? Think about how much our relationships with other people would improve? Real self-esteem is built on developing specific character strengths. Moral character strengths are the foundation of this development and must be in place first, and then fortified with performance character strengths on top.

The strangest thing happened while I was writing this chapter: I literally had the chapter open for editing one day when a new client sheepishly came into my office. I asked him what was up and he said he had overstated his revenue and profit numbers to me. I told him I was working on this chapter, and that he would most likely be added to it as an example. He said he was fine with that. I asked why he exaggerated, and he said he felt embarrassed by them and often overstated them to potential clients and partners so he would earn their business. He apologized to me and indicated it would not happen again. After discussing how this behavior impacted him on a personal basis, we began to create a plan for his business based on the realities of the situation so he would not feel compelled to lie again. This reality baseline, while albeit a lower one, was actually a very solid position from which to start. How can we make meaningful progress against a fantasy, with no grounding in reality? Like the biblical parable, build your moral character on a solid base of rock, not shifting sand[28].

Impact of Low Moral Character Strengths

The good news is that moral character traits can be improved upon (performance character traits can be improved as well). The fact is we all have moral and ethical deficiencies that need correcting. No amount of money can buy better trust, honor, or respect. But the good news is these characteristics are not bought and sold, but rather, are attributes we can obtain if we simply choose to do so. But it starts with accepting your flaws. The biggest issue is being in denial about our deficiencies. The definition of denial is lying to ourselves. So it is important to start with a basis in reality. Here are some questions to help us in this area:

1. How can I be a kinder person?
2. In what areas of my life can I improve my honesty?

28 Matthew 7:24-27

3. How can I be more truthful? Where have I deceived someone?
4. Where can I improve my integrity? How well have I done at keeping my word?
5. How can I be more just and fair to others?
6. Am I generous enough? Do I share enough credit with my team members?
7. With whom can I show more patience?
8. Where can I improve my honor?
9. What areas, if found out, would bring shame to me and my organization?

Those questions should help you identify areas to improve your moral character strengths. I have taught the course "Professional Ethics" to many different audiences. I find that A Players are usually the most self-aware of where they need to improve. I am always very skeptical about any person who is closed and guarded about areas for improvement in this area. So much so, that a person who claims to be of high standards in all these areas usually has something to hide. Watch out for the sanctimonious. Beware, the mightier they are, the harder they fall! If someone does claim to have high integrity, then my recommendation is to watch very carefully how they hold their integrity and learn from them.

A Players develop a scorecard that contains both performance and moral character strengths. To be balanced, it must contain elements of both. As we showed above, in today's society, performance character attributes are more outwardly celebrated than moral character traits. Over the last decade or so, we have given our celebrities and sports stars a pass despite letting us down with ethical lapses. We are so enamored by their performance that we overlook their misdeeds and allow them to become narcissists.

Former Florida State star quarterback Jameis Winston is a prime example. Despite numerous sexual assault, shoplifting, and other suspensions and allegations, Winston was awarded the 2013 Heisman Trophy and was the number one overall draft pick in the 2015 NFL draft by the Tampa Bay Buccaneers. Sports pundits rationalized that the general manager who passed on the athletically talented Winston would be doing his team a disservice. Their sentiment was,

"The general manager's job is to put the best athletes on the team. They owe it to their fans to put the best players on the field."

Now, these violations would not get overlooked and tolerated if we really prioritized moral character traits over performance character traits. We teach what we tolerate. We hear things such as, "it's just business." If a sports or business team gets busted for an infraction, we hear "everyone is doing it, we just got caught." However, without moral character strengths, performance successes are meaningless, as the achievements are hollow without any true moral substance.

Fortunately, it seems that people are finally standing up to this "win at all cost" mentality. How many times have you heard "it's not personal, it's just business?" One of the tenants of *Conscious Capitalism* states that there should not be one set of principles for business and another for personal conduct. The Container Store CEO Kip Tindell calls this "business is personal." I agree. Where along the way did it become acceptable to hang up our personal values when we entered work? Why would it be proper to treat business transactions differently from personal transactions?

There is more evidence of increased focus on moral character. In the fall of 2015, starting Ohio State quarterback JT Barrett was arrested for driving under the influence. It is easy to rationalize his behavior as that of a normal 20-year-old college student. But Barrett is anything from a normal college student. He is the leader of the reigning national championship Buckeye football team, and the only player in that storied program to be elected captain as a sophomore. I have now lived in Columbus for ten years, and Ohio State football is treated with reverence and sanctity. As an outsider, I have an unbiased view of the program. In the past, any Buckeye missteps would be rationalized away in an "us versus them" mentality, and "all teams do this, we just got caught" excuse.

Interestingly enough, since his arrival in 2012, head coach Urban Meyer has been cranking up the moral character strengths of the team. In a town where any critique of the Buckeyes was once considered heresy, Meyer not only benched Barrett, he also suspended his scholarship for a semester. Meyer cited that the two-time captain needed to be held to a higher standard.

This is a far cry from the 2010 Buckeye "Tattoogate" team whose members sold their football awards to pay for discounted tattoos. Then starting quarterback Terrell Pryor even sold a *sportsmanship* award from the 2008 Fiesta Bowl, along with his 2008 Big Ten championship ring! These infractions cost head coach Jim Tressel his job, and caused the eventual departure of president Gordon Gee because the university was lax on enforcing NCAA rules relative to the sale of awards by athletes. Some are arguing that Meyer's punishment of Barrett for such a serious offense as driving under the influence is not strict enough given that drunk driving can kill people, but it does mark a positive change in the program's culture.

So where does this leave us? For one thing, I hope this discussion has caused you to self-evaluate the level of your own moral character strengths. In his very instructive book *Cowboy Ethics*, author James P. Owen summarizes it wonderfully. To paraphrase Owen, when you boil ethics down, other people only need two things from you:

1. Someone they trust
2. Someone they can count on

When you really think about it, these characteristics are sorely missing in many of our business relationships, both on an organizational and personal level. The true A Players are people who uphold this level of integrity in their actions.

Thus, to have a truly successful life, development and mastery of the moral character strengths represent the summit of personal human development. In short, our moral character ultimately defines us. Are you substantially becoming a better person by improving your moral character strengths? Only a fool would claim to be perfect. We are all fallen men and women who are less than perfect. The A Player is aware of his or her deficiencies and is constantly striving to be a better person of stronger character. After all, our character becomes our legacy and epitaph when we are gone. What traits do you want people to remember you by?

As mentioned above, the good news is that character can be enhanced. Here is how:

1. *The first step is to stop rationalizing our bad behaviors and understand when we come up short.*
2. *The second step is to become incrementally better.*

Stop stretching the truth. Cut back on those little white lies. Be aware of how often we all make these small transgressions. You will be amazed how many times you catch yourself in a week's time. There is another additional benefit to getting better in character traits. Best-selling author Jack Canfield shares that when we improve our integrity and keep our agreements, our self-esteem actually improves on a foundational basis. This is exactly in line with Dr. Loehr's findings on character development. The benefit to performance as an A Player employee is that as our self-esteem increases, we are willing to take the risks that lead to even greater success.

To grow our teams of A Players, on the executive recruiting side of my business, we are constantly assessing candidates for high moral and performance character strengths. Identifying and hiring employees with high character are so important that we use a variety of sophisticated "truth serum" interview techniques and assessments as well as extensive background checks to separate the pretenders from the contenders. One key tool we use is the four-hour Topgrading interview. Let's put it this way: it is virtually impossible for a candidate to embellish their accomplishments over this length of interview. The B or C Player cannot keep up the façade for that long and withstand our very specific questions. One recent executive candidate we interviewed tried to leave our interview team with the impression he had closed a multimillion dollar deal with a huge corporation. My executive interview panel was ready to accept it as face value and move on when I added the question, "When did the deal close?" The candidate's jaw dropped and he said it hadn't. He was more than willing to deceive us that it had. Obviously we passed on that candidate.

Nothing is more important in our search for top people than high character, since character drives both ethical and performance traits. With the preponderance of candidates to exaggerate their performance, we dive deep into what we can prove they have actually done. The A Player candidates we see maintain stellar moral character strengths coupled with strong performance character attributes. In addition, they are refreshingly candid about their opportunities to improve their character strengths and other shortcomings. As I mentioned, only the poser claims to be perfect. The A Player has humility, which drives honor.

A Players have a certain tangible luster about their character. They say what they mean and mean what they say. I've had the pleasure of leading a large number of high performing A Players over the years. I particularly like what a high performing A Player employee said about character in response to her commitment to high-quality work and punctuality: "Rick, it's far more than just trying to please you as the boss, it's just who I am to meet commitments. I would just not feel right if I did not."

A Players have an abundance of both moral and performance character strengths. B and C Players do not. As an A Player you should have that inner feeling that "It's just who you are." You will also have the self-awareness and humility to know how much more you have to improve. In conjunction with the questions asked above, here is a short test to gauge where your opportunities are:

Key:	1	2	3	4	5	6	7	8	9	10
	Liability	Poorly	Not often	Seldom	Not enough	Occasionally	Sometimes	Often	Most of the Time	Always, Role Model

Truthful: Tells the whole truth. Does not deceive nor hide the truth.

1	2	3	4	5	6	7	8	9	10
☐	☐	☐	☐	☐	☐	☐	☐	☐	☐

Integrity: Do what you say you will do.

1	2	3	4	5	6	7	8	9	10
☐	☐	☐	☐	☐	☐	☐	☐	☐	☐

Honor: Do actions that enhance, not shame the reputation of self or the organization.

1	2	3	4	5	6	7	8	9	10
☐	☐	☐	☐	☐	☐	☐	☐	☐	☐

Commitment: Keep your word and promises

1	2	3	4	5	6	7	8	9	10
☐	☐	☐	☐	☐	☐	☐	☐	☐	☐

Kindness: Treats others as you would want to be treated

1	2	3	4	5	6	7	8	9	10
☐	☐	☐	☐	☐	☐	☐	☐	☐	☐

Humility: Modest, lower view of one's importance

1	2	3	4	5	6	7	8	9	10
☐	☐	☐	☐	☐	☐	☐	☐	☐	☐

Just: Treats others impartially based on abilities and contributions.

1	2	3	4	5	6	7	8	9	10
☐	☐	☐	☐	☐	☐	☐	☐	☐	☐

Generous: Shares credit, money, profits and time.

1	2	3	4	5	6	7	8	9	10
☐	☐	☐	☐	☐	☐	☐	☐	☐	☐

Patience: Accepts delays and trouble without getting upset

1	2	3	4	5	6	7	8	9	10
☐	☐	☐	☐	☐	☐	☐	☐	☐	☐

As you can tell, it takes very high scores for these to be considered strengths. Weaknesses in your moral character are like a speck of debris on a glass of drinking water, where just a small piece of dried residue fizzing up is enough to taint the entire glass of water and make it nasty to drink. Whether you have some lower scores to improve dramatically, or some areas where a small improvement can make a big difference, in either case there are huge benefits to you if you choose to improve your moral character strengths. Not only will you find your own true north and improve your real self-esteem by becoming the person you were meant to be, but also your performance character strengths will be more enduring, as performance and wealth gained without character are only temporary. You will also lead a happier, stress-free life by shedding the burdens of moral character flaws.

We just got really deep into the components of character! This should have really got you thinking! As someone striving to be an A Player, these concepts are vital to your success. They will serve as a critical foundation as we build upon these principles in our next chapter on A Player leadership.

Chapter 14

A PLAYER LEADERSHIP AT ALL LEVELS

"Be the change that you wish to see in the world."
—**Mahatma Gandhi**, Father of the Indian Independence Movement

Theodore Roosevelt, the 26th President of the United States, said, "It is not the critic who counts; not the man who points out how the strong man stumbles, or where the doer of deeds could have done them better. The credit belongs to the man who is actually in the arena, whose face is marred by dust and sweat and blood; who strives valiantly; who errs, who comes short again and again, because there is no effort without error and shortcoming; but who does actually strive to do the deeds; who knows great enthusiasms, the great devotions; who spends himself in a worthy cause; who at the best knows in the end the triumph of high achievement, and who at the worst, if he fails, at least fails while daring greatly, so that his place shall never be with those cold and timid souls who neither know victory nor defeat."

The above referenced quote uttered by one of the greatest leaders of all time should demonstrate to you that leadership is not based on title, or accolades, or even responsibilities. Leadership is about doing. In fact, a little talked about truism is that you don't actually need to have a formal position or title to be a leader. This is called *leading at all levels*. A Players innately understand this, and assume leadership roles naturally and effortlessly in all situations.

But that doesn't mean they always jump to the front of the line by standing up and asking that the formal title of leader be bestowed upon them before they start leading. Often, A Players demonstrate leadership by actually being a follower, especially when the situation dictates this as the appropriate approach. One such example is when a leader supports a team member and follows his lead in order to develop that person's leadership ability. Often, we just need to support and validate a good idea that comes from a teammate so that idea gets supported and gets the chance to develop. Being a leader is not always having to be right or get our own way. It's really about encouraging and channeling collaboration so the best ideas get the chance to shine and succeed. Many times, the most junior person in a room actually shows the most leadership due to making hands-on actions to the situation at task.

Make no doubt about it, any group of people or team can immediately sense who the real leaders in the group are. The oft quoted phrase "leadership abhors a vacuum" rings true. Whether you have a formal leadership title or not, you lead with the following characteristics: vision, action, results, alignment, clarity, credibility, congruence, character, challenge, and supporting your teammates.

A Player Tip: The 5 Cs of Leadership

I have developed the 5 Cs of Leadership to help leaders boil down the critical elements of leadership in an easy-to-understand action model:

Clarity: What is the vision? What is the goal? Do we have a clear sense of the strategies needed to get us there?

Credibility: Am I credible as a leader? Have I produced the results so others trust my ability to lead in this area? What actions can I take to improve my credibility?

Congruence: Do I walk the talk? Others will not follow me if I don't follow my own leadership myself. How can I show that my actions are consistent with my own plan?

Character: Is my character sufficient enough that people would follow me even without formal authority? Do I have integrity? Do I do what I say I am going to do? Do I maintain commitments?

Challenge: Am I challenging the status quo? What does a better future look like? Am I challenging myself? How effective am I at challenging my teammates?

As stated above, great leaders are often great followers because they align with organizational objectives and support others in making them happen. To give you a clear picture of this dynamic, think about a time when a colleague who did not report to you in your organization provided excellent support to you to help achieve your initiative. Remember the feelings of gratitude, respect, and admiration you had for that person? That is the leader by follower dynamic we are talking about. This powerful form of leadership is also known as *servant leadership*. Servant leadership is most correctly defined as helping others develop and become their best selves.

Then why is leadership apparently so desperately lacking in so many organizations? I think it is because despite the thousands of leadership books written, the concepts of leadership at all levels and servant leading that we just introduced are widely misunderstood. The 2014 Global Human Capital Trends survey published by the Deloitte University Press cites that "leadership remains the No. 1 talent issue facing organizations around the world," with 86% of respondents to the survey rating it as "urgent" or "important." However, only 13% of respondents in the survey say they do an excellent job of developing leaders at all levels. This means that this area has the largest "readiness gap" in organizations.

The notion of *Leadership at All Levels* is very real, but as I just said, also a very misunderstood and rare element of the overall concept of leadership. A Players understand it and flourish in this regard.

The definition of leadership itself is often obscured. I had the opportunity to be a founding member of leadership expert and best-selling leadership author Dr. John C. Maxwell's Leadership Team. As part of the program, John hosted a reception at his house. During the tour of his library, I asked John what he considered to be his top resources on leadership. He pointed to a special nook right next to the computer where he authors his books, and prominently shelved among six or so titles was *The Leadership Challenge* by James M. Kouzes and Barry Z. Posner. *The Leadership Challenge* is widely considered to be the foremost resource on leadership in the world, and also happens to be my favorite book on developing leadership acumen.

There are three foundational principles from *The Leadership Challenge* that are fundamental to the definition of leadership and to the A Player's leadership skillset. The first revolves around being a leader at all levels:

> Leadership is not about organizational power or authority. It's not about celebrity or wealth. It's not about the family you are born into. It's not about being a CEO, president, general, or prime minister. And it's definitely not about being a hero. Leadership is about relationships, about credibility, and about what you do.

Notice Kouzes' and Posner's emphasis on not needing a title or formal power to be a leader. Remember, leaders are born or developed; they are not crowned. The other key point in their definition is on "what you do." Leadership is about doing. As my telephone greeting states, "talk is cheap, results are priceless."

The second theme is based on the notion that leadership is a 24/7 business, never knowing exactly when you will be called on. Aligned to this, great leaders must always consider their motivation. Are you leading for yourself or for others? Here are some thoughts from leaders interviewed in *The Leadership Challenge*:

> What makes the difference between being a leader or not is how you respond in the moment.
>
> Sometimes we imagine leadership to be something majestic—about grand visions, about world-changing initiatives, about transforming the lives of millions. While all are noble possibilities, real leadership is in the daily moments.

Then it occurred to me—I was thinking selfishly. What I envisioned was instant gratification, recognition for my skills and talent…[instead] I found that every day I had an opportunity to make a small difference. I could have coached somebody better, I could have listened better, I could have been more positive towards people.

Those quotes point directly to the notion of servant leadership. It's not about the grandiose office, nor the title, nor the perks. It is about quietly leading in the day-to-day situations and aligning and supporting your teammates, so they achieve their goals and become the best they can be.

The Leadership Challenge also contains a third profound definition of leadership. I will paraphrase it as follows:

Creating an environment in which people provide their best and most heartfelt effort to turn challenging opportunities into remarkable successes.

The key aspect here is that life is filled with challenges, and it is the leader's responsibility to make a better situation out of every challenge. In the study of human history, it is interesting how many of the most famous leaders were actually forged out of times of war, strife, and turmoil. Believe it or not, I often hear people use the excuse for not having the opportunity to be a great leader as being that they did not have the *opportunity* to face a crisis or personal adversity themselves!

The fact is that leadership is all about taking the initiative in the face of a tremendous challenge. It does not mean you are excused from taking a leadership initiative just because you may not have had to overcome a particularly dire personal obstacle like a disease, disability, war, or company turnaround. Often, the test of true leadership is in challenging the status quo. Often challenging or changing the status quo is amazingly difficult. Look for your opportunities here:

Where can you make something better, despite how good it may already be? The two areas to look for are:

1. Where an area is good and comfortable.
2. Where a situation has been bad for so long, it becomes tolerated.

The less popular the stance the more determination and effort required. A Players have an obligation as leaders to improve the current scenario, especially when it is an unacceptable one. As Kouzes and Posner point out, the work of leaders is change!

Here is the summary of how A, B and C Players affect making things better:

Instant A Player Assessment: Leadership—Making Things Better

A Player	B Player	C Player
A Vision for a Better Future	No Vision/Status Quo	Complacency

Boiling it down, leadership is not about ourselves, but in making those around us better. That singular notion is truly what servant leadership is all about.

Instant A Player Assessment: Servant Leadership

A Player	B Player	C Player
Focus on Other's Goals	Focus on Own Goals	"Me" Focus

Let's pause a moment to point out a critical nuance in servant leadership. An oft-misunderstood concept about servant leadership is that it is about *making things better for others*. A much more powerful tenet of servant leadership is *making others better*.

My definition of servant leadership is: **Servant leadership is not about making others' lives more comfortable; it is about making them better**. Let me share with you a couple of examples to illustrate this important and powerful distinction.

When you think about servant leadership, the immediate notion is about serving others. The critical variable is in *how* this serving is being done. Conventional wisdom is that the organization exists to serve the members of the organization. This is actually not the case. The organization actually exists to serve the noble purpose of the organization. Since I am a Boy Scout leader, let me use the Boy Scouts of America as an example. The noble purpose of the Boy Scouts of America is to prepare young people to make ethical and moral choices over their lifetimes by instilling in them the values of the Scout Oath and Law. One thing that people not directly affiliated with the Boy Scouts may not realize is that the troops should actually be boy led. This means that as leaders we need to step back and actually empower the scouts to make the decisions and execute their campouts and activities. Sometimes this means letting them fail and experience temporary periods of discomfort if they forgot to pack a needed piece of gear, or their food for a trip.

We often hear that failure is good, but try explaining that to an overprotective Cub Scout parent whose boy is cold and hungry because he was not responsible enough to pay attention when the patrol leader, who is a boy himself, went over the packing list and instructed them to pack a winter coat and snack. You see, what scouting fundamentally teaches the boys is how to be responsible. If we had served the boy in the conventional sense, we would have given him a coat and given him food. Instead, we instruct the boy to find their patrol leader or senior patrol leader. These patrol leaders are boys who are trained to serve by helping these younger scouts solve their own problems. Instead of always being *dependent* on the adults, these boys learn to be *resourceful* (which is an overriding A Player trait). Instead of getting a coat and food handed to him, the patrol leader challenges the boy to use his resources to solve his own problem.

The result? The boy finds that he did pack a thermal top and a fleece, and layers it with another boy's rain poncho to create an improvised coat. Instead of giving him the proverbial fish, the patrol leader teaches him how to fish by supervising him opening the patrol box, lighting the camp stove and preparing not only his own meal, but also the meal for the other scouts in his patrol as well. So the moral of servant leadership in this example is that as servant leaders, we did not make things better for that young scout, but instead we did something much more powerful. We made that scout *better*. We actually served just by facilitating the process through our leadership mentoring and allowing the events to happen through logistics and by volunteering our time. We set the parameters and boundaries so to speak, and the boys do the rest. Trust me, that scout will pay better attention next time and will not forget his coat on the next campout. Even better, if the coat he brings next time gets soaked by the rain, he will be resourceful enough to improve his situation on his own.

In business organizations we often see a similar dynamic with team members. They often don't take the initiative to figure it out themselves. If you get frustrated with them as a leader, nothing positive happens. The key as a servant leader is not to give him or her that fish, but teach them to fish, and then furthermore challenge them to become better fisherman and to fish more often. The important skills here as an A Player servant leader are inspiration, coaching, clarity, and challenge.

Where in your organization can you serve others by making them better?

As a servant leader it is important to make this distinction to the people that you serve. This happens in charity all the time. In his book *Toxic Charity,* author Robert Lupton, a forty-year veteran of urban ministries cautions:

That the people "we serve," are not to be viewed as "the people we serve"—but as partners, collaborators, leaders in their own communities. In other words, "they" have to be the solution. We are just helping in some way to help them be/become their own solution…

Likewise, in a company setting, make sure that your teammates are aligned around the organization's noble purpose and not their own selfish agenda of being served themselves. Be on the lookout, as many team members have this entitlement mentality. They lose focus on why they are at the organization. Many think they are there for a paycheck or for their own gratification. If your servant model is to do it for them, they become dependent on you and in the process disempower themselves. Your job is to serve your team by equipping them so that they develop into the best version of themselves and become more empowered and less dependent on you.

There is one final tenant of servant leadership that needs to be reinforced. And that is *"Anyone who wants to be first must be the very last, and the servant of all[29]."* This is literally leadership wisdom of biblical proportions! What this means is that those of us who want to become leaders must do it with the purest motives. We must want to lead because we want to serve, not because we want to be leaders. The Marine Corps has a saying "leaders eat last." You literally need to put your team's needs before your own. If you are leading because you want the power, prestige, and glory, you better rethink your motives, as you are likely thinking about yourself and not others. The best leaders want to lead because they believe they are the most capable of doing the job and achieving the team's result.

Leading Without A Title

Servant leadership is just one step in the staircase. And now that we have a fundamental understanding of servant leadership, let's further explore the notion of leading at all levels. A Players embrace the *Lead Without Title*, or LWT philosophy, explained in Robin Sharma's #1 bestselling book *The Leader Who Had No Title*. LWT is akin to Leaders at All Levels. Robin's book should be mandatory reading for both the current and aspiring A Player. B and C Players often lament they do not have any power or authority in the organization. In my extensive work with organizations, I find that nothing is farther from the truth. B and C Players often use the lack of title as a convenient excuse for not taking on leadership responsibilities for their organization's success. However, as Robin points out, the best organizations are filled with very high percentages of A Players, and for an organization to excel, every employee should see themselves as a member of the leadership team. Hence, Leaders at All Levels.

Leaders at All Levels is a very real, but unfortunately very rare phenomena. In Leaders at All Levels, it is no longer an excuse to say you don't have power because you don't have a high rank or title. Everyone needs to show leadership in the LWT model. Everyone needs to drive innovation. Everyone needs to inspire others. Everyone needs to embrace change. Everyone needs to take responsibility for results. Everyone needs to be positive. Everyone needs to be devoted to

29 Mark 9:35 New International Version

reaching his or her absolute best.[30] As we will cover in more detail in *Chapter 16*, A Players, also known as Leaders at All Levels, have huge numerators of ownership, accountability, and responsibility. These are what I call "above-the-line" behaviors.

A Players do not lament the situations they find themselves in. They leave that for their B or C Player counterparts. Rather, A Players instead utilize what many consider to be the highest form of all human abilities, which is the ability to choose how we respond to the environment in which we find ourselves. When we chose to respond with above-the-line behaviors of ownership, accountability, and responsibility, we develop solutions. When we chose to respond with below-the-line thoughts of blame, excuse, and denial, we get nowhere. How do you typically choose to respond? Where B and C Players find problems, A Players develop solutions. When confronted with challenging situations, below is a summary of how A, B and C Players respond to leadership opportunities at all levels:

Instant A Player Assessment: Leadership at all Levels

A Player	B Player	C Player
Brings Solutions	Brings Problems	Brings Chaos

Let's conclude this chapter on leadership with a different perspective on how A Players help improve leadership. Much is discussed about the need for better leadership in organizations. I was on a recent conference call with the aforementioned Jim Kouzes and he quoted a client who said, "Good people deserve good leadership." While this is certainly true, the flipside is rarely considered. That is, don't great leaders deserve great people? In fact, the quickest way I have found to increase a leader's leadership acumen is to upgrade the people around them. Why? It's simply easier to lead better people!

Not all teams are created equal. I have seen plenty of capable leaders being frustrated by team members who either really didn't buy into the organization's mission, didn't want to be on the team, or felt an entitlement mentality and did not want to contribute. In fairness, I have also seen some teams of good

---

30   Directly adapted for *The Leader who Had No Title* by Robin Sharma

people stymied by poor leaders. This is why it is so critical to understand the concept of leadership at all levels, so we can identify it. We need to be very surgical in understanding where deficiencies in leadership exist. Is the problem with the leadership of the leader or the team members? Now back to upgrading these teams.

There are two very apparent and crucial benefits to upgrading team-members. First, the need for low-end leadership "skills" [sic] like babysitting and micromanagement are immediately eliminated. Second, and even more exciting, is that the responsibility of leading better people naturally raises our leadership game, as we are able to work on more strategic issues. This is in part because these better employees intrinsically require better leadership. It's akin to performance cars requiring premium gasoline and careful maintenance. We must be more strategic in our interactions with A Player employees to challenge and help them to develop as both people and future leaders. In short, A Players simply inspire us to be better leaders due to our responsibility to grow and cultivate leadership. If you think about it, just as we take better care of a luxury performance car vs. a mainstream car, leaders take the best care of their best people. They are the ones that deserve the extra care and attention.

The sports world shows us an excellent illustration for the benefits talented teams provide. In most cases, legendary coaches were successful because they attracted better talent. In fact, many of the famous teams resembled All-Star teams in terms of the great players on their rosters. They were attracted to the better leadership of the coach, and in turn they won, and more great players wanted to join the team creating a virtuous cycle. The lesson here is that the best leaders are also the best recruiters and coaches of talent.

A Players must have A Teams. Dr. Brad Smart is one of the pioneers in the field of A Players. He developed the Topgrading® interviewing methodology. One of Brad's contributions to the field of A Players has been the leadership rule that: you cannot be an A Player yourself if you have Bs and Cs reporting to you. In his groundbreaking book *Topgrading*, Brad outlines this concept in detail. In my work with countless organizations, this notion drives excellent leadership improvement as we conduct talent reviews, and helps to deliver a reality check when assessing the A, B and C Players in each leader's division.

For leaders to be A Players themselves, they will need to have 100% A Player talent in their own organizations. As I explain to leaders, if you look at an organization whose leader has Bs and Cs reporting to them, then the math just does not add up to A Player performance. This is strong medicine to be sure, but as you consider it, it makes no sense that a true A Player leader can harbor and protect Bs and Cs on their team and expect to be called an A Player themselves.

Visually, this looks like:

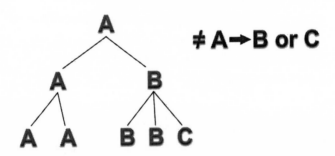

"A" Leaders Must Have "A" Teams

The remedy and action step is to coach the Bs and Cs up to full A Player level, or replace them with true A Players. This is what I call the "Reform or Replace" strategy.

Leadership is such a critical element to both organizations and A Players that I hope I imparted some valuable leadership insights that you can apply as an A Player leader regardless of your level in the organization. Let's summarize what we learned:

Leadership starts with us. As the famous Mahatma Gandhi quote at the beginning of the chapter indicates, we have to be the change we wish to see in others. Instead of complaining about others' lack of leadership, A Players model the type of leadership needed. As we saw at the start of the chapter, sometimes being a great leader means we become a great follower and take a more supporting role and help another's great idea take flight.

You don't need a formal title to be a leader. As an A Player, you have the great attributes of a positive attitude and a solution mindset to make great things happen. This is all about empowering yourself to make it happen. Your organization is begging for you to step up and make improvements a reality. Which ones can you progress in the coming month?

Then we covered the often misunderstood, but tremendously powerful concept of servant leadership. As servant leaders we need to understand who we serve. Ultimately we serve the beneficiary of the organization's noble purpose. Remember, to be first we must be last, but in the process you don't need to do it for your teammates, but instead equip them so they can do it themselves. Your goal of the servant leader is actually to make them better, not necessarily make it better for them.

Next, examine who is on your team. An easy way to think of this is that you cannot be an A Player leader if you have Bs and Cs on the team. The math just doesn't add up. How are you going to upgrade your team to an All-Star team of A Players? Which Bs and Cs are going to make the journey all the way to A? Who do you need to be recruiting to enhance the talent level on your team?

This fortification of A Player leadership principles will be essential as we tackle the topic of teamwork in the next chapter. A Players use their great leadership qualities to be great team members, despite whatever their role may be on the team.

Chapter 15

A PLAYERS ARE
TEAM PLAYERS

"The way a team plays as a whole determines its success. You may have the greatest bunch of individual stars in the world, but if they don't play together, the club won't be worth a dime."
—**Babe Ruth**, Hall of Fame Major League Baseball Player

On the evening of April 13, 1970, United States astronauts Fred Haise, Jack Swigert, and Jim Lovell were en route to the moon in their Apollo 13 spacecraft. The spacecraft was comprised of two independent vehicles docked by a tunnel: the orbiter Odyssey and lunar lander Aquarius. Already 200,000 miles from Earth, they received word from mission controller Sy Liebergot in Houston that there was a low-pressure warning signal in the Odyssey's cryogenic oxygen tank. Odyssey's pilot Jack Swigert flipped the switch to perform a routine maintenance on the tank and the entire spacecraft shuttered with a bang as the oxygen pressure fell and power disappeared. Swigert informed mission control of this with the famous words: "Houston, we've had a problem[31]."

---

31 The quote you may recognize as "Houston, we have a problem", was actually Hollywood taking a little creative license for the movie *Apollo 13*.

The NASA team at mission control in Houston immediately partnered with the three astronauts to develop solutions. There was a strong possibility the spacecraft and its crew was doomed. The big issue was conserving enough oxygen, water, and power to survive long enough to navigate the spacecraft around the moon in a slingshot trajectory to provide the opportunity to attempt a re-entry to the earth's atmosphere. With the Odyssey command module damaged, this poised a major problem.

To save precious energy, this command module needed to be shut down cold. Instead of panicking, Haise, Swigert and Lovell teamed up and divided the multitude of tasks needed to survive. They had to accomplish these tasks in a fraction of the time in which they had trained. Time was of the essence. Gene Krantz, the flight director at mission control in Houston, platooned his engineers off their regular rotations to work around the clock in order to calculate the precise slingshot return path of the spacecraft around the moon and back to earth. Another team planned how to conserve the much needed water, oxygen and power. And yet another team came up with the brilliant solution of having the crew live in the undamaged Aquarius lunar lander module as a makeshift "life raft" right up until re-entry, when they would then transfer back to the Odyssey capsule. Only the command module Odyssey was designed for re-entry due to its heat shield and conical construction, which could withstand the 5,000 degree Fahrenheit temperatures and extreme pressures caused by the Earth's atmosphere.

The ground controllers in Houston faced a nearly impossible task. Because the makeshift spacecraft was not being used as intended, completely new procedures had to be developed and tested in the simulator before being beamed up to the astronauts. In fact, the flight controllers redeveloped the critical procedures to restart the cold Odyssey command module in only three days, versus the three months taken to write the original protocol. Precise and precious pulses of power from thrusters not intended for that purpose were needed to set the course back to Earth. Any mistakes would prove fatal.

The astronauts pulsed the spacecraft with a critical "burn" to set the course back to Earth, and then they shut down power and endured freezing temperatures and skipped meals. Due to the cold temperatures, some food became inedible.

Despite the utter fatigue of working around the clock, both the Apollo astronauts and the mission control team stayed in constant communication. Transcripts of these communications showed that even with the dire circumstances, communications stayed fact based, calm, cool, and collected. Four days later at 17:53:45 GMT on April 17th, with the condition of the Odyssey capsule's heat shield uncertain from the oxygen tank explosion, Apollo 13 made the critical re-entry into the Earth's atmosphere and by 18:07:41 the crew had splashed down safely in the Pacific Ocean thanks to this incredible display of teamwork by the entire Apollo 13 team both in the spacecraft and at ground control. This was a pinnacle of leadership and teamwork in action!

As an A Player, hopefully the Apollo 13 team's story of teamwork inspires you to want to partner with your own team to tackle the challenges your organization faces. As we just covered the topic of leadership in *Chapter 14*, it is very fitting that leadership plays a huge role in being a great teammate. You saw it firsthand in the story above. The entire Apollo 13 team, whether the astronauts whose lives were at risk, or the mission control team on the ground in Houston, were 100% aligned and focused on getting those three men safely back to earth. Nothing else mattered to the mission. Team members did whatever it took. They worked tirelessly around the clock developing solutions and performing critical calculations. There is essentially no evidence in the archives of any significant political infighting to taint the mission of saving the astronauts. Sure, some of the discussions were heated, but all were focused on problem solving. This alignment of purpose and outstanding execution with a "failure is not an option" mentality and "do whatever it takes" attitude serves as one of the most successful and famous examples of teamwork ever. How does the teamwork at your organization compare to that of Apollo 13's?

One common and unfair misconception of A Players is that they are lone wolfs and not team players. Nothing can be farther from the truth! In developing this book, best-selling author Mark Sanborn was kind enough to share his thoughts on A Players with me. Mark started off our interview by recalling a quote from the great collegiate coach John Wooden: "A player who makes a team great is much more valuable than a great player." Coach Wooden also stated "The main ingredient of stardom is the rest of the team."

A Players shine the most as great teammates and by helping others around them succeed. Directly from his book *TeamBuilt: Making Teamwork Work*, Mark's advice is to hire ACES (see definition below). I really like how Mark's definition of ACES provides a great framework for how the A Player needs to use servant leadership principles to be a great teammate to his or her team. The acronym ACES stands for:

Attitude:	An intrinsic quality that you can't really teach
Cooperation:	We are interdependent on others for success
Energy:	Talent without effort is latent
Service Orientation:	Subordinating others' needs before our own

Humility plays importantly into ACES and the DNA of the A Player. I have been fortunate to meet some pretty important and famous people over the years. What I have found is that these people are not just successful, but are also extremely humble. Dr. Norman Vincent Peale, the author of *The Power of Positive Thinking*, said, "humble people don't think less of themselves. They just think of themselves less." I've found this to be true of some of the most impressive celebrities I have met over the years. Some years ago my flight was cancelled after attending the NCAA Final Four Basketball Championship in St. Louis. Upon my return to the airport, the Hall of Fame college basketball announcer Dick Vitale approached me in the hotel lobby to make sure I had a place to stay and that everything was alright. I'll always remember this famous man's concern for my well-being. As busy as he was, he found time to check in on me. Dick is always the center of attention at every Final Four in which he has participated. The fact that he was concerned about my well-being speaks volumes about his character. This goes to show the greatest always display this servant leadership mindset that is inherent in any true A Player.

A Players don't showboat, claim credit for other's accomplishments, or overstate their contribution to a project. As David DeWolf states on his website, *Humble Confidence:* "The best leaders and employees typically give credit to others." He adds: "These types of individuals are the true all-stars in your organization. They probably have plenty of great successes themselves, but you won't hear about it from them. Each of us must make the effort to contribute to the best of our ability according to our individual talents. And then we put all the individual talents together for the highest good of the group... Understanding that the good of the group comes first is fundamental to being a highly productive member of a team."

In working with organizations, I find that it is usually the B and C Players who tout their accomplishments. The underlying reason is they crave the attention and accolades because they lack the intrinsic results and self-esteem. Look at the true greats in any field. With few exceptions, you will find that most of those professionals are very humble about their accomplishments. A Players let actions and results speak louder than words. In an organization working to transform itself into a team of 100% A Players, I ironically find it is the B and C Players who are campaigning that they are As. A true A Player has no need to do this. I am amazed by how many people in their daily work life exclaim, "I'm so smart" or "I'm so good." Unfortunately they end up woefully short. I recently taught a group of project managers and a C Player in the audience said, "well I think I'm an A Player." I told her what she thought of herself really didn't carry a lot of credibility. I suggested she ask her manager and teammates what they felt. She apparently did not like my answer as she scowled and skipped out of some key exercises over the course of that day. If you feel the need to self-promote, you are not an A Player.

In contrast, A Players let their results and actions speak for themselves. If for some reason you think you are being underappreciated, just schedule to conduct a presentation and share your good work with your manager or department. I'm sure others will find value in the good work you do, and they can leverage your value to help their own department. Just to be sure to focus on how the work can help the team, and not focus solely on yourself. Kip Tindell, CEO of the The Container Store, who is a very humble leader, uses the term "leadership equals communication," which emphasizes that communicating wins and valuable information is always appreciated.

This focus on humility reminds me of two terms that I have used for years, but had almost taken for granted. These terms are: "showdog" and "workdog." I was recently teaching a workshop on how to be an A Player and one of the participants asked me about flashy coworkers who were very effective at schmoozing leaders and always got the credit. That would be a "showdog." This participant was in a technical field and went on to describe how she works tirelessly, and correctly identified herself as a "workdog." I had not used these terms in years and was amused by how they gravitated to the concept and how productive the discussion was with that group talking about these two different types of employees.

Which one would your teammates consider you to be? I will say that real work does beat show any day, so I consider "workdogs" to typically be the real A Players. What I did advise this group on was how they could learn from the "showdogs." What they can learn from them is how they can improve their interpersonal and emotional intelligence skills to connect better with others. They all agreed this would be a great way to improve their leadership acumen with their managers and teammates in addition to the intrinsic results they produced as "workdogs."

Instant A Player Assessment: Teamwork

A Player	B Player	C Player
Focus on the Team	Focus on Themselves	Self-Promoting

Aligned with this notion about being a "workdog" is David DeWolf's conclusion that: "Your true A-players are more than happy to share the spotlight. For them, it's about the success of the team, of the whole unit, of the entire company. It's not about themselves." Well said, David! These are the individuals you want on your team! The first day on my job at the Ford Motor Company my manager gave me some excellent advice, which still guides my approach to being a good teammate. He said, "be the person everyone wants on their team." I have found over the years that this advice has served me very well, and I highly recommend it to you as an A Player.

Unfortunately, despite this, A Players are often maligned for not being team players because they call self-serving B and C Players out for not contributing their fair share. In weaker organizations, this is considered impolite and not representative of team play. However, championship teams and organizations consider this true leadership, as A Players are willing to accept the responsibility of being unpopular and still hold underperforming team members accountable for better results. This happens in sports all the time when an Aaron Rogers or LeBron James holds his teammates accountable to performance. The result is worth the price they pay, as the entire team benefits from accountability and beating goals. Everyone acts as a professional by not taking the constructive criticism personally. The most skilled A Players hold others accountable through an amazing amount of love, skillful communication, resolve and tact. You can recognize these transformational individuals because you feel like you are really letting them down if you don't carry your weight and don't deliver.

In his the best-selling book *The Five Dysfunctions of a Team*, Patrick Lencioni calls this concept "healthy conflict." Too many organizations get stalled because they won't address the elephant in the room. The key is to attack process, not people. Healthy conflict is also about respecting other people and their opinions in order to find true north on a solution. You can't argue with results, and people will soon get over the discomfort they perceive with healthy conflict when the clarity, communications, and results improve. I really like how Gino Wickman expands on this culture of accountability in his book *Traction*:

> Most leaders know that bringing discipline and accountability in the organization will make people a little uncomfortable...What usually holds an organization back is the fear of creating this discomfort.
>
> As with all steps along the way, this one requires a total commitment from the leadership team. There will be far too many opportunities to pull back and retreat. If your leadership can stay the course, however, within months your people will appreciate the increased accountability, improved communication and solid results. The discomfort you were concerned about turns out to be not nearly as bad as you thought. And truth be told, the people who continue to resist are either the wrong people or in the wrong seat.

If you are an A Player who is truly pulling your own weight, it is appropriate to build accountability systems in your organization to hold others accountable. I find that a weekly report-out, where all team members audibly report their progress on their goals in a group setting, is the best way to achieve the type of accountability described above. Business expert Verne Harnish is also a big advocate of team-based reporting meetings: "in one-on-ones there's no Greek chorus singing out when the untruths begin to fly" as a lot of private negotiating is going on as people will offer up excuses that they would never serve up in a group setting for fear of embarrassment.[32] In contrast, with the entire team reporting results together, natural peer pressure increases the rate of deliverables. B and C Players like to hide from being accountable to a team, but true A Players relish accountability and show true leadership by walking the talk, delivering performance, and demanding that their teammates do the same.

If you think about it, the best team performance happens when a team is 100% aligned on the achievement of a goal or objective. That was clear in the exemplary teamwork that occurred in the famous Apollo 13 team at the beginning of this chapter. How aligned is the team you are on in achieving its objectives? If you are not aligned, how can you get better?

Immediately beneath alignment on goals is agreeing on the strategies taken to achieve the goal. Since opinions can vary greatly, this is an area ripe for discourse within teams. The key here is for the A Player to remain fact based. Teammates can take their positions very personally; so remember to focus your discussions on process, not people. I once had a teammate who had a large facsimile dollar bill in his office that said, "In God we trust, all others bring facts and data." This is a poignant reminder of the importance of bringing facts and data into a team decision. I have found that nothing cools down a heated debate like bringing in the facts. Your team will recognize your A Player leadership for this.

One misconception about teams is that all seats at the table have the same vote. This is not true. The opinions of those that have better results carry far more weight. As an A Player, make sure you enter the team meeting with all of your commitments and assignments completed. This is called congruency. A Players report out with numbers, while B and C Players try to tap dance with a story. If you hear a B or C Player start their report out with "Well…", then you know you are in trouble! Politely keep the meeting on track by asking what his or her results were in terms of numbers and timing. Also, teams need to keep in

---

32   In a Greek chorus, the company of performers sings out answers in unison.

check the comments from people without a vested stake in either the funding, execution, or outcome of an action. Those who have "skin in the game" get a bigger say in the decision.

If you reflect about it, you joined a team to be part of something bigger than yourself. To be candid, for years I would hear statements similar to this, about "people wanting to be part of something bigger than them," and they always sounded very cliché to me. The person saying that would never explain why. I have a very practical mind and hearing that carte blanche was never enough. And then one day it sunk in. In a discussion with an executive I asked her why she was at a company. She responded: "I couldn't do what I do by myself. I couldn't achieve these results without the support and resources of the organization." The light bulbs went on in my head. Of course that was it! The reason we are on any team is that the team enables us to do things we could not do by ourselves. There are two levels to this of course, the practical side as well as the emotional side. The practical side of teams is that they allow us to play on a bigger stage than we can by ourselves. Let's face it; in many cases we could not make as much income on our own as we can as part of a team. The team brings support and resources we cannot muster on our own. Remember this when we start to get full of ourselves. The emotional side is that we are all social beings. We intrinsically need to be a part of a team as part of our human needs. Winning feels best when we have someone to share the process with, and teams fulfill this role.

Speaking of winning, I'd like to conclude this chapter with a story about a team that pulled together. This team was undergoing a transformation to a team of 100% A Players. They were en route to a record year, but as part of this transformation, they lost both a B Player and a C Player during a critical period right before the end of the year. A couple of the team members were bummed they had lost people and the workload would increase, but another team member correctly pointed out that since they had not lost any A Players, they had really not lost anything at all. The team was in a very seasonal construction-based business, so they discussed that replacing these two positions at that point in the season would add costly headcount that would not be productive due to the training ramp-up and seasonal slowdown.

As team members, they knew this was not in the best interest of the business. The team literally looked at one another and one of the junior members of the team suggested a plan where each of the team members picked up a piece of the departed member's responsibilities for a brief two-month period. The team quickly agreed that they could all handle additional workload for a limited amount of time and that it would be the best for the business. The leader appreciated their willingness and created a bonus structure for the extra hours they would put in, which would be funded from the open salaries of the two departed employees. As the result of *the leaders at all levels* plan, the team hit their goal during this critical two month period. In fact, despite the extra work, they were very happy because they were all pulling in the same direction, partnering on projects, and growing in their capabilities. In addition, the teammate who had proposed this plan thrived in his elevated responsibilities and ended up getting promoted based on his ability to contribute. The team felt a tremendous sense of accomplishment for beating their goals with a shorthanded group, and they all learned new skills from having to step up and fill in the gaps. Finally, the team culture was further improved with the departure of the B and C Players. There is nothing quite like the feeling of winning with great teammates!

We will learn more about this winning mindset of ownership, accountability, and responsibility in the next chapter.

Chapter 16

THE "A" IN *A* PLAYER
IS FOR ACCOUNTABILITY

"The ancient Romans had a tradition: whenever one of their engineers constructed an arch, as the capstone was hoisted into place, the engineer assumed accountability for his work in the most profound way possible: he stood under the arch."

—**Michael Armstrong**, Former Chairman and CEO of AT&T

*A*s I continuously study teams and individual employee performance, I am amazed by the truism that perhaps the greatest part of successful performance hinges on personal accountability. Inevitably, almost every resounding success and every tragic failure comes down to whether an individual took personal responsibility and accountability for his or her actions.

In fact, perhaps no other single attribute defines the A Player like accountability.

Thus, the "A" in *A* Player very well stands for Accountability.

Instant A Player Assessment: Accountability

A Player	B Player	C Player
Accountability and Results	Selective Accountability	Excuses

Let's take a look at accountability in more detail:

Several years ago, when I became a professional executive business coach, one of the first success tenets that I learned was called the Line of Choice[33]. This concept is also known as "Above or Below the Line." This idea has proven to be so powerful that I have a firsthand experience of seeing it transform organizations for the better. It is actually even a guiding principle within my own family, which helps us to stay accountable to one another.

As my clients and I can personally attest, the line of accountability is extremely thin and can be the difference between resounding success or complete mediocrity. Since I learned of this concept there has not been a day that is gone by when I don't challenge my thinking and actions against this powerful model. Here's how it works:

First, start by drawing a horizontal line. This is called the Line of Choice. From the time we are born, every human being needs to realize that we make choices in our lives and we need to be responsible for those choices.

The Line of Choice

Ownership
Accountability
Responsibility

Blame
Excuses
Denial

---

33   A lot of people would like to claim credit for this concept. However, after extensive research, the exact origins and original author of the Line of Choice remain unclear. Apparently the concept dates back to at least the 1980s and is widely used by executive coaches and self-development experts.

This line illustrates that we make all of the choices in our lives. Think about that for a moment. We chose how well we did in elementary school, what we studied in college, whom we dated, how much money we invest, and how we spend our time, etc. As you consider this, it's actually a pretty sobering responsibility we have for our own personal decisions! When a situation or opportunity emerges, we always have a choice on how we respond to that challenge. When it comes down to our choice of response, we have complete freedom.

Now write the acronym BED vertically below the Line of Choice. This is where the mnemonic phrase of getting out of BED will come in.

B is for Blame

The B is for Blame (this is where you start filling out the acronym!). When a situation, challenge, or opportunity occurs, do you find yourself blaming someone or something for that outcome? If so, you are wasting valuable energy when you should be taking action. To illustrate this point, during the depths of the Great Recession of 2007 to 2010, how well did blaming the economy for your business or career advancement woes work? Not so well, right? A Players condition their minds not to blame others or events for their circumstances. They simply look for solutions.

E is for Excuses

The E is for Excuses. Think of when we don't achieve our sales, production, or profit goals and we craft an elaborate reason why we did not hit our targets. Or we make excuses for perpetually being late. Reasons are just the politically correct term for excuses. Excuses get us nowhere. Start to listen for them and shut them down to get an immediate improvement in results. Again, A Players continually work to purge excuses from our lives. This is just like exercise. We get better at it with daily discipline and practice.

D is for Denial

The last Below-the-Line condition is D for Denial. Denial is where we ignore the true condition of a situation. With business professionals, I most commonly see denial manifest itself in terms of someone claiming to have business skills or results that they do not really possess. They cannot progress until they come to grips with the fact they do not have these skills or results and need to get better. A Players are realistic with their current skills and abilities, and recognize that there is always room for improvement. Because they are successful, they actually celebrate when they uncover a developmental opportunity because this allows them to take their game to a new level.

The other denial situation I frequently see is when people ignore or deny the existence of an upcoming or existing problem. Many employees are in denial regarding business conditions. For example, I've also had countless sales executives claim they were doing everything to hit their sales goals, but they still were falling short. We quickly rectified the sales situation and got back to hitting goals once we confronted denial and addressed the real issues to the problem. A Players don't ignore problems, but instead address them head-on before they grow in magnitude. Remember, confronting the truth early on is always far less painful than handling a problem that has exploded out of control later on.

Collectively, Blame, Excuses and Denial represent Below-the-Line responses to situations, even tough ones. Sometimes we are dealt a really bad hand. Whether it is fair or not does not matter. This is bitter medicine for many of us to swallow. We are conditioned as a society that it's expected and acceptable to be Below-the-Line. We are taught that it feels good and it is right to blame, make excuses, and be in denial. An oft quoted phrase that drives this point home is that Below-the-Line responses "have never solved a problem, achieved a goal, or improved a relationship." But this doesn't cut it for A Players. The fact of the matter is that Blame, Excuses, and Denial responses get us nowhere in improving the situation. Actually, these behaviors are the silent killers of human achievement.

The reality is we are all human beings, and even as A Players, we spend some time Below-the-Line. The key is to make our journeys there as short as possible. The first step is to recognize when we are down there and ask, "What should I do right now to move towards what I really want? How can I get Above-the-Line?"

Remember, as A Players, we control and have choice in our response to any given situation. Also, as A Players, we spend the least amount of time Below-the-Line compared to B or C Players.

Live Above-the-Line

Above-the-Line is where all of the positive action occurs! This is where A Players spend 99% of their time. This is because only positive responses will get us either out of our bind or towards the goals we aspire to. The acronym for being Above-the-Line is OAR. Think of it as putting your oar in the water to help propel you forward.

O is for Ownership

The O is for Ownership. We have to own up to the reality of the situation. We also need to recognize that we own both the problem and the solution. Shareholders and owners own the business. However, everybody in the organization owns a piece of it, whether it is a department or a role and the results that go with it. Empower yourself with this.

As an A Player, ownership thinking is the absolute highest level of thinking for both your business and personal life. When you think and act like you *own* it, you are working at your absolute most strategic and optimal level. A critical area here is to take ownership of your own mistakes and problems. This is one way to quickly identify a true A Player. Where B and C Players blame, make excuses or deny their mistakes, A Players immediately own up to them and make solutions.

A is for Accountability

A is for Accountability. Accountability is all about keeping score of our results. How well do we (and our teams) declare goals and then hold ourselves accountable for achieving them? Are you and the people on your team accountable enough to report your results on a weekly scorecard? When an organization knows the score and faces the music on achieving them, it takes off! To do this, everyone on the team must embrace the notion and power of accountability. A Players take the leadership role in spreading a culture of accountability throughout the organization.

R is for Responsibility

Finally, R is for Responsibility. Responsibility is all about owning and taking the actions required for the results you want and those required by the organization.

Responsibility can be identified by the action of someone stepping up and stating a plan of action and then following through with the actions. Writing down, declaring, and then executing your plan is an absolute breakthrough in achieving results. A Players taking individual responsibility is infectious for your organization, and is the fastest path to filling your team with other A Players and achieving high performance levels.

Another important outcome of Above-the-Line Behavior is that your personal relationships will improve. How so? Well think about how you interact with people who are Below-the-Line with you. When others serve up Blame, Excuses and Denial to you, it doesn't go over so well with the relationship, does it? If you are like me, I tend to avoid those people in my relationships. Flipping over the coin, we fortify our relationships with others as we live more Above-the-Line with Ownership, Accountability, and Responsibility.

The Line of Choice is thin! However, the results of being Above-the-Line are priceless! Get out your OAR and start reaping the results immediately in both business and your personal life. You'll be glad you did!

As an A Player, you have the leadership responsibility in creating an Above-the-Line culture in your organization.

How A, B and C Players Respond to Accountability:

A Player	B Player	C Player
Accountable	Blame and Borderline	Can't Spell Accountable

Let's face it: we are all human, and A Players occasionally make mistakes.[34] An acid test of A versus B and C Players is how they respond to those mistakes when they are inevitably made. The A Player is apologetic when a goal is missed or mistake is made. A Players publicly take ownership of that same mistake and are usually even harder on themselves than their managers or peers would be. This is in stark contrast with B Players who tend to deflect accountability through denial or C Players who flat out blame others or cower and hide. Look for these behaviors; they are telltale signs of A versus B or C Player behavior.

---

34   It's just that A Players tend to make far fewer mistakes than B or C Players.

Instant A Player Assessment: Accountability when a mistake is made

A Player	B Player	C Player
Acknowledge, Ownership and Results	Denies and Deflects Accountability	Blames and Cowers

One key area of accountability within organizations that usually encounters resistance is the act of holding people accountable for hitting specific numbers and measurable goals. *Traction* author Gino Wickman has a great perspective showing the dynamic of the awesome cultures accountable A Players create:

Accountable people appreciate numbers. Wrong people in the wrong seats usually resist measurement. Right people in the right seats love clarity. Knowing the numbers they need to hit, they enjoy being part of a culture where all are held accountable. It creates an esprit de corps with everyone pitching in to make the company a success because [the] right people want to win.

Instant A Player Assessment: Accountable People Appreciate Numbers

A Player	B Player	C Player
Accountable People Appreciate Numbers	Balks	Cowers

How *A* Players Respond to SMART Goals and Accountability

Having goals that are Specific, Measurable, Achievable, Relevant, and Time-bound is critical to success. Goals that have these attributes are known as SMART. Many business people will claim to know how to construct and execute SMART goals, but few actually do. SMART goals are so important that Appendix 2 of this book provides a comprehensive guide to creating them.

Numerous CEOs and senior leaders were interviewed as part of the research for this book. One of the key takeaways from these interviews with top executives was how appreciative these leaders are of the enthusiasm A Players show for their accountability to achieve SMART goals. What really struck me was how the CEOs and senior leaders gushed with enthusiasm as they spoke about the joy of working with A Player employees and the tremendous accomplishments they generated. They also shared how easy and effortless it is to have results and accountability discussions with A Players. Both leaders and employees are accountable for setting and achieving SMART goals. If you lead others, make sure the goals you give your teammates are always SMART. A Player employees love a challenge and are appreciative of well-thought-out SMART goals. SMART goals lead to SMART execution and SMART results.

Best-selling business author Jim Collins's view on self-motivation and accountability accurately describes the intrinsic motivation that defines the A Player:

The right people will do the right things and deliver the best results of which they are capable, regardless of the incentive system…

The right people don't need to be tightly managed or fired up; they will be self-motivated by an inner drive to produce the best results and to be part of creating something truly great.

This is the exact sentiment the CEOs and senior leaders shared with me. You bring much to an organization as an A Player. This value is both in terms of results and offering support to others to create a super positive work culture. Speaking of culture, I think the perspective The Container Store executive Amy Carovillano has to share about the real driver of a great corporate culture really speaks to the importance of fantastic A Player employees:

Do you want to work here because it is a great place to work, or is it a great place to work because you work here?

Amy makes a profound point here! Most people want to work at a great place to work, but is it a great place to work (and becoming an even better one) because you are an awesome A Player employee, or are you a B or C Player who will dilute a great place to work? Are you a builder or a destroyer? Are you bringing Above-the-Line or Below-the-Line behaviors to work? Don't be the employee other employees need to carry their weight all the time. In fact, in a culture of A Players, freeloaders are not tolerated by the other employees.

Achieving results creates a great culture of accountability. In addition, a culture of accountability and results is also personally rewarding and fun. To capture this dynamic and value, here is the model that I have developed to illustrate the partnership an A Player leader has with an A Player employee on the accountability of delivering SMART goals. This model was inspired by the excellent work on accountability done by Roger Connors and Tom Smith in their best-selling book, *How Did That Happen?*

Notice that this model is radically different from conventional wisdom on management and accountability:

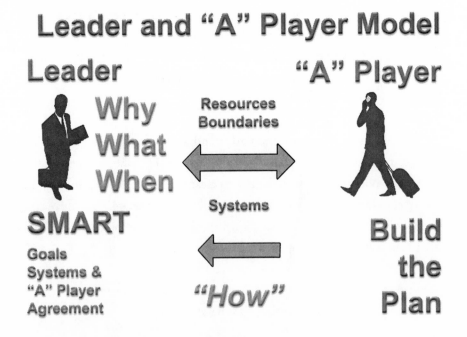

Leader and "A" Player Model

Leader   "A" Player

Why   Resources
       Boundaries
What
When
       Systems
SMART   Build
Goals   the
Systems &   Plan
"A" Player   "How"
Agreement

Here is how this A Player leadership and accountability model works:

1. The A Player leader develops SMART goals for his or her organization.
2. In sharing the SMART goals with his team, the leader shares three critical elements:

a) Why achieving the goal is important;

b) What is the exact deliverable; and

c) *When* is the goal due (time-bound)?

3. The A Player leader is also responsible for creating systems for the A Player employees to follow. This includes the A Player Agreement, which is a job description on steroids that we will cover in detail in *Chapter 19.* These systems enable the organization to get consistent results without the need for the leader to micromanage.

4. Notice what is notably absent from the leaders' briefing is the *How.* We will come back to this in a moment.

5. The A Player employee readily accepts the accountability of achieving the SMART goals and builds the plan to accomplish them. As an A Player, they have acquired the acumen and skills needed to achieve the goals. They are also following the systems created by the leaders of the company to do the job properly. Therefore, the A Player employee generates the specific *How* for a particular situation. There may be several viable ways and alternatives to achieve the *How,* and since the A Player is empowered, they pick the path they want to take to achieve the goals. They enjoy more empowerment, freedom, and creativity. This makes work fun, interesting, and joyful to them.

6. The A Player leader coaches the A Player employee on what *Resources* are available to them and what *Boundaries* they need to stay within while completing the goal.

7. The A Player is then *Responsible* for providing feedback and progress reports back to the A Player leader.

8. Once the A Player masters the company system created by leadership, they will apply their learnings to innovate and improve the system even more. Their enhancements become the basis for the improved and updated system.

Notice that this model of accountability is radically different from conventional wisdom on management and accountability. There are several huge advantages of it over conventional management models.

First, it works better. Every goal is SMART, and creates better results.

Second, it is a much more innovative and creative place to work. In this culture, A Players are constantly making improvements to the organization's systems. Think of it as harnessing all of the brains in the organization much like parallel processing in computing. It is literally like an ongoing Six-Sigma process improvement culture.

And finally, it brings out the best in people and makes work a fun and rewarding place.

Instant A Player Assessment: In Response to a SMART Goal

A Player	B Player	C Player
"I'll build the plan"	"I'll give it a try"	"Just tell me what to do"

Accountability is the fundamental axiom for being an A Player. Becoming a more accountable person and becoming more accountable as an organization are absolutely the fastest paths to more results, more success, and more happiness.

Realize that every area of your life is touched by the Line of Choice. Whether to live above or below that line is the most fundamental choice you make each day of your life. Recognize: it is a constant battle to stay Above-the-Line. It requires continual discipline. Actively purge the Below-the-Line behaviors of Blame, Excuses, and Denial from your thinking. Replace those behaviors with the Above-the-Line behaviors of Ownership, Accountability, and Responsibility. These are learned skills that can absolutely be improved. Remember that living Above-the-Line is the fundamental pathway to success in all areas of your life. We will need this fortification in accountability as we tackle A Player hard work and discipline in the next chapter.

Chapter 17

A PLAYER HARD WORK
AND DISCIPLINE

*"For attaining wisdom and discipline; for understanding words of insight;
for acquiring a disciplined and prudent life, doing what is right and just
and fair; for giving prudence to the simple, knowledge and discretion to the
young, let the wise listen and add to their learning, and let the discerning get
guidance, for understanding proverbs and parables, the sayings and riddles
of the wise. The fear of the Lord is the beginning of knowledge, but fools
despise wisdom and discipline."*
—Proverbs 1:2-7 (NIV)

We live in what sociologists call the "Microwave Society." This is because we want instant gratification all the time. We expect to see exactly what we want and then immediately obtain it! Researchers report the average adult has an attention span of only eight seconds, and that number may be dwindling. We all require constant entertainment or we get bored and impatiently move on. Couples going on dates these days are often entertained by their smartphones and not one another. We live in a culture of entitlement. New employees with only fair performance have the audacity to ask for a raise just three months into a new job. People over-order when eating out and then half of their order gets thrown away. And no self-respecting parent would dare think of firing up the minivan without the decency of first amusing their precocious offspring with the latest video release from Disney. Entitlement is the new norm!

As an A Player talent expert and executive coach, I see this same microwave mindset with employees, particularly those of the millennial generation. People want the nice salaries and the perks, without first putting in the hard work and generating the results. I often say that the current generation entering the workforce is the first one whose parents would simply lower the hoop if they could not reach the rim with the basketball. Not like the old days when we persevered only after days of practice and suffering through finding the ball ricocheting off the bottom of the rim and hitting us smack dab in the face, until one day we got strong enough to find the ball swish through the basket. What a feeling of accomplishment when you made your first bucket the good old-fashioned way! Overcoming failure is great for building character. Sadly, those days seem to be quickly disappearing.

The Basketball Tree in Nantes France. Cute, but does this build character?

Renowned Stanford University psychologist Dr. Carol S. Dweck feels the same way. In fact, in her best-selling book *Mindset* she laments:

Are we going to have a problem finding leaders in the future? You can't pick up a magazine or turn on the radio without hearing about the problem of praise in the workplace. We could have seen it coming.

We've talked about all the well-meaning parents who've tried to boost their children's self-esteem by telling them how smart and talented they are. And we talked about all the negative effects of this praise. Well, these children of praise have now entered the workforce, and sure enough, many can't function without getting a sticker for their every move. Instead of annual bonuses, some companies are giving quarterly or even monthly bonuses.[35] Instead of employee of the month, it's the employee of the day. Companies are calling in consultants to teach them how to lavish rewards on this overpraised generation. We now have a workforce full of people who need constant reassurance and can't take criticism. Not a recipe for success in business, where taking on challenges, showing persistence, and admitting and correcting mistakes are essential.

What Dweck is arguing for is that leaders need to stop praising employees with the wrong kind of praise for their innate abilities of intelligence and talent, or simply for meeting baseline expectations. This leads to entitlement, dependence, and fragility. Instead, praise should be given to employees for actions like taking initiative, accepting constructive criticism, showing resilience, beating a goal, or making a significant breakthrough. This latter type of praise engenders hard work, grit, a true sense of self-worth, and personal growth.

---

35 I actually am a big proponent of quarterly or monthly bonuses to put rewards in closer proximity to when the goal achievement is made. I advise clients to pay a very fair base salary with the opportunity to make fantastic money when goals are met. I find this approach actually creates more satisfied employees, because they are empowered to earn the great money they want, are focused on the right things for the business, and the satisfaction is derived by actually hitting goals and being rewarded for achievement. This is actually more powerful than "entitlement compensation," where everyone gets a reward, regardless of team or individual accomplishment towards achieving goals.

As cited in *Chapter 11* on A Player Acumen, Dweck characterizes two types of primary mindsets: Fixed and Growth. The fixed mindset is the domain of the B and C Player. They believe that they are naturally talented. Because they have been praised all their life for their natural abilities, they rest on their laurels, and don't learn how to handle challenges or setbacks by working harder. When the hard stuff is thrown at them in the normal pressures of work, and they can't perform up to par, these B and C Players suffer from paralysis and respond by hiding, trying to divert the topic, making excuses, or simply throwing their hands in the air and giving up. Worse, they try to ignore you or pretend the situation does not exist by acting like you did not tell them or they misunderstood. They would make you think they are the victims. In their minds they are too "talented" to lower themselves to do the nitty-gritty grunt work that actually gets results. As covered in the last chapter, this is actually denial, which is the farthest point away from ownership, accountability, and responsibility. They are too scared to stick their necks out. They are more concerned about looking good.

On the other hand, A Players have a growth mindset. When faced with one of life's inevitable and numerous challenges or setbacks, the growth-oriented A Player faces them directly and with responsive action. They understand that almost every important skill is learnable. Where a B or C Player tends to start a pity party complete by labeling themselves with self-limiting titles like "I'm technology illiterate" or "I'm no good at this" and then diverting or giving up, A Players who possess a growth mindset dig in by not labeling themselves, and confronting the challenges by simply working harder to achieve goals.

I really like this column investment expert Malcolm Berko wrote in response to a father asking if he should invest in a Sonic restaurant franchise for his son who was struggling to find a job.

If your college-educated son does not have the drive to find a high-paying job, then he may not have the drive to be a Sonic franchisee, which is hard work. Most college degrees today aren't worth a miser's coin, because very little of what kids learn grooms them to be attractive to employers or prepares them for the reality of making a living. Managing a Sonic restaurant with success requires more brains than earning a college diploma.

Malcolm's advice is spot on. In my vantage point of helping companies recruit and develop talent, we find that many new college graduates lack the work ethic and fundamental knowledge of how businesses run and how they can add value to those same organizations. With that said, the formula to add value in a business is:

Value=

((# of Customers x What they Pay per item x How many times a year they Pay) - Cost of what they Bought) - Overhead Expenses = Value

As an employee, if you are helping to increase the three variables on the left and decrease the two on the right as directly as possible then you are adding value to the organization. Basically this formula is about delivering products and services that delight customers who will come back time and time again. Sadly, way too many employees do not consider that it is the customer who is paying the bills. Every person and function in an organization must be either directly or indirectly supporting the improvement of one of these variables.

For example, if you are in engineering, you are developing new products that keep the company competitive and drive revenue. Or perhaps you are value engineering an existing system to take out variable costs, which improves gross profit. Or you may be a customer service representative. You add value to the organization by adding to the customer experience that encourages customers to remain loyal to your business and buy in the future. Be sure you know how you are adding value to the business. If you think I am being too literal on this, please think again. You are there to provide value, not just have a job. I'm sure your CEO will agree with me, as value needs to be centered towards customers. Remember, it's the customers who pay the bills! The more directly you add value, the better for all concerned, and the more you will be rewarded for your efforts.

What Hard Work Looks like

The first factor of hard work is doing work that is relevant and high-value to your organization. This does not mean you have to be a robot. Initiative is highly prized by organizations. A Players see the need and take the initiative. In fact, it is a frequent occurrence that A Players see the need before their managers do. They just confirm that they are solving a relevant problem with their leadership team before they embark, and that the baseline work the organization is expecting from them is being done as well. Just please make sure you are not doing superfluous projects on a whim.

The second factor of hard work is good time management. According to placement firm Robert Half International, the average employee wastes about 50 percent of his or her time on non work related activities. This amounts to nothing short of time theft and it is exactly the same as stealing money from your employer.

On the other hand, the A Player employee manages his or her time wisely. A Players enjoy what they do and almost always have more projects to do than time available. This focuses their work and allows them to wisely use their time. Watching A Players at work, you will see they are very focused on the tasks at hand with little or no time for idle chitchat with coworkers. They also make room in their schedules for strategic time and production time. In this strategic time, they will do activities like setting goals, strategic planning, and personnel actions (including their own), to name a few.

Paradoxically, A Players are far less "busy" than B Players. In fact, Gillian Harper, an A Player senior executive with ShelfGenie Systems and I are fond of calling the B Players the "Busy Bees." Trust me; A Players are being far more productive than the Bs. They just don't obsess with being "busy" like the Bs. In fact the Bs use being "busy" as a sort of crutch, although they never seem to be able to specifically tell you what they are working on and accomplishing. They're just busy! In contrast, A Players are profitable, productive, and focused.

Instant A Player Assessment: Time Management

A Player	B Player	C Player
"All on Track"	"Busy"	"Can't Do It"

Hard, focused, and productive work is what produces dividends. Business expert Brian Tracy has seven key recommendations for success in his excellent book *No Excuses!* These align exactly with why hard work is so valued.

1. Focus on the "Law of Three." This law says there are three things that you do that generate 90 percent or more of the value you provide to your company or organization. Determine what these three things are in your role that provides the most value to your organization. Focus on excellence on these three things and don't be distracted by other tasks. Your leadership will also value you doing three things with excellence rather than four or more things with mediocrity.

2. Do the work your boss values. A Players respect their boss. B and C Players tend to disrespect their boss. Respect your boss and work on the tasks your boss deems most important. Aligning with your boss to move both of your careers in the right direction is a very rewarding experience. Being misaligned with your boss is sheer misery.

3. Work all the time you are at work. Work is about working, not chatting with coworkers, doing family business, or drinking coffee.

4. Be the hardest working employee. Forget about having the reputation to be the one. Actually do the work that makes you the one. Results speak volumes over reputation. Per the A Player growth mindset, hard work can overcome almost any obstacle. Everyone values hard workers on their team.

5. Speed matters. When your boss gives you an assignment, do it immediately. In today's fast-paced world, speed can be the difference between winning a deal and losing out.

6. Ask for more responsibility. As you do more high-quality work quickly, you have earned the right to ask for more responsibility. Be sure you are all caught up on your deliverables before asking for projects of more strategic and financial importance.

7. Pay the price. Another three-part formula: come in earlier, work a little harder, and stay a little later. 40 hours a week is just table stakes. Come in an hour earlier, work over lunch, and stay an hour later. This will

give you a 15-hour per week advantage over the average employee. This equates to over 735 additional hours per year, which is equivalent to having 3 more months at your disposal to contribute to you and your organization's success.[36] If flextime is yours and your organization's culture, that's fine. Work out a flex arrangement that works for both of you. Just remember there is no substitute for focused working time.

A good way to think about hard work is to adopt an Immigrant Mindset. According to Glenn Llopis, in an August 2012 *Harvard Business Review* on the topic of Immigrant Mindset, it consists of equal parts optimism, staying on your toes, being entrepreneurial, working with generous purpose, and having the desire to leave a lasting legacy. This mindset really works, as he cites a study revealing that immigrants or their children founded more than 40% of Fortune 500 companies operating in 2010.

Why Self-Discipline Wins

Early twentieth century American writer Elbert Hubbard provides one of the most useful definitions of self-discipline. He described it as: "the ability to do what you should do, when you should do it, whether you feel like it or not." Think about it. Everything you repeatedly do becomes a habit, whether positive or negative.

As mentioned in *Chapter 3: Make a Decision*, Robin Sharma's instruction is extremely compelling: "If you want to get the same results the top 5% do, then you have to do things only people in the top 5% do."

A Players realize that excellence is the direct result of discipline. On the other hand, B and C Players lament that they "should have, could of, and would have." There is a price to be paid for everything worthwhile.

Discipline is a key element of the A Player's success. I had a discussion with my colleague and fellow executive coach Rob Garibay about this. Rob used his daily workout routine to illustrate his view on discipline: "Each morning my mindset is 2 hours from now, will I be glad I worked out or wish I had?" Rob's comment is particularly poignant. Since discipline is fundamentally what

---

36   As reported by Brian Tracy in Chapter 8 of his book, *No Excuses!*

is good for us versus what is convenient or easy, when we look back on our activities, we will either be pleased with our focus and efforts or disappointed with ourselves.

Rob's point on discipline is very aligned to the great boost in self-esteem people feel when they honor their commitments with integrity. When we are disciplined, it feels both spiritually and physically amazing. Remember, the Lilliputians of B and C Player mediocrity will try to bring you down to their level by encouraging you to abandon your disciplines. Successful people do the things that unsuccessful people are unwilling to do. Therefore, it is critical that we surround ourselves with other A Players, who also lead disciplined lives.

That being said, this is where the rubber meets the road. Here is an extensive list of some of the key A Player disciplines:

1. **Do the Things Only People in the Top 10% Do.** Pick your percentage here. If you are already an A Player and in the top 10%, then, as Robin Sharma suggests, set your sights even higher for the top 5%, or an even higher percentage like doing what the top 2% or 1% do.

2. **Sacrifice by Delaying Gratification.** A Players have superior performance when compared to average people. The critical factor in this is the ability to sacrifice in the short term for a longer-term gain. While B and C Players are busy seeking shortcuts, the A Player realizes that sacrifices in practice and preparation are needed to earn greater results and returns in the long term. Doing what is right and necessary ahead of what is fun and easy is the key to success.

3. **Be Prepared.** Take a tip from the Boy Scouts of America motto: "Be Prepared." A Players don't suffer from hubris and don't "wing it." Instead they meticulously prepare for every meeting and business review. Take more data and materials than you think you'll need. Inevitably you'll need the information, and you'll be glad you were prepared.

4. **Practice.** Like top athletes, A Players always practice their craft. This is a fundamental discipline that separates the As from the Bs and Cs. A Players love the chance to practice their skills or presentations, while Bs

and Cs resist practice with an "I know it all" attitude. Raw talent is not enough. Talent plus Practice equals Skill.[37]

5. **Review Your Numbers and KPIs Daily.** A Players are disciplined and study their key performance indicators (KPIs) daily. In fact, they develop a routine to review these critical numbers at a similar time each day. From this daily discipline, A Players are always informed and able to make good decisions and actions based on facts and data.

6. **Practice "Lombardi Time."** A Players know the value of punctuality and practice "Lombardi Time" by being 15 minutes early to meetings and events, a requirement of legendary Green Bay Packers coach Vince Lombardi of his players. By doing this you value other's time and put yourself in a situation to interact with other A Players who also practice this discipline. You will be amazed by the amount of critical connections and key business you will engender by practicing this discipline.

7. **Self-Control.** A Players can certainly "work hard and play hard." But they do it with a degree of self-control not exhibited by the B or C Players. A Players tend not to overindulge by consuming too much alcohol and getting sloppy. The same goes for coarse language and being inappropriately outspoken. You are being evaluated at all times, and lack of self-control in these areas can be a career limiter.

8. **Fitness and Sleep.** In general, A Players take better care of their bodies, minds, and souls than B and C Players. A Players watch their weight, diet, and get enough sleep so they are optimal performers each and every day. The best have amazing daily exercise rituals as well. They also have the discipline and self-control to pass on extra calories or late night revelry.

9. **Be a Disciplined Learner.** With innovation increasing at an exponential pace in many industries, A Players realize their knowledge can soon become obsolete and that learning is the key to winning and remaining ahead of the curve. A Players are disciplined in their learning approach. Best practice for A Players in this area is to scan news relative to your field daily, read your industry periodical weekly, read two technical,

---

37 Inspired by Ohio State head football coach Urban Meyer

self-development, or business books monthly. Audiobooks also count in this area and are a great way to maximize your drive time with a valuable activity.

10. **Be Responsible for Your Own Training.** With the advent of the Internet, training on any required system is available to you within seconds via a few keystrokes. A Players train themselves. They also read the training manuals that B and C Players are "too busy" to read. A Players also train on their own watch, so that working hours are preserved to produce the results they were hired for.

11. **Turn Information into Intelligence and Insights.** Information only goes so far. Actively scan information to derive trends and patterns. These trends and patterns become intelligent insights that are far more valuable than the information itself.

12. **Ask Insightful Questions.** Questions are the answers. Be known by the great questions you ask. The interrogative form of speech is more powerful than the declarative.

13. **Writing and Systems Development.** The timeless adage of "if you really want to know something then teach it" applies here. A Players are disciplined in writing down their thoughts in presentations, white papers, business cases, and systems. The discipline of writing enhances the quality of your thinking as a result of the psycho-neuro-motor activity that occurs when thoughts are translated to paper through either a keyboard or pen. This discipline also creates enduring, valuable documents that create leverage in the organization.

14. **Become a "Collector of Jewels."** A mentor of mine suggested this metaphor to me years ago and it is a powerful visualization of how A Players view all of the knowledge available to them on a daily basis. These jewels are available to all of us. There is no limitation on access to them. Strive to add a couple of jewels or pearls of wisdom to your collection each day.

15. **Practice Gratitude Daily.** Discipline yourself to take a few moments each morning to think about all the things for which you are grateful. Add in a prayer each morning as a great antidote to combat the inevitable

struggles that we all face in life. You will be amazed at the difference gratitude and prayer will make in your life.

Evaluate how well you are doing on each of these A Player disciplines. This list is extensive but not inclusive. There are many more disciplines, some of which you may formulate on your own. Apply what works best for you and make it a routine. You will inevitably find areas of opportunity for yourself. The benefit of improvement in these areas is enormous. You will create better results through more self-discipline. And you will then gain more self-esteem through having better results. With more self-esteem you will become a more powerful person who can add more value to others. Creating value to others is the currency of the A Player.

As Brian Tracy says in his book *No Excuses! The Power of Self-Discipline,* "the ability to practice self-discipline is the real reason some people are more successful and happy than others."

There is no free lunch in creating success. It is a well-documented fact that genius and expertise have been created by over 10,000 hours of hard work, discipline, and sacrifice[38] by those practicing their craft. A Players are willing to pay this price.

Are you?

---

38   In his best-selling book, *Outliers* author Malcolm Gladwell promotes the "10,000-Hour Rule", claiming that the key to success in any field is, to a large extent, a matter of practicing a specific task for at least 10,000 hours so mastery can occur.

Chapter 18

BE COACHABLE

"These guys [NBA Basketball Players] are extremely smart! And being smart means knowing they can't do it alone. They all want an edge to get even better. Therefore they surround themselves with other smart people and actively seek their opinions."
—**Mike Krzyzewski**, Hall of Fame Basketball Coach, Duke University

*P*erhaps Hall of Fame Basketball Coach John Wooden said it best: "It's what you learn after you know it all that counts." That is the attitude of A Players. They are highly coachable. It does not matter if they are in sports, business, or the great game of life. A Players always want to improve and are constantly seeking advice from credible people.[39] In fact, the sports world provides one of the best learning laboratories for successful coaching models. After all, where is coaching more formalized than in sports? Think about it. No self-respecting team in their right mind would field a squad without a coach. In fact, on most sports teams there is a whole cadre of specialized coaches for every imaginable skill. In fact,

---

39 My colleague Steve Leach, a fine business coach from Brisbane, Australia, has the rule of only taking advice from people he aspires to be like. Many people will offer you advice. A lot of them are clueless and not congruent in following their own advice. Make sure they are credible and that you aspire to be like them.

most teams also have access to top leadership coaches and sport psychologists to ensure their superstar A Player athletes are also focused and thinking straight. The best teams are the ones that are well coached on many levels.

So, what if you have already achieved a lot in your life and your career? What if you think you have already achieved A Player status? This is exactly the conversation I had a couple years year ago with legendary Missouri basketball coach Norm Stewart at the 2013 Final Four in Atlanta. "Rick, an A Player is someone who wants to get better. If they don't want to get better, I can't help them. If a kid is a #30 draft prospect and is happy with that, I can't help him. I want a kid who is a #30 draft prospect who wants to improve to #10." Sounds familiar to the "I Know" attitude we covered in *Chapter 12* on A Player Acumen, doesn't it? Sadly, too many people in business have a fixed mindset and don't want to grow or develop.

From my experience in working with hundreds of clients, I have an instant A, B and C Player test that can be applied to any individual to determine that person's coachability. Here's a sample of the conversation I typically have with CEOs and other senior leaders about how the instant A, B, and C Players test goes:

Rick:	"Allan, want to know how to instantly tell your A, B and C Players?"
Allan:	"Sure Rick"
Rick:	"A Players *love* coaching. They want any edge they can to get better. I just coached an A Player team member this morning who has already sent me two e-mails on how much she enjoyed her coaching session and the results she has achieved. B Players who want to be A Players *like* coaching. They are still a little sensitive about not yet being A Players, but they want to get better. B Players who want to be C Players *don't like* coaching. They try to squirm out of it and their actions say, "I'm stale and I know it all." In contrast, C Players *hate* coaching. Their actions say, "I suck and it was a mistake to hire me."
Allan:	"Sounds right to me!"

Rick: "OK Allan, so who's on your team?"

Instant A Player Assessment: When Given Coaching

A Player	B Player-Wants to Be an A Player	B Player-Wants to Be an C Player	C Player
Loves Coaching	*Likes* Coaching	*Does Not Like Coaching*	*Hates* Coaching

In addition to the above-referenced test, there are very predictable results and feedback that you get between A, B, and C Players in which you invest professional coaching.[40] They are as follows:

Instant A Player Assessment: Results from Coaching

A Player	B Player-Wants to Be an A Player	B Player-Wants to Be an C Player	C Player
Shares great results gained from the engagement.	Somewhat reluctant. Tends to try to evaluate the coach, but you see progress in their leadership.	Misses and puts off coaching sessions. Tells you as the manager that he/she knows all that is being covered. Is too "busy."	Tells you the coach is bad and you are wasting your money on him or her.

I found these truth serum tests to be so revealing that I now begin with the tests when interviewing new clients. It limits the time and aggravation I spend on trying to coach B Players who really want to be Cs, and C Players who don't care at all and should not have any development resources invested in them. As Matthew 22:14 instructs, "For many are invited, but few are chosen."[41]

A Players are highly coachable. As Coach Stewart advises: "Are you willing to get better? If not, then you are not coachable." I often advise clients to look at their own hobbies and pastimes for areas they have a lot of passion to improve. I often find that employees will devote a lot more developmental time and be more coachable on their hobbies than their daytime profession. The avid golfers

---

40 The absolute best investment in coaching is working with an existing A Player to elevate performance. They appreciate the investment you are making in them and respond by using the coaching tools to achieve even higher levels of performance.
41 New International Version (NIV)

among us will go to great lengths to take two strokes off their handicap. The tennis player will subject himself to a lot of coaching, critiques, and conditioning to get another 5 mph on the speed of his serve.

The fact is, when we are in the heat of battle, whether in business or sports, we cannot see our own game. When we are in the arena, we are often stressed or fatigued and/or the issues are only inches in front of our nose. Coaches help us see a greater perspective on where the opportunities lie from their usually more strategic vantage point. Also, the business of winning is hard work. I am fond of saying that if you take the hard road now, the easy road follows. If you take the easy road now, an even harder road or perhaps no road at all lies in front of you. We have explored A Player discipline, and as legendary NFL coach Tom Landry of the Dallas Cowboys said, "a coach is someone who gets you to do something you don't want to do, so you can be somebody who you want to be."

As a business professional, if you get the opportunity to work with a professional coach, it should be viewed as a major career benefit and not as a remediation. A little known fact is the best investment of professional coaching is actually on the A Player, followed by the B and then the C Player. Why? Getting an A Player to even higher levels of performance produces the best return on investment. As we saw above, the A Players are also more coachable, which produces faster and more elevated results. Want to know who has a coach? CEOs!

> CNN.com reports that "Once used to bolster troubled staffers, coaching now is part of the standard leadership development training for elite executives and talented up-and-comers at IBM, Motorola, J.P. Morgan, Chase, and Hewlett Packard. These companies are discreetly giving their best prospects what star athletes have long had: a trusted advisor to help reach their goals."

In fact, there is hardly a CEO in the Fortune 500 who does not have an executive coach. Marshall Goldsmith, who has kindly contributed to this book and serves as a mentor to me, has coached high profile and successful CEOs such as Alan Mulally of Ford Motor Company. Eric Schmidt, the Chairman and CEO of Google, also has an executive coach. Although initially resistant to getting a coach, here is what Mr. Schmidt had to say in a Fortune interview on the best advice he ever got:

> The advice that sticks out I got from John Doerr, who in 2001 said, "My advice to you is to have a coach." The coach he said I should have is Bill Campbell. I initially resented the advice, because after all, I was a CEO. I was pretty experienced. Why would I need a coach? Am I doing something wrong? My argument was, How could a coach advise me if I'm the best person in the world at this? But that's not what a coach does. The coach doesn't have to play the sport as well as you do. They have to watch you and get you to be your best. In the business context a coach is not a repetitious coach. A coach is somebody who looks at something with another set of eyes, describes it to you in [his] words, and discusses how to approach the problem.
>
> Once I realized I could trust him and that he could help me with perspective, I decided this was a great idea. When there is [a] business conflict you tend to get rat-holed into it. [Bill's] general advice has been to rise one step higher, above the person on the other side of the table, and to take the long view. He'll say, "You're letting it bother you. Don't."

Whether you have the opportunity to work with a professional executive business coach, or have the occasion to work with managers and executives who are willing to coach and mentor you, the key thing is that you have a coachable, growth oriented mindset that you can always improve. Coachable people never rest on their laurels, and welcome critique and constructive criticism that will help them improve. They are always looking for and seeking that winner's edge.

What are the areas of your business and professional life where getting better would produce a huge return? To that end, here are six great questions to ask yourself that will help you to identify your preferred areas of improvement:

1. What areas of my professional life would create the most benefit if I were to improve them?
2. What area of my professional life would be easiest to improve?
3. What actions can I immediately take to improve areas of my professional life?
4. What area of my personal life would create the most benefit if I were to improve it?
5. What area of my personal life would be easiest to improve?
6. What actions can I immediately take to improve areas of my personal life?

The bottom-line is that A Players are the most self-aware and most coachable. We have a growth mindset and not a fixed mindset. We know there are always areas for improvement and we are always growing. We seek input from those whose opinions we trust, and we actively seek critiques and even criticism.

Jeff Haden, Inc., Magazine Columnist and LinkedIn Influencer, offers this advice on his LinkedIn blog:

> *"Be grateful for criticism:*
> *When you get feedback, at least someone cares enough to want you to improve: Your product, your service, your work, your life... You only need to worry when no one cares enough to criticize you.*
> *Criticism creates an opportunity. Embrace that opportunity."*

A great example of this occurred with one of my CEO clients. While traveling abroad, she asked if I would use the time we normally spent together to coach two of her A Player employees. Of course, I obliged. Coaching a leader's A Player employees in a skip-level coaching session is always a great return on investment. At the conclusion of a very productive session, an A Player named Kendra asked the following question: "Rick, what feedback or constructive criticism do you have for Jennifer and I so we can get even better?" As you can imagine, I sat there with a smile on my face. Kendra was an A Player not just for what she does for her boss and her team, but for her continued desire to develop and further improve.

As an A Player employee, embrace the same question Kendra articulated. As good as you are, that singular question may be the most important one you will ever ask. The answer will absolutely make you better when you act on the advice given. Take the attitude of any professional athlete and seek coaching in your professional life. Your profession may not be to throw a football or catch a baseball, but maintaining that same attitude and dedication to your trade will help you to perfect your special skillset. Be coachable and you will recognize a substantial return on your investment. Seek coaching in your professional life as an elite athlete seeks coaching in theirs. We will now use the skills we learned from being coachable to produce A Player level results in the next chapter.

Chapter 19

A PLAYERS DELIVER RESULTS

*"Results are the name of the Game…Results! What other game is there?…
Results!"*

—Jim Rohn

When it comes right down to it, A Players deliver results! They have that no-nonsense bottom-line mind-set that delivers the results that truly matter to any organization.

I often have the pleasure of leading corporate planning sessions and retreats. One of the exercises I love to kick off the sessions with is to ask each participant to succinctly summarize his or her results for the past quarter and then declare if he or she is either an A, B, or C Player based on those results. The amazing point of this exercise is the difference in both the language and results of the A Players versus the Bs and Cs.

A Players are concise and to the point when discussing results. They speak in terms of activities and numbers that matter to the bottom-line, and reference the aligned goals of the organization. For example, instead of saying "very good" when articulating their performance, A Players use specific numbers such as "120% of goal" or "2 days ahead of schedule." This specific, crisp and concise speech makes it very easy to understand the results they have achieved. They are excited to share performance versus goals, and are highly accountable if they were a little short in some areas by sharing plans to recover and hit the numbers in short order. In turn, review meetings with A Players become specific and exciting. There is a vivid texture to their results and plans. It feels like we have a front row seat on the action. They confidently proclaim they are A Players based on the *specific* achievements of the past quarter, not ghosts of Christmas past! I find that their peers and leaders agree with their self-assessment.

On the other hand, B Players begin with a song and dance routine. They typically start off their recap with a weak word like, "Well," or a non-word like "Um…" Then the *story* starts. Because they don't have concrete results they feel obliged to waste time with a story outlining all the "Below-the-Line" *reasons* why they don't have *measurable results*. These excuses and lack of specifics make attending the meeting virtually unbearable. Our mind is not built to pay attention to vagueness and fables. Because they kill so much of our time and energy, my colleague Nancy Richison refers to B Players as the Killer Bs!

I'm pleased to say that there seems to be a trend amongst shrewd A Player managers and peers not to fall for these B and C Player shenanigans. Instead of having to waste valuable time suffering through all of the context-building drivel and excuses that B and C Players use as smoke screens, they are now mercifully cutting off this nonsense at the onset and asking for results. In addition, results are driven by great execution, so A Players ensure that there are clear-cut action steps detailing who does what and by when.

As the well-known business philosopher Jim Rohn was fond of saying: "I don't want a story, I want a number! That's why I made this little box so small, so a story won't fit!"

A Player Tip: Act on Lead Measures

To achieve results, A Players act on lead measures. As defined in the excellent book *The 4 Disciplines of Execution*, lead measures are those actions that are predictive of achieving the end result and those that can be directly influenced by the team. Typically, employees only track lag measures and pray that the results come in. A Players take a proactive approach by identifying predictive lead measures, which they can actually influence, and then acting on these. To provide a quick illustration on the power of action on lead measures, let's use weight loss as an example. The lag measure for losing weight is standing on a scale and reading your pounds. The lead measures that are predictive of losing weight are the amount of calories your burn by exercising, the amount of calories you intake by eating, and the hours of sleep you get each evening. First you influence and control these lead measures, and then achieving your weight loss goal becomes the lag measure. What predictive lead measures should you be identifying and influencing in your business?

How *A* Players Have Integrity For Results

Often times, there is a misalignment between the activities an employee is doing and the results the organization needs in business. There are numerous reasons for this misalignment. Here is a list of some of the most commonly encountered ones:

- Mistaking activity for results
- Focusing on the things you like to do rather than the important things that need to be done
- Lacking a clear focus on the goals and results needed (the onus can be on either the management or the employee in this case)
- Not following the proven system developed by your organization to deliver results
- Taking shortcuts and missing key process steps
- Negligently denying facts and reality
- Lack of clear cut next steps regarding responsibility

Recently, I was assisting a client in doing a performance review on the return of investment for their prior quarter's marketing plan. In the past, the marketing manager had actually performed quite well, developing integrated programs that exceeded the lead generation objectives for campaigns. These campaigns required painstaking planning, coordination, and execution. The highest lead generating parts of the campaign involved fairly unglamorous, but effective campaigns including data mining, direct marketing, and telemarketing—old school "sweat equity" marketing if you will. These campaigns worked exceedingly well and the leads generated from the marketing produced a handsome return on investment (ROI) that drove the company's bottom line. In turn, the marketing manager was rewarded with handsome performance bonuses. She was definitely performing as an A Player during this time period.

However, apparently the marketing manager decided that she enjoyed working on "new age" marketing better than the proven methods. She got caught up with the romance of "building the brand" through relatively hard to quantify strategies like social media and sponsorships, and eschewed the results-oriented marketing that predictably generated valuable leads, the lifeblood of any business. During this process she ignored her management's caution to make sure the ultimate results were still there. The problem with "building the brand" strategies is they are difficult to measure. These marketers tend to talk down to others with haughty terms like "brand equity" and "mind share." The reason they do is because they struggle to provide a quantifiable result or ROI from their efforts. Therefore, they try to baffle you with "you know what!"

In a business context, I'm fond of saying "If you can't measure it, it does not exist." Skeptical? Then ask your social media or sponsorship marketer how many leads their last campaign yielded for the company, or how many they will commit to on their next campaign.[42] If they can provide a concrete, validated number please call me so I can hire them!

Anyway, this became a classic case of employees working on their own personal interest, rather than measurable business practices. In the world of marketing, a relatively little taught fact is that marketing is actually about lead

---

42 Some very sophisticated companies can actually provide the return on investment from brand building activities like social media or sponsorships. This is because they have highly developed lead attribution systems. The problem is that less sophisticated marketing people only guess at the results of these actions and therefore play the "brand building card". Please don't be fooled by their lack of results. Most likely, you can better deploy your funds to directly build your brand through activities like employee training or product upgrades that the customer will actually see and feel.

generation.[43] Everything else in marketing is superfluous to that singular and crucial goal. As this employee lost focus on results and instead got caught up on what she wanted to work on, her results dramatically suffered. Despite being immediately coached to focus on results, she instead focused on extraneous activities. Unfortunately, she defiantly worked on the wrong activity and her leadership team immediately recruited an even better marketing manager who had the track record and aligned focus to exceed at the task of lead generation. The former A Player, who demoted herself to B Player, was let go. Within two weeks this new A Player was outperforming the former marketing manager's results, and management was thrilled that they had upgraded the position. As is often the case, this is one of those instances where the new A Player is so good we had a very hard time remembering the former employee's name after a couple of weeks.

The morals of this story:

1. Results tell the story.
2. Focus on the results that matter most to the business.
3. Keep your skills sharp and your A Player status current, as a great company will readily be able to assemble a talent pool to challenge or even upgrade the position.

A Player Tip: Never Mistake Activity For Achievement

Don't get me wrong—activity is good! When results are needed, A Players take action. The key with A Player activity is that it is 100% aligned in obtaining the results needed. B and C Players on the other hand are notorious for avoidance behavior activities that are not aligned with generating results. I call these behaviors "rearranging the sock drawer." To use an analogy from the home front, it's kind of like when you have guests coming over and your wife needs you to mop the floors, so you decide it is a great time to clean your golf clubs!

---

43 Also known as Demand Generation.

As employees, we all have the same amount of time in a week. It's amazing that in weekly reviews A Players are investing their time into actions that yield results. Unfortunately, B and C Players are wasting that same precious time on superfluous activities that do not yield results. Funny how the Bs and Cs are always the busiest—the Busy Bs! Never mistake activity for achievement!

How *A* Players Have Integrity for Achieving Results

In *Chapter 4*, I cited Jack Zenger and Joseph Folkman's excellent article posted on the Harvard Business Review blog, *The Behaviors That Define A-Players*, when discussing how CEOs and senior leaders view A Players. The results of that study are worth repeating. By studying over 4,158 individuals, they concluded that integrity for committing to and producing results is the #1 hallmark of the A Player. CEOs and senior leaders value that A Player employees set high goals, commit to them, and then follow through on their commitments by doing what they said they would do. This is a very rare trait in today's society and business world. As A Players, we have a sense of sworn duty to honor our commitments to results with a "do whatever it takes mentality." To not follow through would be what Zenger and Folkman view as "dishonest behavior." Please think about that for a moment. How often do others let us down on commitments by being disingenuous in making them? A Players do not engage in this intellectual dishonesty, as they always display excellent follow-through on their commitments.

It is my observation that A Players have an innate alignment with the organization's purpose and therefore see the line of sight between the result required of them, the benefit to the organization, and the ultimate benefit to them. The benefit to the organization transcends their own monetary, prestigious, and positional rewards within the organization. Although these benefits are real and meaningful, it appears that the even more powerful drivers are more innate and influence the A Player's deep sense of integrity, personal ownership, and duty to others and self. The result of this alignment represents true symbiosis between the A Player and their organization. Their commitment has meaning, and can be taken at face value. In essence, *integrity* is just who they are.

They don't worry if they are giving too much to their employer. They never feel like they are being taken advantage of. They know that in the long run their rewards will be recognized and that there is always a market for A Players like themselves. As business guru Robin Sharma writes in his leadership fable *The Leader Who Had No Title,* "The more I let go of needing all the things most people worry so much about and focused on doing brilliant work and reflecting some real leadership in my behavior, the more all those things just seemed to appear in my life almost by accident." In other words, you reap what you sow!

A Players do the right things with a sense of purpose and joy all the time. They find a way to deliver on their commitments despite hardships or obstacles. Call it a result of a great upbringing if you will. This integrity for results is real and it is one of the most valuable resources on the planet. Your personal track record in this area is what makes this tangible and measurable. Many will claim to have integrity for results, but only real A Players deliver the goods!

Performing to Your *A* Player Agreement

One of the first steps taken to improve performance in organizations is to define what A Player performance looks like. One of the tools we use to do this is to craft an A Player Agreement for the position. Think of the A Player Agreement as a job description on steroids. Most job descriptions are far too vague and candidly are not worth the paper on which they are printed. In contrast, the A Player Agreement is the blueprint on how to get an "A" in the job. They are very specifically written as to the daily, weekly, monthly, quarterly, and annual critical drivers that lead to A Player performance. In addition, they spell out both the lead measures and key performance indicators (KPIs), or lag measures, and results that define success. It needs to be in writing and be reviewed and signed off by both the employee and the manager. When you perform to the A Player Agreement you are clearly an A Player. It is the responsibility of the A Player employee to ensure they are performing to the A Player Agreement.

If you do not have a performance document like this, I suggest you craft one and take it to your manager to align on. If you manage other people, a well-crafted A Player Agreement is one of the quickest ways to get a performance improvement from your team members. A Players will appreciate the clarity and alignment this document provides. Also, having this document to share with candidates as they are interviewing allows you the amazing opportunity to align on the performance expectations of the role *before* the candidate is hired. You will find this alignment will yield better hires who hit the ground running because they are clear on the expectations for results. You can request a sample A Player Agreement at the A Player Advantage website: www.aplayeradvantage.com/resources.

In summary, results are the name of the game! As the old adage goes, "don't tell me how good you are, show me." Results drive everything. Of course it goes without saying that results must be ethically obtained. It is not win at all costs, but with results everything does seem to fall into place.

Remember, when A Players report results, they express these as numbers and not stories. Leave the tales to the B and C Players. If in a report out, someone starts out with a "well…" it's time to summon the Greek chorus to stifle the novel that is about to take place as the excuses begin to fly. Seriously, do your organization a favor and demand crisp results and clear action steps. Define who does what and by when.

A Players are also scrupulous in their integrity for meeting their commitments for achieving results. They consistently do what they say they will do. B and C Players casually commit to assignments, hoping that you will forget to follow-up. Having integrity for results is one of the most critical qualities an A Player brings to the table, and it is a priceless attribute that nobody can take away from you. CEOs and senior leaders highly value this quality, and it will certainly pay dividends for you.

A Players are also crystal clear on which lead measures and results are aligned to organizational objectives. They work on the critical things that truly drive the business, and not their own agenda. I recommend you align with your boss on an A Player Agreement. This document breaks down the 3-5 major functions of your role into daily, weekly, monthly, and quarterly activities that drive results. It provides tremendous clarity on what it takes to obtain the results necessary to be an A Player in that role.

Results are the currency of the A Player. B and C Players simply don't have the fortitude to produce them. But even as A Players we cannot rest on our laurels.

The forces of global competition make us only as good as our last performance. We should be both proud and grateful for our results. We'll discover how to have an attitude of gratitude in the next chapter.

Chapter 20

DEVELOP AN ATTITUDE
OF GRATITUDE

"The talent for being happy is appreciating and liking what you have, instead of what you don't have."
— **Woody Allen**, American Playwright

In the last chapter we took a deep exploration of how A Players achieve results. While A Players certainly achieve great results, they also possess stellar attitudes. Too often, mangers hire employees with prior experience in a given field rather than hiring for great attitude. One of the axioms that I stress with my clients is to hire for attitude and character over aptitude. It is easy to develop a greater aptitude. But in stark contrast, it is extremely difficult to change an attitude and to shape character. There is simply no substitute for a person with great attitude, character, and the intelligence to learn new skills. In his excellent book *True Professionalism*, David H. Maister, who specifically advises lawyers and CPAs, aptly points out, "those who win are not necessarily smarter than their competitors, but they show more energy, excitement, enthusiasm, drive and commitment." I'd also add positive attitude to Maister's list. This awesome illustration on attitude literally sums it up!

Attitude: Coincidence or Not?

If...

A B C D E F G H I J K L M N O P Q R S T U V W X Y Z

EQUALS...

1 2 3 4 5 6 7 8 9 10 11 12 13 14 15 16 17 18 19 20 21 22 23 24 25 26

THEN...

K + N + O + W + L + E + D + G + E

11 + 14 + 15 + 23 + 12 + 5 + 4 + 7 + 5 = 96%

H + A + R + D + W + O + R + K

8 + 1 + 1 8 + 4 + 23 + 15 + 18 + 11 = 98%

Both are important, but fall just short of 100%

BUT...

A + T + T + I + T + U + D + E

1 + 20 + 20 + 9 + 20 + 21 + 4 + 5 = 100%

How true these words ring! Great attitude, energy, excitement, enthusiasm, drive and commitment are exactly what our leaders' desire from each of us. These attributes are the currency of the A Player. The question is: on a daily basis, how well do you deliver on these attributes? On a scale of 1 to 10, how would your boss score you on each of these factors? You are not currently performing as an A Player employee if you are not scoring 9s and 10s. The good news is if you are not currently at this level, at least you are self-aware enough to recognize it and to do something about it.

People without great attitude, energy, excitement, enthusiasm, drive and commitment are a drain on the organization. I routinely advise CEOs and other top executives to either coach up or out of the organization those employees who lack these attributes. One simple tool that we utilize is simply informing the employee if they are performing at an A, B or C level. Provide this feedback on a very frequent basis, like weekly one-on-one meetings and monthly or quarterly reviews. As you may expect, A Players are happy with the calibration and motivated B players take the feedback well and tend to improve their performance to A grade level. It surprises many outsiders that we provide this level of candid and immediate feedback to employees, but we have found it is by far the fairest and most effective way to go. In fact, we found that regular feedback produces the best and most immediate results.

David Maister has a very interesting take on where the issues fall in relation to A, B, and C Players. In his parlance, he refers to As, Bs and Cs as Dynamos, Cruisers, and Losers. Maister contends that most organizations do a pretty good job of either turning around or firing the Losers. However, he contends that the biggest problems are the Cruisers, those employees who lack the fantastic attitude, energy, excitement, enthusiasm, drive and commitment to learn new things and to develop their skills. These are employees who potentially have the talent, but settle for the status quo rather than to realize their true potential. There is a huge waste of self and economic potential here because they lack the attitude of improvement. As the great physicist Albert Einstein observed: "Weakness of attitude becomes weakness of character."

I totally agree with Maister; the B Players are the real bane of existence for an organization. Often, they don't work to their full potential, and most leaders and managers will settle or tolerate them. Therefore, they are the Killer Bs, AKA the silent killers of the organization. As Dr. Brad Smart says, "bad breath is unfortunately viewed as better than no breath." In short, they take up space that should be occupied by an A Player employee. Specifically, we are taking about the B Players with tepid attitudes and fixed mindsets. We have the time and energy to develop those with the desire to improve to A Players. Please remember there is an A Player ready to replace every jaundiced B Player out there. It is your job as a teammate or manager to recruit these A Players and upgrade your team.

Instant A Player Assessment: Attitude

A Player	B Player	C Player
Awesome	Borderline	Cancer

While writing this chapter, I happened to take a break to check in on my social network channels. A colleague of mine had just posted the following chart:

WINNERS	LOSERS
SAY "IT MAY BE DIFFICULT BUT IT IS POSSIBLE."	SAY "IT MAY BE POSSIBLE BUT IT IS TOO DIFFICULT."
SEE THE GAIN.	SEE THE PAIN.
SEE POSSIBILITIES.	SEE PROBLEMS.
MAKE IT HAPPEN.	LET IT HAPPEN.

Some may say it would be too harsh to define everybody as a winner or a loser. However, in my experience this simple chart defines how A Players think. This is the essence of the *Possibility Thinking* I wrote about in *Chapter 12* when discussing A Player Acumen. The interesting thing is it takes a similar amount of effort, no matter which side you are on. By using *Possibility Thinking*, the winner, or A Player employee, takes into account attitude, energy, excitement, enthusiasm, drive, and commitment, plus a singular focus to get it done.

Instant A Player Assessment: Attitude

A Player	B Player	C Player
Appreciate	Blame	Complain

Want more on this? My colleague, and fellow Gazelle's International coach, Andy Bailey recently sent out a postcard on the differences between successful and unsuccessful people. This card summarized an article authored by *New York Times* best-selling author Dave Kerpen on his LinkedIn blog. This summary of sixteen difference-making attitudes listed below is a great comparison of the attitudes A Players need to foster versus the ones they need to purge:

1. **Embrace change vs. Fear change**

   Embracing change is one of the hardest things a person can do. With the world moving so fast and constantly changing, we need to embrace what's coming and adapt rather than fear it, deny it, or hide from it.

2. **Want others to succeed vs. Secretly hope others fail**

   When you're in an organization with a group of people, in order to be successful, you all have to be successful. We need to want to see our coworkers succeed and grow. If you wish for their demise, why even work with them at all?

3. **Exude joy vs. Exude anger**

   In business and in life, it's always better to be happy and then exude that joy to others. It becomes contagious and encourages others to exude their joy as well. When people are happier they tend to be more focused and successful. If a person exudes anger, it puts everyone around that person in a horrible, unmotivated mood, and results in little, if any, success.

4. **Accept responsibility for your failures vs. Blame others for your failures**

   When there are ups, there are most always downs. Leaders and successful businesspersons always accept responsibility for their failures. Blaming others solves nothing; it just puts other people down and absolutely no good comes from it.

5. **Talk about ideas vs. Talk about people**

   What did we all learn in high school? Gossip gets you nowhere. Much of the time it's false, and most of the time it's negative. Instead of gossiping about people, successful people talk about ideas. Sharing ideas with others will only make them better.

6. **Share data and info vs. Hoard data and info**

As we all learned in kindergarten, sharing is caring. Sharing is important to being successful in social media, in business, and in life. When you share your info and data with others, you can get others involved in what you are doing to achieve success. Hoarding data and info is selfish and short-sighted.

7. **Give people all the credit for their victories vs. Take all the credit from others**

Teamwork is a key to success. When working with others, don't take credit for their ideas. Letting others have their own victories and moments to shine motivates them. Remember, the better they perform, the better you'll look anyway.

8. **Set goals and life plans vs. Do not set goals**

You can't possibly be successful without knowing where you're going in life. A life vision board, 10-year plan, 3-year forecast, annual strategic plan, and daily goal lists are just a few of the useful tools of the mega-successful people in your life. Get your visions and goals down on paper!

9. **Keep a journal vs. Say you keep a journal but don't**

Keeping a journal is a great way to jot down quick ideas and important thoughts you don't want to forget. Writing them down can lead to something even greater. You can even use mobile apps or your notes function in your phone. But don't fool yourself by saying you keep a journal and not following through.

10. **Read every day vs. Watch TV every day**

Reading every day educates you on new subjects. Whether you are reading a blog, your favorite magazine, or a good book, you can learn and become more knowledgeable as you read. On the other hand, watching television may be good entertainment or an escape, but you'll rarely get anything out of TV to help you become more successful.

11. **Operate from a transformational perspective vs. Operate from a transactional perspective**

Transformational leaders go above and beyond to reach success on another level. They focus on team building, motivation, and collaboration across organizations. They're always looking ahead to see how they can transform themselves and others, instead of looking to just make a sale, generate more revenue, or get something out of the way.

12. **Continuously learn vs. Fly by the seat of your pants**

Continuously learning and improving are the only ways to grow. You can be a step above your competition and become more flexible because you know more. If you just fly by the seat of your pants, you could be passing up opportunities that prevent you from learning (and growing!)

13. **Compliment others vs. Criticize others**

Complimenting someone is always a great way to show you care. A compliment gives a natural boost of energy to someone, and is an act of kindness that makes you feel better as well. Criticizing produces negativity and leads to no good.

14. **Forgive others vs. Hold a grudge**

Everybody makes mistakes; it's human. The only way to get past the mistake is to forgive and move on. Dwelling on anger only makes things worse, for you.

15. **Keep a "To-Be" list vs. Don't know what you want to be**

A "To-Be" list is a great way to strategize for the future. For instance: I want to be a best-selling author. I want to be a TED speaker. I want to be the CEO of a public company. I want to be a great father and husband. Unsuccessful people have no idea what they want to be. If you don't know what you want to be, how can you achieve success?

What do you want to be?

16. **Have Gratitude vs. Don't appreciate others and the world around you**

Each moment of gratitude can transform lives and unquestionably make people happier. The people who you are grateful for are often the ones who have a huge part in your success. Be sure to thank everyone you come in contact with and walk with a spirit of gratitude, appreciation, and wonder about the world around you. Gratitude is the ultimate key to being successful in business and in life.[44]

To summarize these points above:

1. Successful people tend to look inside for solutions.
2. Less successful people tend to look outside for problems.

Author Glenn Shepard, in his very instructive book, *How to Be the Employee Your Company Can't Live Without,* addresses a topic that comes up a lot with B and C Player employees. That issue is the notion of employees saying they will work better, faster, smarter, harder etc. if only they were paid more. Glenn

---

44 Graphic Source: Andy Bailey-Petra Coach

points out that when employees say to him that they would do a better job if they were paid more, he asks if they are grateful for the money they already have. He says most people will not directly respond with a simple yes or no. That indicates to me that people who are not grateful for what they have now, are not grateful for what they will get in the future. Glenn advises: show your gratitude first and the money will follow later. Showing gratitude for your job creates a very predictable cycle:

The Attitude of Gratitude Model[45]:
1. **Be Grateful➔Value Your Job More**
2. **Value Your Job More➔Do It Well**
3. **Do Your Job Well➔Become More Valuable**
4. **Become More Valuable➔You Become Worth More**
5. **You Become Worth More➔You Get Paid More or Get Promoted**

An attitude of gratitude is the polar opposite of an entitlement mentality. We are only grateful for what we value. As Glenn points out: "People are only grateful for things they value. Things that are valued are taken care of, while things that aren't valued get neglected. Neglecting something causes it to deteriorate until it's ultimately lost." The same applies to our job. As the Attitude of Gratitude Model instructs: the only way to be paid more money is to become more valuable. To become more valuable, we need to do our job better. To do our job better, we need to value it. To value it, we need to start with an attitude of gratitude. This is the domain of the A Player employee. Managers like employees who are grateful for their positions and compensation, and dislike those with an entitlement mentality who think they are always owed something.

Surprisingly, I find that very few employees see the correlation between the value they provide to the organization and their total compensation.

This basic correlation looks like this:

---

45 Inspired from Glenn Shepard: *How to Be the Employee Your Company Can't Live Without.* Pages 104 to 106.

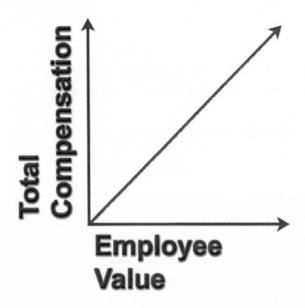

Aligned to the Attitude of Gratitude Model, those who are scientifically oriented will discern that Employee Value is the independent variable on the X-axis, which then drives Total Compensation on the Y-axis. The correct question the A Player asks if they seek more compensation is: "What else can I do to become more valuable?"

Notice I say total compensation instead of salary, because I am a big believer in Ownership Thinking as outlined in *Chapter 8* of this book. Remember, Ownership Thinking entails being paid like an owner, as opposed to being paid like an employee. What's the difference? Owners are paid a relatively conservative salary, with performance-based bonuses (profit-sharing) when profits are good. As you might expect, I am also not a proponent of annual cost-of-living adjustments. Instead, I'd rather reward high performers with bonuses and merit increases. Salary increases are driven when employees demonstrate sustained increases in value, and when their jobs become bigger due to company growth. I am also a big fan of paying out these increases to A Player employees on a quarterly basis, so they can more immediately see the fruits of their labors. Notice that the A Player bonus is twice the size of the B Player's, while C Players don't participate in the payouts. This matrix looks like:

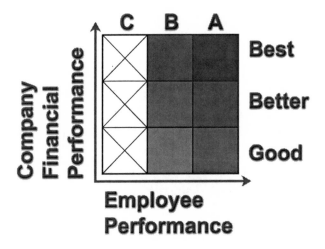

I talk about compensation and income relative to happiness and gratitude because people often think there is too much of a direct correlation between the two. If you are not grateful for the job you accept, and take it only as a temporary paycheck until something better comes along, you are being both fraudulent and unethical. You knew the terms of the job, including compensation and expectations, when you signed up.

To help my clients remember to have an attitude of gratitude, I often remind them that a bad day in the First World is still likely better than a great day in the Third World. I do this myself. When I see a tough or challenging day ahead, I'll take stock of all that I have to be grateful for, and almost miraculously my attitude improves and I can feel myself shifting into a more powerful solution mode. I do this all the time, especially when approaching situations that I forecast to be more challenging or confrontational. By applying this method, the confrontation or challenge almost inevitably melts away and the situations that I thought were going to be tough become some of the best in terms of outcomes. Remember, people pick up on your cues of gratitude. If things start getting heated, use your leadership to back people up to what is really important, then re-set and drive forward. At this stage, I literally ask people to take stock of all we are grateful for. Once we have had a chance for everybody to share, we can then embark onto our daily agenda. You will be amazed at how this simple exercise can drive powerful and effective outcomes.

My colleague, Heather Christie, also a top executive business coach, has a similar technique that I also employ on a regular basis. She calls it the "Gratitude Snooze." The Gratitude Snooze is simple: when your alarm goes off in the morning, hit the snooze button and for the ensuing five minutes or so give thanks and be grateful to your Creator for all the blessings and good things in your life. Like the technique I shared above, the Gratitude Snooze has the amazing ability to set your day off on the right track by aligning your attitude to the right priorities. Heather has told me that this simple but powerful step is always one that her executive clients say is a key takeaway that they put to immediate use.

In closing, having an attitude of gratitude will not only make you an A Player, but it will also make you a happier person as well. Brian Tracy reminds us, "Develop an attitude of gratitude, and give thanks for everything that happens to you, knowing that every step forward is a step toward achieving something bigger and better than your current situation." Only when we are grateful for what we have now, can we be grateful for what we will receive in the future.

Having a grateful attitude will serve us well as we put Emotional Intelligence into practice in the next chapter.

Chapter 21

A PLAYER EQ/EI, PUTTING EMOTIONAL INTELLIGENCE TO USE

"Any time you give a man something he doesn't earn, you cheapen him. Our kids earn what they get, and that includes respect."
—**Woody Hayes**, former Ohio State Football Coach

*E*Q stands for Emotional Quotient. Think of EQ as *people smarts*, while IQ or Intelligence Quotient measures *book smarts*. Among other positive things, people with high EQ are those who connect extremely well with the needs of others. However, to more accurately denote its far-reaching impacts, many practitioners of EQ actually prefer the term *Emotional Intelligence*, so you may also hear it referred to as EI. Research psychologists John Mayer of the University of New Hampshire and Peter Salovey of Yale University gave birth to the concept of Emotional Intelligence in 1990 in the seminal article of the same name. Then, in 1995, in his best-selling book *Emotional Intelligence: Why It Can Matter More Than IQ*, Psychologist and *The New York Times* science writer Daniel Goleman popularized the findings of the article. Thus, the concept of emotional intelligence came to the forefront of both the self-improvement and leadership development worlds. For our purposes, and in deference to the work of Mayer, Salovey and Goleman, I will use their preferred term of EI.

Remember, as recently as the 1990s Intelligent Quotient (IQ) was considered the gold standard in terms of predicting success in life, not the "softer" skills relating to interpersonal people and emotions. This is because the tools measuring EI/EQ were not yet developed. Whether we knew it or not, many of us were administered an IQ exam somewhere along the way of our schooling. However, it turns out that for vocations requiring human interaction (which is most of them), a far more important ingredient and predictor of success is emotional intelligence (EI). Even in highly technical fields, the people who rise to the top of the organization have higher EI skills. This is because the barometer for success becomes interacting with and motivating other people in an organization setting. As Goleman points out: "Emotional intelligence trumps IQ primarily in those "soft" domains; your intellect is relatively less relevant for success—where, for example, emotional self-regulation and empathy may be more salient skills than purely cognitive abilities."

Think about it: with computers handling big data and artificial intelligence, the premium going forward will be on how you relate to others more than on pure cognitive horsepower. Many of the interpersonal and leadership principles written in this book are directly related to the skills of emotional intelligence. A Players tend to have more developed EI skills than average employees. In fact, as Goleman points out in his 1998 book *Working with Emotional Intelligence*, EI skills matter more than IQ or technical skills as the competencies that best predict leadership ability and career advancement. It turns out that IQ and technical expertise are more valued at entry-level jobs, while EI competencies matter more at the senior and executive echelons of companies. However, even at the entry level, you may find your advancement options limited without EI skills.

Time and time again, I have found in my own work, as an executive business coach and A Player talent expert, that the emerging high performance employees, so valued by senior leaders and CEOs, possess these high EI skills and abilities.

So with that said, what are these EI skills and abilities?

At its root, EI is composed of six major sets of factors:

1. Self-control
2. Compassion and empathy

3. Managing emotions
4. Delayed gratification
5. Zeal and persistence
6. Self-motivation

Below you will find a discussion of each…

Self-Control: Self-control is based on the ability to regulate impulses. As Goleman cites, the ability to control impulse is the basis of will and character. Strong will and character, as well as the ability to regulate and control your impulses, are fundamental A Player attributes. These are the specific traits any sophisticated employer will measure through psychometric assessment tools when you go through the hiring and advancement processes. They will also be assessing these factors through intensive reference interviews with prior employers to determine if you possess high self-control.

Compassion and Empathy: The second set of factors, compassion and empathy, account for our ability to see the world through others' eyes. Compassion and empathy allow us to read peoples' emotions, which in turn allow us to be caring and altruistic towards others. Practically speaking, this is rooted in the old adage, "to get what you want, help others get what they want." In business, in particular, too often we encounter people with a "me, me, me" attitude. These people inevitably have a low EI. They are the "takers" of the world. Fortunately, business cultures tend to flush these people out and neutralize them.

A Player employees, who inevitably have higher EI skills and abilities, more often see their personal and professional lives through the lens of others. This is personified by the pure, compassionate and humanistic interactions A Players have with others.

Managing Emotions: There are two stages to the ability to manage emotions. The first stage is actually knowing our emotions. This means our ability to truly know our own feelings, so we can accurately know how we are feeling about situations within the moment. This ability greatly helps in our decision-making process. The second stage is the management of these emotions. People with poor coping mechanisms cannot avoid and move past feelings of distress, anxiety, gloom, and depression, which creates less resiliency to rebound from setbacks, uncertainty, and challenges. Unfortunately, their negative emotions can cast an aura over an organization like a plague. These people are very poor at the *Possibility Thinking* covered in *Chapter 12* on A Player Acumen. Everything tends to be a negative, unsolvable, or insurmountable challenge. On the other hand, A Players have either an innate or developed way to manage positive attitude and self-talk to soothe, control, and contain their emotions. The attitude of gratitude examined in the prior chapter is a useful tool to develop this skill.

Delayed Gratification: The notion of delaying gratification of a short-term reward in exchange for a more strategic and perhaps more satisfying long-term reward is closely tied to impulse control. This will be one of the biggest predictors of your success. Daniel Goleman cites the famous marshmallow study that was conducted in the 1960s at Stanford University. This study provides a very illustrative example about the power of delayed gratification. A pre-selected number of four-year-olds were given a choice: they could either eat one marshmallow immediately, or restrain from eating the marshmallow and wait 15 to 20 minutes for the researchers to return. Upon the researchers' return, they would be rewarded with two marshmallows. Approximately two-thirds of the students were able to exhibit self-control and delay gratification for the larger reward of the two marshmallows. Those students were again studied after graduating from high school, and were found to be more trustworthy and dependable, more likely to take the initiative on projects, and more resilient in the face of challenges, pressure, and difficulties than the one-third of those students who could not control their impulse and ate the first marshmallow. In fact, the students who could not delay gratification tended to be more stubborn and indecisive, became easily upset by frustrations, had lower self-esteem, were resentful about not "getting enough," were prone to jealousy and envy, and tended to be irritable and argumentative.

These latter traits are exactly many of the same characteristics we see in C and B Player employees. At the root cause is their need for "microwave" gratification. In reference to the quote from the legendary Ohio State University football coach Woody Hayes that started this chapter, they are far less concerned about actually earning the rewards than they are simply getting them quickly. A Players realize that all worthwhile rewards take an investment of focus, energy, excellence, and time. They are then willing to put off a quick saccharin-like prize for a more satisfying long-term reward.

As you recruit people for your team, be sure to ask behavior-based questions that assess the candidate's ability to delay gratification. Delaying gratification is one of the hallmarks of an A Player.

Zeal and Persistence: Zeal is tangible. It is a passion not only for the task at hand, but also for life itself. It is what the French describe as "joie de vivre," translated as the joy of life. Excellence in your work requires both zeal and passion for what you do. I describe this to clients as the same kind of passion in their work that they have for their hobbies, family, recreation, and sports pursuits. Employees with high EI simply love what they do. Of course, there will certainly be setbacks, frustrations, bad calls, roadblocks and even some unfair situations in the pursuit of something that we are passionate about and love to do. In addition, even in jobs and careers that look glamorous to others, there are unpleasant aspects. For example, most of the CEOs that I have worked with take home a satchel of projects and correspondence every weekend, while a mid-level executive may be able to enjoy a weekend free of any office work. The same applies to responding to e-mails late at night while at home. In the sports world, this means grueling workout schedules filled with pain and injury, possibly including restrictive diets and the inability to even participate in a nice leisurely pursuit like a weekend out with friends or a ski vacation. My best friend is a well-known sports anchor at ESPN. Seems like a sexy job, right? Well the truth is that few people would have endured the low pay and terrible hours associated with lugging a camera around rural Oklahoma during his formidable years. To low EI employees, they only see the glamorous sides of the job and forget the extra sacrifice inherent in them. For A Player employees with high EI, they tend to absolutely love what they do with both zeal and passion. This is particularly important because any meaningful job typically means we spend more of our time at work than at home with the family.

As covered in the previous chapter, resilience and drive are two of the most important and predictive competencies of A Players. Drive will be covered on the sixth EI factor on self-motivation. Resiliency is directly aligned with persistence. Directly supporting the research of psychologist Carol Dweck of Stanford

University on the benefits of a growth mindset over a fixed mindset, persistence and resilience are the abilities needed to have a positive outlook and to try again and again to improve and get a better result.

As pointed out by authorities Goleman, Dweck, and Malcom Gladwell, whether it is music, dance or sports, the masters in any given field have put in a minimum of 10,000 total hours of lifetime practice to develop their expertise. Practice makes the skill both perfect and permanent. In other words, the solution to most problems is some combination of persistence and hard work with a touch of strategic thinking. I find that the great employees and leaders actually have more hard work and determination than raw brilliance in their success formula. How much practice are you putting into the key skills of your profession?

Let's go back to possibility thinking. When a tough goal exists with a client, one technique I use is to ask, "Given unlimited resources, what result can we get?" Using an example in marketing, say the marketing team needs to develop an action to generate 500 leads based on the marketing plan. I may ask, "Would a Super Bowl advertisement generate over 500 leads?" If the answer is that it would generate tens of thousands of leads, then it opens up *Possibility Thinking* for far more affordable and creative marketing strategies that will meet our goal. In other words, every goal is solvable with some combination of persistent effort and strategy. Whether it is manufacturing, engineering, or customer service, this works in other fields as well. Typically, developing great strategies takes great persistence. These are both the purviews of the A Player employee.

Self-Motivation: As mentioned in the prior section, drive, which can be measured by both prior documented results as well as psychometric assessments, is one of the most predictive competencies of the A Player. Drive is vital to self-motivation. Who can start an initiative and bring it to a successful completion? Self-motivation becomes one of those x-factors that make the A Player employee extremely valuable to the organization. Why? In a dynamic organization with multiple initiatives simultaneously carried out, it is simply beyond the bandwidth of even the most talented managers to choreograph every move that every one of their employees should make. In fact, this would be undesirable, as we need empowered A Player employees to fill in the gaps and deliver the multitude of initiatives necessary for a successful execution at all levels of the organization.

There are several good emotional intelligence assessments you can take yourself. For people striving to increase their A Player acumen, taking a good EI assessment provides a deep "look under the hood," as these attributes and their implications are rarely explored otherwise. You can start to unmask areas of your EI that are either strong, or need improvement by taking a formal EI assessment or through asking your confidants for some unfiltered feedback in these specific areas. With that said, I have found that the quickest way to develop is actually by improving a weakness. This is contrary to the popular opinion that we simply need to maximize our strengths. The reason we should work to clean up our weaknesses is because there are things we unconsciously do that drive others crazy. Let me share an analogy to drive this point home: It would be like me pouring you a glass of expensive Dom Perignon champagne into a dirty glass and then serving it to you. No matter how good the champagne, the dirt on the glass contaminates it. The same is true with weaknesses, as they prevent others from seeing your true strengths.

On my own A Player journey, my leadership team at Ford Motor Company hired an executive coach to help me get to the next level. Harry Cohen was his name. The first thing he had me work on was improving my emotional intelligence. In fact, he recommended that I read Goleman's EI book to start. The results were almost instantaneous. I was always viewed as an A Player employee in the organization, but now I was also viewed as the employee at my salary band with not only the best results, but also the best leadership potential as well. It was all because I improved my skills of connecting with others and allowed my IQ to be channeled more effectively through my EQ.

High EI skills are prized in any organization. Given that you have a reasonable intelligence, in today's day and age, they have become even more important than IQ. Understanding the components of EI and how to improve your own emotional intelligence will serve you well as an A Player.

Chapter 22

PARTING WORDS

"*As I grow older I pay less attention to what men say. I just watch what they do.*"

—**Andrew Carnegie**, American Industrialist

*C*ongratulations on reading *The A Player*! It is exciting to think we are nearing the end of this part of your journey. Completing a rigorous book is always satisfying. But the end here marks the beginning for you. By virtue of reading this book and making it this far, you are likely on your way to becoming an A Player. But it takes time, energy, and endless effort to maintain that status. We have covered a lot of ground on our A Player journey together. I hope you have enjoyed it as much as I have, and I hope you revisit the lessons from this book on a regular basis. These imparted lessons are the products of years of working with literally thousands of A Players. As a high performer, they should resonate deep within your fabric. Not only can you reach A Player status, but you can also maintain this high level through the teachings within this book. It is my heartfelt hope that the content of this book has done for you what it has done for numerous employees and leaders at all levels, which is helping them to obtain and sustain the greatness and intrinsic joy that being an A Player and working with other A Players brings.

The truth is that A Players are everywhere! They exist in the form of the CEO who is an incredibly transformational leader followed by legions of people. Or they appear as the visionary entrepreneur who built his or her company from literally nothing to a 100 million dollar enterprise now employing over 300 people. Or it can be you, working as the key person on a team that the entire organization counts on to make it all happen.

The great thing about A Players is they are easy to spot by their terrific leadership at all levels, attitudes, and excellent service, like the A Player Pizza Hut employee I purchased an eleven dollar pie from tonight who fastidiously checked to make sure I was not waiting too long and that every one of the eight toppings on my custom Meat Lovers pizza was correct! Seriously, I think that guy was the *Undercover Boss* CEO of Pizza Hut, but I doubt the CEO could have even been that good. I can tell you this: only an A Player cares as much about pizza and his customers as that guy did! I'm sure that guy will go far in whatever career he puts his energy into. In reality, no amount of money buys that amount of service and heart. It is ingrained in the fabric and the DNA of certain people. They are born with it, and then work to nurture it through their professional lives.

My point is that A Players literally make the world go around. Without A Players, the world would hopelessly regress into B and C Player mediocrity. It is safe to say that all meaningful progress in the world is made by A Players. American futurist Joel Barker's well-known quote rings true here: "Vision without action is merely a dream. Action without vision just passes the time. Vision with action can change the world."

Being an A Player is simple, but it is not easy! This book lays out the formula, but like all great things in life, talking a good game versus taking action are two complexly different things. As the great English philosopher John Locke said: "I have always thought the actions of men the best interpreters of their thoughts." Growing into and performing at an A Player level is very obtainable with the correct focus, drive, and attitude. In fact, the recipe is quite simple. The ingredients are easy to understand. The challenge lies in applying these tried and true principles to your life in an extremely prescriptive, disciplined, and consistent manner. It requires you to focus on doing the small, important things that produce big results with persistence and determination every single day. A Players reach this level because they apply a high level of discipline to every single behavior and action within their lives.

You can make a difference. If you are already solidly an A Player, then you well recognize that champions never rest on their laurels. Since you are already at the top 10% of your field, why not shoot to be in the top 5%, 2%, or even 1%. Author Earl Nightingale said that one hour of study per day will put you at the top of your field within three years. Imagine what you can accomplish in five years with this course of action! A Players do all the little things (as well as the big things) to the best of their ability. And they do so all of the time. This is what sets them apart from the B and C Players. Be sure to be diligent and purge yourself of B Player tendencies that may try to creep in from time to time.

If you are a B or C Player who desires to be an A, I want to give you a shout out for having the courage to make it this far! Everyone has patience and respect for people who are committed to self-development. What makes the difference here is being an earnest person as opposed to being a poser, because there is a substantial and quantifiable difference. Everyone wants the benefits of being an A Player, but who is truly willing to pay the price? In working with teams, one of the most exciting moments is when a B or C Player faces up to the reality that they are not truly giving 100%, and commit to being an A Player. The transformation that occurs within the person as well as at the organization's culture is almost nothing short of miraculous! Mostly because as A Players grow, so does the organization in which they reside. I have literally seen people's lives changed from mundane to exceptional by making this decision. Making the transformation from B or C Player to A Player takes hard work and determination, and those who persevere in this journey deserve applause. Those who make it show exceptional character and fortitude.

Obviously, as this book instructs, a lot goes into being an A Player. That is what also makes this such a rewarding journey, as there is always something to work on and improve in our A Player DNA. As such, here is a model highlighting the key components of A Player DNA.

A Player DNA:[46]

Summary "A" Player DNA

In sharing the concepts contained in this book with clients and other business people, it is clear that the A Player Movement is definitely taking hold. As the concepts of this book are shared in business forums, within a few months of implementing elements of *The A Player*, CEOs and senior leaders will report stories of how just discussing the concept of 100% A Players with their team showed immediate improvements in terms of better organizational culture and bottom-line results. In short, they are building A Player Cultures.

---

46   ©2016 Rick Crossland

The simple notion of discussing everything in the simple, but powerful context of A, B, or C performance is an extremely meaningful concept. Executives crave discussions about A Players and how to develop and recruit teams of them. CEOs and other business leaders write and respond to blog posts about the virtues of these high performers and the fabulous cultures they create. It is so rewarding that people immediately grasp the enormous power of this simple concept! Team members shoot out e-mails congratulating their peers for A Player attitude and performance. At team meetings, employees ask such profound questions as "who on this team can really say they are an A Player?" or statements such as "I am relishing the opportunity to add more A Players to my team." The A Player Movement is tangible and growing.

Now is the time to join this A Player Movement! As we wrap up, here are some action steps you can take to create an A Player Culture in your organization:

1. **Enroll Your Leaders:** Ask your leaders what a team of A Players would mean to the business? Ask them what an A Player looks like in your business versus a B or C Player? Ask them if they would enthusiastically hire you? Ask them what performance they would like to see from you in the coming quarter or year?

2. **Conduct an A Player Alignment Session:** The absolute best teams are always working on bettering themselves through training. Set aside a half-day, full-day or even two-day retreat dedicated to launching the A Player Movement in your business. Be sure to get outside the office and away from distractions when you do this. Most very good businesses point to this day as the inflection point when they went from "Good to Great."[47]

3. **Make Being a Team of 100% A Players Your Annual Theme:** Being a Team of 100% A Players is a sure-fire theme to rally your organization towards excellence. It is simple to understand and aspirational. Keep it alive by holding quarterly A Player Alignment sessions as described above.

---

47   Also the title of Jim Collins' seminal book

4. **Conduct an ABC Organizational Assessment:** This is very easy to do and very impactful. Start with your department. List on a white board or a sheet of paper the names of those who fall into being an A, B, or C Player. List development plans for everyone to get them to an A in your organization. If they cannot become an A, what is your plan to reassign them within or outside the organization so they can become an A? What is the plan to develop, reward, or promote your A Players even further?

5. **Work on Your Own A Player Developmental Plan:** Regardless of whether you are already an A Player or are in the process of becoming one, you know you still can improve. Be honest where you have opportunities to improve. This is the concept of a growth mindset versus a fixed mindset. Write down your specific plan in the SMART goal format. Include specific education, training, feedback, feedforward and challenging development assignments in this plan.

6. **Spread the Powerful Concept of Teams of 100% A Players:** The concept of everyone performing as an A Player is a tremendously appealing and powerful one. It makes for a stimulating and productive strategic conversation when networking with other business leaders. Share the concept and the results! To be candid, the sharpest executives understand the power of teams of 100% A Players. Only the insecure shun the concept. Otherwise, who would really harbor underperformers on their team and put the rest of the organization at risk?

7. **Decide Where You Can Be an A Player:** Life as a B or C Player would be miserable. An important precept is that everyone has the right to be an A Player. However, it is up to you to determine where you can truly be an A. Find the place where you love what you do, and can be great at it, and you will truly not work another day in your life.

I sincerely appreciate your commitment to being (or becoming) an A Player! The A Player Movement is real and growing. On behalf of your organization, we thank and applaud you for your commitment to excellence. As an A Player you are making work a pure joy for those who work for you, work beside you, and for those that lead you. Thank you for all of your contributions, and the goodness you contribute not only to the economy, but also to building a positive work environment that allows others to enjoy and flourish in what they do. The contributions you make as an A Player truly make a difference to all you encounter. Even beyond that, the benefits that an A Player like you contributes can make not just your company, but also the entire world a better place.

But before we part ways, I want you to take just a few seconds and consider what it means to truly be an A Player. Close your eyes and think about some of those people you admire as A Players. A Players can be everywhere. In fact, they are. You have contact with them each and every day of your life. You may not reflect upon it, but A Players live within every job description in our society. They do not have to hit game-winning jumpers for a living or throw last second touchdowns. An A Player is anyone who does their job at an extremely high level with passion for what they do. Please take the time to thank them for who they are and the contributions they make.

A Player opportunity lives within each of us. This book should help you unlock that status. And if you have already reached that level, this book will help you to maintain it. Who doesn't love an A Player? The truth is that we all do.

I am truly honored to have the privilege to work with A Players. If at any point I can help you or your organization on the journey of being A Players, please do not hesitate to pick up the phone or drop me a line. I'd love to help you get to the next level!

Rick Crossland

ABOUT THE AUTHOR

Rick Crossland is an internationally known expert and thought leader on A Player talent. He works with organizations across the country to transform good companies into great companies with his unique A Player approach. His innovative approach to developing and validating A Players has been published on leading business sites such as Inc.com, Fortune.com, and many others.

Rick genuinely walks the talk when it comes to being an A Player. He has almost 30 years of experience developing, recruiting and leading high performers, and developing high performing cultures at companies. Before founding his executive coaching, leadership, and talent development practice eight years ago, Rick held positions of increasing leadership responsibility at Johnson and Johnson, ICI-Zeneca, Planters-Lifesavers, Ford Motor Company, and Limited Brands. He holds a bachelor's degree in chemistry from the University of Delaware and an MBA from Duke University. In addition to his writing and consulting, Rick is a passionate speaker who loves to captivate audiences with his unique A Player approach.

Rick resides with his family in Dublin, Ohio. In addition to working with A Players, he enjoys scouting, skiing, tennis, golf, cycling, reading, and photography.

He can be reached via www.aplayeradvantage.com

ACKNOWLEDGMENTS

A Very Hearty Thank You!

This book is the culmination of over three years of intense focus, late nights, and early weekends. It is truly a labor of love, and I enjoyed every moment of writing it. I hope it brings value to your life and helps to create a world of A Players!

I would first like to thank my wonderful wife Jennifer. For our over 25 years of marriage, she has been the love of my life, and a constant source of inspiration, devotion, and strength. Every time I sat down to write, she was always very supportive, and there is no telling how many household chores she let me off the hook for during this endeavor. Jenny is a bona-fide A Player and she is the hardest working and most accountable person I know.

I would also like to thank my daughter Ashley for being such an amazing daughter to me from infancy to adulthood. Her dedication to her studies at Butler University is incredible. As a young businesswoman, she has contributed significantly to my firm, A Player Advantage, and in addition she edited several chapters of this book. You are one of the most reliable people I know and you are truly a role model! You are an A Player and have a fine future ahead of you!

And to my son Kevin who, at 18, shows signs of becoming an amazing engineer. Due to his intense early college course load at Ohio State University, he constantly labored on his homework late nights and weekends and kept me company while I wrote. Keep living Above the Line as an A Player and the sky's the limit! Congratulations on your lifetime achievement of becoming an Eagle Scout!

My parents and in-laws also played an amazingly supportive role in the book. My father, Dick, died just over 20 years ago while we were skiing at Val-d'Isère, France. My dad was an A Player, and not a writing session went by without me wondering what he would think of this book. Dad: I hope I have made you proud!

Thank you to my mother Mary, who always challenged me to be my best while growing up and helped me see my potential early on.

And a thank you to my mother-in-law, Sara, who also directly contributed to the completed project by professionally proofreading this work. My father-in-law, Gordon, also provided critical encouragement by understanding the importance of writing about A Players.

My clients provided not only support, but also a wonderful learning laboratory to validate how well the A Player methodology works. And boy does it work! You adopted it and executed it brilliantly. Congratulations on transforming your cultures!

These past and present clients include: Tracey Adams, Jeanette and Mark Armbrust, Phil Baker, Otto Beatty, Krishna Bobba, Alisha Booher, Lora Boukheir, Carrie Briskin, Brian Brooks, Lisa Busch, Matt Butzier, Kate Cosgrove, Jason Cromley, Heidi and Kevin Crouse, Teresa Crye, Brent and Lori Davis, Patti DeMatteis, Chris DiSilvestri, Jim Dixon, Tony Durieux, Vic Enis, Michael Farrell, Kevin Fleahman, Steve Fischbach, Brett Fry, Srikanth Gaddam, Jeff German, Cindy Getter, Pete Gilfillan, Chad Goldsberry, Scott Gosselin, Mary Griffith, Gil Harris, Todd and Danielle Hays, Trent Heer, Pat Hernon, Doug Howery, Dawn Jacobs, Sumithra Jagannath, Sarah Joyce, Mike Kent, Shawn Loevenguth, Tom Marks, Doug Maynard, Rob Martin, Dave Mead, Mel Meyers, Jon McKay, Andy Michel, Jared Miller, Jennifer Mills, David Moore, John Moore, Ira, Joey and Sam Nutis, Brian Osborne, Randy Overly, Shankar Ramachandran ,Cody Ramey, Rusty Ranney, Shawn Richard, Grant Ripp, Paul Rockwell, Harsha Roddam, Chris Ruch, Mike Saunders, Patrick Scott, Steve Scott, Matt Seiler, Yoshimasa Sekigucki, Joel Stephens, Ray So, Kevin Taylor, Anil Vadhi, Jim Vaive, Jim, Nancy and Andy

Wasserstrom, Tom Wood, Koji Yamamoto, Ranjith Yengoti, Allan Young, Kory Young, and Dave Zuppo.

Thank you to my longtime executive coach Jennifer Hines, who contributed greatly to the marketing and launch strategy of the book, and provided insightful ways to share its content through a variety of media. In particular, Jennifer was a key contributor to helping me develop the *Prosperity Principles*®.

I would like to express particular gratitude to best-selling authors Brad Smart, Marshall Goldsmith, and Mark Sanborn for allowing me to interview them for the book and for their specific insights and the sharing of their intellectual property, which is included in this book. You'll find this book benefited immeasurably from their contributions.

I would also like to thank Brad Sugars, for helping me parlay my corporate skills into creating a successful business. Additionally, market leaders Craig and Annette Hohnberger provided terrific on-the-ground support for me as I scaled up. Creating my own business brought new meaning to the terms ownership, accountability, and responsibility!

Special thanks to the Gazelles International Team of Verne Harnish, Keith Cupp, and Ron Huntington for immediately seeing the unique perspective this book provides in the marketplace and urging me to write it as quickly as possible. Verne provided some invaluable edits as the book entered completion. I really appreciate the faith these gentlemen have in me.

Also, special thanks to my A Player editor Justin Spizman. Justin's considerable editing talents improved the final product, and as an A Player he was a joy to work with.

In addition, Greg Schmidt, my longtime graphic artist, pulled out all the stops to finalize the graphics in the book, as well as develop the unique cover image.

I am grateful to the publishing team of David Hancock, Jim Howard, Rick and Scott Frishman, Kim Spano, Margo Toulouse, and Nickcole Watkins for immediately recognizing the power of the A Player concept and making this book a reality.

Finally, I would like to thank the great leaders and mentors I had the opportunity to work for: Barker Keith, Mike Barone, and Bill Long at ICI Americas; Bill Clay and Joy Hatch at RJR Nabisco; Brian Miller, Joe Castelli,

Rich Stoddart, Marty Collins, Beth Donovan, Elena Ford, Joe Pierucci, Chuck Sullivan, Jim O'Connor, and Martin Inglis at Ford Motor Company; and Brian Beitler at Limited Brands. Thanks to each of you for seeing the A Player in me!

Appendix 1

A PLAYER ASSESSMENT

Are You an A Player? Let's Find Out...

So the question is: Are you an A Player? This assessment will give you a very accurate picture of where you stand. Please be honest in rating yourself, so you can pinpoint your areas of development in order to make the biggest improvements. Most of us have room for improvement; so do not let yourself feel discouraged if you are not quite there. Remember, the behaviors and attitudes needed to attain A Player status can be developed.

Let's use the following scorecard to determine where you stand:

Comprehensive A, B, or C Player Assessment:

Please select the answer that best reflects your natural and honest response to each question. Use the scoring key at the end of this chapter to score your answers once you have completed the entire assessment.

1. ***When you receive critique or criticism, you take it:***
    a. With gratitude and as an opportunity to improve. "Thank you, great to know; I see the value of doing better."
    b. Somewhat defensively. "Didn't they see all the good I contributed?"

236

c. "This is no fun, I'm trying my best."

d. Unwanted. "I know what I am doing better than them."

e. "My supervisor is an idiot."

2. ***You are offered the opportunity to work with an executive coach as an investment the company is willing to make in you. Your first reaction is:***

a. "Awesome! I'm excited for the experience and the opportunity to learn skills and tools to get even better."

b. "I probably don't have the time. Let's see what this person can do."

c. "I probably know more than the coach."

d. "What a waste of time."

3. ***You are given a very challenging assignment. You are asked to produce a result beyond what has been achieved to date. Success is by no means guaranteed. Your reaction is:***

a. "Failure is not an option."

b. "Thanks for the confidence in me. I'll figure out a way. I'll build a plan to achieve the results."

c. "Wow, that's challenging, I'll see what I can do."

d. "I'll think about it."

e. "I don't see the benefit."

f. "I don't agree this is the right goal to go after."

g. "It can't be done."

h. "Just tell me what to do."

4. ***Expertise in your career:***

a. "I know all there is to know."

b. "I teach people how to do this."

c. "I'm actively learning and making improvements."

5. ***You have a better way to do a project or process than your manager. You:***

a. Salute the flag and do it your manager's way.

b. Tell your manager that they should listen to you and do it your way.

c. Ask your manager if they are open to better results, and if they will allow you to prove to them your method is better.

6. *The results of a project come up short. Your first tendency is to think:*
   a. "The goal was probably wrong."
   b. "Who screwed up?"
   c. "Where did others come up short?"
   d. "I wasn't really on-board with the goal anyway."
   e. "My company is doing the wrong actions."
   f. "What could I have done better?"

7. *A crisis comes up. Your tendency is to:*
   a. Critique the situation.
   b. Take personal action.
   c. Hide and avoid the action.

8. *Your leader comes in with an assignment that seems unrealistic. You:*
   a. Salute the flag and attempt to do it.
   b. Push back on the assignment.
   c. Partner with your leader to make the assignment SMART[48] and then build the plan and hit the goal.
   d. Ask to discuss underlining assumptions before embarking.
   e. Go through the motions and let the project run its course.
   f. Stall and hope it goes away.
   g. Tell them why it won't work.
   h. Tell your boss s/he's an idiot.

9. *Your company needs a solution to a major opportunity or problem. You offer:*
   a. Your opinion on how to solve.
   b. A detailed plan and business case and what you can do to help.
   c. Nothing, you are too busy on your other priorities.
   d. Nothing, it is somebody else's job to do.

10. *A project blows up. You are culpable for some strategic and execution errors. Your instinct is to:*
    a. Find something to explain the shortcoming.
    b. Feel insecure. Figure out who or what to blame.

---

48 SMART = Specific, Measurable, Achievable, Relevant, and Time-bound; covered in detail in Appendix 2

    c.   Stand up and take responsibility.

    d.   Take your vacation days and wait for it to blow over.

11. ***To what extent do you do the things that nobody else wants to do to become successful?***

    a.   "I only work on big picture things."

    b.   "They are below my pay grade; I delegate them to others."

    c.   "I'm in a position where I can work only on the things I like to."

    d.   "I relish the unsavory tasks because I understand their value."

    e.   "If my competitors aren't doing them, then I should."

    f.   a and b

    g.   d and e

12. ***If you are a leader, what percentage of your team is made of A, B and C Players?***

    _____ % A Players

    _____ % B Players

    _____ % C Players

    = 100%

13. ***How do you feel about your current job?***

    a.   "I am fully engaged at work. I love what I do."

    b.   "I am not at all engaged. I am actively looking for a job somewhere else."

    c.   "I am somewhat engaged. I may look for something better."

14. ***How do you feel about your current supervisor?***

    a.   "S/he is providing terrific experiences and opportunities for me."

    b.   "S/he is a workaholic."

    c.   "S/he has unrealistic expectations."

15. ***When you are presented with a SMART Goal:***

    a.   "Show me how you want it done."

    b.   "I'll build the plan and deliver results."

    c.   "Just tell me what you want me to do."

16. ***Your beliefs about follow-up and micromanagement are generally:***

    a.   "I hate it when they check up on me."

    b.   "Don't they trust me?"

    c.   "I like to give my supervisor updates."

17. *I believe my role in the organization is to:*
    a.   "Earn a living."
    b.   "Do my job."
    c.   "Drive improvements and efficiency to increase value."

18. *The responses you hear from your manager are:*
    a.   "You are amazing…I love having you on the team."
    b.   "You're OK…would not lose sleep if you left."
    c.   "I'd like to see you move on."

19. *I'd work harder if:*
    a.   I was paid more.
    b.   I'm already working 100%.
    c.   I could see the results of my work.

20. *The purpose of a job is to:*
    a.   Make an income.
    b.   Do something that I am great at that provides value to a business and its customers and receive good compensation for providing that value.

21. *Results: This quarter I am:*
    a.   Beating my goal.
    b.   90% or better of my goal
    c.   Less than 90% of my goal

Now, if you were like many of us, you may have been tempted to score yourself with what you thought was the correct answer versus how you really respond in that given situation. If so, please go back and be candid with yourself. Before we get to the scoring of the assessment, let's pause to consider the ramifications of some of the questions posed above. Perhaps you think that some of the questions had clear A Player responses. Perhaps some of the responses hit hard and were obvious B or C Player behavior. Did you take ownership and fess up to that thinking, or were you in denial and chose a more politically correct answer? I would hope you take the steps to A Player behavior and answer these honestly, as great self-awareness and integrity are the first steps in becoming an A Player.

In addition to the probing questions above, you should always remain in constant assessment mode, considering the answers to powerful questions like:

Have you thought about whether or not you've been an A Player this last quarter or last year? Would your manager agree with your assessment? How would your peers rate you? Have you had a great quarter of fantastic results and leadership? How has your attitude and teamwork been?

Have you been beating your goals?

Have you achieved A Player employee status in the past? If so, are you now resting on your laurels and prior accomplishments? Is your A Player status current or is it outdated? Who besides yourself is calling you an A Player?

Or are you a consummate B Player, and just want recognition from your organization for doing a decent job?

Do you want to be and are you committed to being an A Player?

Are you willing to expend the 10 to 20% more effort and focus it takes to achieve 2 to 3 times the results?

These are examples of just some of the questions you should be continually asking yourself on your journey of being an A Player. You can always come up with your own questions to add, so long as they are consistent with the goals of constantly assessing and working to improve.

Now let's look at the actual scoring of your assessment. Remember that these scores correlate to how top managers and CEOs assess A, B, and C talent. A Players are very self-aware, so if your score is not to your liking, the best thing you can do is "own" your result and work to make those improvements necessary to elevate your game.

A, B, or C Player Assessment Scoring:

Please circle the response you made earlier in the chapter and add up your score. Note: With the exception of question 12, there is only 1 score per question.

	Score
1. When you receive critique or criticism, you take it:	
a. With gratitude and as an opportunity to improve. "Thank you, great to know; I see the value of doing better."	8
b. Somewhat defensively. "Didn't they see all the good I contributed?"	4
c. "This is no fun, I'm trying my best."	3
d. Unwanted. "I know what I am doing better than them."	2
e. "My supervisor is an idiot."	1

	Score
2. You are offered the opportunity to work with an executive coach as an investment the company is willing to make in you. Your first reaction is:	
a. "Awesome! I'm excited for the experience and the opportunity to learn skills and tools to get even better."	8
b. "I probably don't have the time. Let's see what this person can do."	4
c. "I probably know more than the coach."	2
d. "What a waste of time."	1

	Score
3. You are given a very challenging assignment. You are asked to produce a result beyond what has been achieved to date. Success is by no means guaranteed. Your reaction is:	
a. "Failure is not an option."	8
b. "Thanks for the confidence in me. I'll figure out a way. I'll build a plan to achieve the results."	8
c. "Wow that's challenging, I'll see what I can do."	6
d. "I'll think about it"	5
e. "I don't see the benefit."	3

f. "I don't agree this is the right goal to go after."	4
g. "It can't be done."	1
h. "Just tell me what to do."	2

	Score
4. Expertise in your career:	
a. "I know all there is to know."	3
b. "I teach people how to do this."	6
c. "I'm actively learning and making improvements."	8

	Score
5. You have a better way to do a project or process than your manager. You:	
a. Salute the flag and do it your manager's way.	4
b. Tell your manager that they should listen to you and do it your way.	6
c. Ask your manager if they are open to better results, and if they will allow you to prove to them your method is better.	8

	Score
6. The results of a project come up short. Your first tendency is to think:	
a. "The goal was probably wrong."	5
b. "Who screwed up?"	3
c. "Where did others come up short?"	2
d. "I wasn't really on-board with the goal anyway."	1
e. "My company is doing the wrong actions."	4
f. "What could I have done better?"	8

	Score
7. A crisis comes up. Your tendency is to:	
a. Critique the situation.	5

b. Take personal action.		8
c. Hide and avoid the action.		1

		Score
8. Your leader comes in with an assignment that seems unrealistic. You:		
	a. Salute the flag and attempt to do it.	5
	b. Push back on the assignment.	3
	c. Partner with your leader to make the assignment SMART and then build the plan and hit the goal.	8
	d. Ask to discuss underlining assumptions before embarking.	7
	e. Go through the motions and let the project run its course.	3
	f. Stall and hope it goes away.	2
	g. Tell them why it won't work.	3
	h. Tell your boss s/he's an idiot.	1

		Score
9. Your company needs a solution to a major opportunity or problem. You offer:		
	a. Your opinion on how to solve.	6
	b. A detailed plan and business case and what you can do to help.	8
	c. Nothing, you are too busy on your other priorities.	4
	d. Nothing, it is somebody else's job to do.	2

		Score
10. A project blows up. You are culpable for some strategic and execution errors. Your instinct is to:		
	a. Find something to explain the shortcoming.	4
	b. Feel insecure. Figure out who or what to blame.	3
	c. Stand up and take responsibility.	8

	d. Take your vacation days and wait for it to blow over.	2
		Score
11. To what extent do you do the things that nobody else wants to do to become successful?		
	a. "I only work on big picture things."	3
	b. "They are below my pay grade; I delegate them to others."	4
	c. "I'm in a position where I can work only on the things I like to."	5
	d. "I relish the unsavory tasks because I understand their value."	7
	e. "If my competitors aren't doing them, then I should."	6
	f. a and b	4
	g. d and e	8
		Score
12. If you are a leader, what percentage of your team is made of A, B and C Players?		
	a. A Players greater than 90%	8
	b. A Players between 80% -89%	7
	c. A Players between 70%-79%	6
	d. A Players between 50-69%	5
	e. A Players between 30-49%	3
	f. A Players under 30%	2
	e. Over 20% of team are C Players (subtract from score)	-5
		Score
13. How do you feel about your current job?		
	a. "I am fully engaged at work. I love what I do."	8
	b. "I am not at all engaged. I am actively looking for a job somewhere else."	1

	c. "I am somewhat engaged. I may look for something better."	4

		Score
14. How do you feel about your current supervisor?		
	a. "S/he is providing terrific experiences and opportunities for me."	8
	b. "S/he a workaholic."	6
	c. "S/he has unrealistic expectations."	3

		Score
15. When you are presented with a SMART Goal:		
	a. "Show me how you want it done."	5
	b. "I'll build the plan and deliver results."	8
	c. "Just tell me what you want me to do."	3

		Score
16. Your beliefs about follow-up and micromanagement are generally:		
	a. "I hate it when they check up on me."	3
	b. "Don't they trust me?"	2
	c. "I like to give my supervisor updates."	8

		Score
17. I believe my role in the organization is to:		
	a. "Earn a living."	1
	b. "Do my job."	5
	c. "Drive improvements and efficiency to increase value."	8

		Score
18. The responses you hear from your manager are:		
	a. "You are amazing…I love having you on the team."	8

	b. "You're OK...would not lose sleep if you left."	5
	c. "I'd like to see you move on."	1

		Score
19. I'd work harder if:		
	a. "I was paid more."	1
	b. "I'm already working 100%."	8
	c. "I could see the results of my work."	5

		Score
20. The purpose of a job is to:		
	a. "Make an income."	2
	b. "Do something that I am great at that provides value to a business and its customers and receive good compensation for providing that value."	8

		Score
21. Results: This quarter I am:		
	a. Beating my goal.	8
	b. 90% or better of my goal	4
	c. Less than 90% of my goal	2

After recording your score by circling your responses, please add your total score here:

Your Score:
Scoring Key:
A Player: 135-170
B Player: 85-134
C Player: 35-84

How did the assessment go for you? Congratulations if you happened to score in the A Player range. But don't stop there. Still take the time to look at your specific responses in the scoring key for opportunities to improve. And remember, repeating this evaluation on an annual basis will help to ensure you maintain your All-Star status.

Now, don't fret if you scored as a B or C Player, as this book was written to help you become an A Player. You will simply need to take a much more dramatic overhaul of your mindset and actions to reach A Player status. During your journey through this book, refer to the scoring key to determine areas of opportunity, new mindsets, and skills that you can improve and elevate through implementing the resources and recommendations within these pages.

Appendix 2

A PLAYERS SET SMART GOALS

"Most 'impossible' goals can be met simply by breaking them down into bite size chunks, writing them down, believing them, and then going full speed ahead as if they were routine."

—**Don Lancaster**, Electronics Pioneer

A Players set SMART goals. You may have even heard the acronym; but what exactly does SMART mean to you? Here is how it is defined:

S-Specific
M-Measurable
A-Achievable
R-Relevant
T-Time-bound

Since you are reading a book about how to be an A Player employee, you likely have been exposed to SMART goals. However, setting and achieving SMART goals are easier said than done. Many executives, business owners, and employees will give lip service to SMART goals, and even claim expertise in the topic, only to struggle mightily when asked to construct goals that are actually Specific, Measurable, Achievable, Relevant, and Time-bound!

The reason for this is simple. While SMART goals appear simple to do, they are actually quite challenging to execute. A Players are not lulled into complacency by the "I Know" factor. Therefore, it is the purview of the A Player to develop their acumen in setting and achieving SMART goals.

To help you become even better at this critical skill, let's break apart the components of SMART:

Specific: Specific means that the parameters of the goal are clearly defined. To set a specific goal you must answer the *six* "W" questions:

Who: Who is involved?
What: What do I want to accomplish?
Where: Identify the location.
When: Establish the time frame.
Which: Identify requirements and constraints.
Why: Specific reasons, purpose, or benefits of accomplishing the goal.

As mentioned above, setting specific goals is an area where even seasoned executives struggle mightily. During a coaching session with a high-powered executive with a degree from the Wharton School of Business, we worked to make his goals more specific. His goal started out as: "meet with new franchise owners biweekly." Not a bad starting notion to be sure, but not nearly specific enough.

One key to making goals more specific is understanding why you really want them. They need to be a means to a bigger end. It was pointed out to this executive that not many people really want a biweekly meeting as a goal (yet mysteriously they write something like that down!). This is not really a worthy goal by itself. There is actually something bigger that you want. So how do you figure out exactly what you want? The key is to keep asking *why* this is important. Why do you really want it? The truth is that we want to achieve the *end*, not the *means* to the end. In this case, the executive *really wanted* better revenue performance from franchise owners during their start-up months.

So with that end in mind, restating this goal to be more *specific* looks like: Conduct biweekly meetings with our five newest franchise owners to review their marketing plans and sales pipelines to ensure they each achieve $30,000 in monthly revenue by May 31st. As you can see, this is a far more specific and useful SMART goal.

Specific goals have a much greater chance of achievement because the rich definition of the six "W" questions drives actions and plans much more effectively than vague general goals do. As noted CPA and business profit expert Greg Crabtree, CEO of Crabtree, Rowe & Berger is fond of saying: "The person who aims at nothing hits it with amazing accuracy." Greg's point rings true, as often executives' goals are far too vague and unspecific. This is important because only *specific* goals drive your mind to create the *specific* actions and plans needed to achieve worthy SMART goals. Investing the time and focus necessary to make your goals more specific yields both major and long-term dividends. This is because creating a very specific goal unlocks the processing horsepower in your mind to do three very important things:

1. First, investing the time to figure out what you really want will create the specificity needed to achieve important goals in the face of challenges and obstacles. If a goal is undefined, it will not be specific or important enough for you to do the hard work necessary to achieve it. As I often say fuzzy goals = fuzzy results.

2. Second, by constructing a very specific goal you will harness both the conscious and subconscious processing power of your brain, and the *specific* action steps needed to achieve this important goal will be almost immediately revealed to you.

3. The third effect is that with specific goals you will be much more creative in the strategies, solutions, and actions required to achieve the result. Many firms get overly caught up in strategy at the expense of goal setting. The consequence of this is they tend to get caught up on the means and not the end. The remedy is to first be very clear on the goals you want to achieve and then the correct strategies to achieve the goal will flow freely.

Making goals more specific and concrete is the first step in getting better results towards better goal achievement. As an A Player, this is an area where you can really show leadership to your team by setting the standard with highly specific goals that answer the key six "W" questions of Who, What, Where, When, Which, and Why. Not only will your own performance improve, but like the great basketball star, Michael Jordan, you will also elevate others around you.

Measurable: As Peter Drucker famously said, "What gets measured gets managed." For a goal to be SMART, it must have a quantitative and measurable outcome. This is one of the biggest areas for goals to be improved.

Objective measures like reducing monthly utility costs from $8,000 a month to $7,250 per month make wonderfully measurable SMART goals. Note that for measurable goals, whole units that can be specifically measured are far better than percentage changes. Why? By using percentage changes it is harder to calculate the actual start and end points to measure success. Weight loss is an excellent example to remind you of this principle: if someone says to you they are going to lose 5% of their body weight by the end of the month, we have to take the steps to not only figure out what they weigh now, but also take the extra step of calculating the ultimate measurable goal of what they will weigh in the future. Better is to declare a finite measurable goal, like getting to 190 pounds by the last workday of the month. The only places that measuring in percentages is valid are intrinsic percentages like financial ratios (e.g., improving net margin from 12 to 14%), or performance ratios (e.g. improving sales conversion rate from 40 to 45%).

What is particularly interesting about this element of SMART is that it is possible and highly desirable to make measures that were previously deemed subjective into objective, measurable SMART goals. In fact, anything that is viewed as subjective can actually be made objective.

For example, in art, it is often said, "beauty is in the eye of the beholder." Let's say we are in an art museum comparing two works of art by the great French Impressionist painter Monet. It is true that we can subjectively enjoy both works of art and legitimately pick our favorite one based on our own individual eye. However, if we were going to purchase one of the pieces, we may want to apply some objective criteria.

We can actually make subjective data objective by simply surveying all of the patrons who visit the museum and derive objective data from subjective inputs to determine which painting the patrons preferred more. We can even gain more objectivity into subjective inputs by asking the patrons which painting has colors they prefer, which has more defined brushstrokes, and even ask them to put a hypothetical bid on the value of the paintings. I use this example of art to illustrate that the evaluation of even subjective, right brain items can be objectively measured.

How can you put this to work in your business or organization? As an example, companies often want to improve their marketing effectiveness. Inevitably, when goal setting with their marketing teams, they will put out something vague and non-SMART like "improve brand awareness." This is an area where the A Player can add a lot of value by adding measurable criteria to the goal. For example, the A Player would refine the above goal into something measurable (and specific and time-bound) like: improve brand awareness of our company with the top 100 target companies within the state of Florida from 23% to 30% by December 31.

Many people try to take the easy cop-out on items typically seen as "soft" and subjective by saying that they cannot easily be measured. Another evasion they take is saying that these attributes should not be measured objectively. A Players realize that actually everything worthwhile can be measured. A Players don't settle for soft or "woolly" goals, but instead dive deeper to add performance metrics like customer satisfaction scores, market data, or timing. Measurement allows for the straightforward determination of whether goals have been achieved or not. Beating measurable goals is the domain of the A Player employee.

Achievable: Some experts who also espouse SMART goals call this attribute Attainable. Both are excellent descriptors of this element of SMART. Goals that are not attainable and that are clearly out of reach actually de-motivate people. Executives often slyly want their people to set and reach "stretch" goals. They seem to almost have a sadistic undertone to them as a challenge to their team members to set and meet goals that are virtually impossible to hit. Too many managers are simply mischievous in setting stretch goals and they end up playing games with people.

Therefore, many experts are not fans of arbitrary "stretch" goals per se, but much prefer achievable SMART goals that have realistic company or personal best levels of achievement embedded in them. To be sure, SMART goals must challenge us and represent substantial and meaningful progress. We should definitely not settle for a goal that is too easy to achieve and not challenging for us, however it does need to be an achievable and realistic goal based on our authority, capabilities, and time frame to achieve.

To be realistic, a goal must represent an objective toward which you are both willing and able to work. For example, a new potential A Player joining a sales team will aspire in the proper time frame to ultimately hit the $250,000 monthly sales figures the veteran A Players are achieving. However, it is not SMART for that person to set their first month goal at $250,000 because they need to build up their customer base to the same level that the veterans enjoy and for which they have tirelessly worked. For example, a SMART first-month goal that builds to their ultimate goal would be to make their first sale of $25,000 within 4 weeks of starting with the new company. Achieving that SMART goal is actually quite credible, and achieving that building block will allow the sales representative to hit his or her ultimate SMART goal of $250,000 in monthly sales. Cain Hayes, president of a major international insurance company, shares: "For the A Player, achieving a SMART goal is their minimum standard."

This brings us to another important aspect of the achievability of SMART goals. Achievable goals have clear-cut actions that allow large longer-range goals to be broken down into a series of highly achievable smaller steps. These smaller steps with clear-cut actions are the secret that enables the achievement of large and complex goals that cannot be achieved otherwise. This is because we simply cannot wrap our heads around the notion that we can start on a goal that large without breaking it down into specific components.

The other aspect of this is that SMART goals actually come in two different strata. I call these the *ultimate* goal level and the *real* goal levels. The difference between ultimate goals and real goals is that ultimate goals are results and cannot be directly attained without the achievement of the real goals. In other words, ultimate goals are dependent on the achievement of the real goals, which directly build up to the ultimate goal.

For example: Most businesses have both ultimate level revenue and profit goals. In fact, they are pretty good at setting these targets, and in most cases sharing these targets with employees on the team as well. Let's say that your organization wants to achieve $5 billion in revenue and $500 million in net profit. Let's assume both of these levels are 10% better than last year's results. Again, these are fine *ultimate* goals and are SMART, but the issue is they cannot be directly achieved without the achievement of the *real* goals. Real goals are goals that we have direct influence and control over. They are critical to goal achievement. In the excellent book *The 4 Disciplines of Execution*, the Covey organization calls them Lead Measures. In this case, the vice president of marketing is responsible for a specific amount of leads coming into the business, while the vice president of sales is responsible for the average dollar sales of the products as well as conversion rate, and the vice president of finance is responsible for containing fixed costs and overhead to a specific level. Achievement of all of these real goals by the specific individuals will lead to the achievement of the ultimate goal of $5 billion in revenue and $500 million in net profit. A Players are adept at translating the ultimate goal of an organization into a number of specific real goals that can be directly influenced and achieved. Think of the real goals as the building block goals that provide the road map to achievement of ultimate goals. This notion is called "line of sight."

Relevant: When goals are relevant and important to you, you become much more creative and innovative in developing solutions to make them become true. Likewise, as an A Player employee, your goals must be relevant to the mission of your organization. Relevancy is important because it is vital to develop direct linkages and alignment between your own personal and department level goals and the goals of your overall organization or business. Think of your own personal or departmental level goals as building blocks towards achievement of your overall company mission. Ask yourself, "Does achieving this goal actually matter?"

Often, employees and executives try to set non-SMART goals that are irrelevant to the overall goals of an organization. Sometimes, relevancy in goal setting can be a rather subtle matter, but it can also be the difference in supporting the overall mission of the organization or missing the mark. Here is an example from the sales and marketing arena to illustrate this point: Let's assume for a moment that sales in your organization are trending at 80% below target for the month. Often, executives work on periphery initiatives like "build the brand" or "build up the database." While building the brand and building up the size of the database are noble pursuits and valuable for just about any business, in the case of the specific SMART goal of returning sales to 100% of plan, they are far too tertiary, vague, and non-SMART to either hit the mark or achieve the objective. Simply stated, they are probably not the most direct actions necessary to achieve the goal.

As they say at Philmont Scout Ranch, the Boy Scouts of America's premier high adventure base, "The most important thing is to keep the most important thing the most important thing and that's the most important thing!" As A Players, we need to seek to set the most relevant goals, and take the most direct and relevant actions to support our organization's objectives. Sometimes this takes the discipline of doing what is most relevant over what may be more enjoyable to each of us. At the extremes of this, people sometimes procrastinate and erroneously prioritize fun or distraction ahead of the relevant, gritty, harder work that really needs to get done to achieve the ultimate goal. The old secret of doing what is more important and urgent to your boss definitely applies here.

As mentioned above, another key aspect in setting relevant SMART goals is to ensure a goal represents an objective toward which you are both willing and able to work. Worthy, relevant goals can be extremely challenging and require perseverance and dedication to achieve. We often hear employees wishing they had the pay and title of higher positions within their organizations. However, only a portion of these people are willing to do the hard work and endure the sacrifices necessary to achieve the goal. Therefore, talking about wanting those positions becomes a wish, not a goal. If you are not really willing to do the work necessary to achieve the goal, then it cannot be relevant to you. In other words, to be relevant, the goal must be something that you intrinsically want, that is important to you, that you are willing to take the arduous task of achieving, and that when achieved represents significant value to you, in and of itself.

Similar to this concept, make sure you know what you really want. I recently worked with an executive who was struggling mightily with SMART goals. I asked him to write down his first 90-day SMART goal and he replied: "Have my performance reviews complete." As his coach, my first question was to ask him how having the performance reviews of his team completed was relevant to him? He reflected for a moment and then replied: "completing and reviewing the performance reviews with all of his direct reports would improve his department's performance." After some more probing, he refined his goal to be SMART: "Complete and review performance reviews for all eight direct reports by December 10th. Through this process, coach each individual on his top two performance opportunities to achieve a 97% customer satisfaction score through the department by March 1. Achievement of this goal will result in achievement of maximum bonus payouts for our entire team and myself." As you can see this is far SMARTer than his starting point.

Drilling down alignment of your goals to ensure they are relevant will greatly enhance your probability of achieving them. A Player employees work for relevancy in setting SMART goals. Drive for maximum alignment of your SMART goals with your organization's major goals.

Time-bound: Perhaps the simplest component of SMART goal setting that is commonly overlooked is setting a time frame for completion of every goal. When conducting strategic business planning sessions with executives who are in the process of developing SMART goals, inevitably the first drafts of their goals are missing timing or the element of a deadline. A non-SMART goal like "Have by performance reviews completed" needs to become, "Have my performance reviews completed by November 30th." "Increase revenue by $400,000" needs to become "Increase revenue by $400,000 by May 31st." Setting a time frame or deadline for goal completion allows for a concrete measure to determine if a goal has or has not been achieved. This is important for several aspects, including that the goal needs to be relevant and meaningful, so having it completed and achieved by a specific time frame usually supports the achievement of other important goals that are dependent upon it. For instance, having an annual marketing plan approved by December 15th will enable successful growth strategies to be executed for the coming year. If timing on having the marketing plan slips, then it puts the following year's growth in peril, as execution on actions will not happen.

Another huge aspect of making SMART goals time-bound is that they immediately set into motion the work plan and action steps necessary to complete the goal, with associated timing needed on the steps. The other benefit of setting a time frame is without a time frame, there is no urgency to complete the goal. As they say on the website *topachievement.com* "someday won't work."

In summary, developing and achieving SMART goals are one of the most important skills the A Player has. Excellence in this attribute is vital to your success and the success of your organization. After all, the successful execution of goals is how organizations win. Setting and beating SMART goals through great execution are the gold standard for the A Player.

Appendix 3

SUMMARY OF THE CORE COMPETENCIES OF *A* PLAYERS

60 A Player Competencies

I am an ordinary man who worked hard to develop the talent I was given. I believed in myself, and I believe in the goodness of others.
—**Muhammad Ali**, World Champion Boxer

A lot goes into being an A Player. It may even be fair to say the list is exhaustive. A lot of human resource professionals are fond of building sophisticated competency models. While this is certainly an honorable notion, I've got to say I've never seen a competency that was not very important. When I asked to see the models, I was told they were still under development and validation.

Since the models were never ready, I was simply searching for a complete list of attributes the A Players needed to be skilled at. I was very pleased to find a comprehensive list of 48 competencies in *Topgrading*, Dr. Brad Smart's seminal work on how to identify A Players. Brad's list covered the key elements you'd expect to find in A Players and was straightforward and practical to assess.

In my practice we adapted the 48 competencies from *Topgrading* and edited and expanded this list to 60 A Player competencies that we work with high performers on. Is 60 a long list? It certainly is! Is it a list that A Players are expected to show proficiency on, absolutely! Is 60 a manageable number? It actually is!

The reason that 60 competencies are actually a reasonable number to evaluate is that A Players need to be excellent at a wide range of skills and behaviors. 60 is also a number of competencies that can be evaluated by a supervisor or peer within a reasonably short period of time. This is also a very manageable number of competencies to be self-reflective about and work on refining areas that need improvement.

Key:	1	2	3	4	5	6	7	8	9	10	N/A
	Detrimental	Caution	Weak	Needs Improvement	Opportunity	Acceptable	Good	Very Good	Excellent	Exemplary-Role Model	

Attitude: A tendency to respond positively towards ideas, people and situations.

1	2	3	4	5	6	7	8	9	10	N/A
❑	❑	❑	❑	❑	❑	❑	❑	❑	❑	❑

Comments: _____

Ownership: "Owns" their results. Takes actions in the organization as if they owned it themselves.

1	2	3	4	5	6	7	8	9	10	N/A
❑	❑	❑	❑	❑	❑	❑	❑	❑	❑	❑

Comments: _____

Accountability: Is forthcoming in achieving and showing measurable results in their position. Does not make excuses.

1	2	3	4	5	6	7	8	9	10	N/A
❑	❑	❑	❑	❑	❑	❑	❑	❑	❑	❑

Comments: _____

Responsibility: Takes actions that improve a situation. Takes care of things. Does not blame others for one's own failures.

1	2	3	4	5	6	7	8	9	10	N/A
❏	❏	❏	❏	❏	❏	❏	❏	❏	❏	❏

Comments: _____

Learning: A change in behavior through experience, instruction, or study. Exhibits continual improvement through reading, seminars, networks and professional organizations.

1	2	3	4	5	6	7	8	9	10	N/A
❏	❏	❏	❏	❏	❏	❏	❏	❏	❏	❏

Comments: _____

Speed: Fast to respond. Efficient at completing tasks. Beats deadlines.

1	2	3	4	5	6	7	8	9	10	N/A
❏	❏	❏	❏	❏	❏	❏	❏	❏	❏	❏

Comments: _____

Execution: Demonstrates good planning, implementation and performance.

1	2	3	4	5	6	7	8	9	10	N/A
❏	❏	❏	❏	❏	❏	❏	❏	❏	❏	❏

Comments: _____

Promptness: Ready in action; quick to act as occasion demands. Is on time, ahead of time. Respects other's time.

1	2	3	4	5	6	7	8	9	10	N/A
❏	❏	❏	❏	❏	❏	❏	❏	❏	❏	❏

Comments: _____

Judgment/ Decision Making: Ability to reason and reach educated conclusions. Makes good decisions.

1	2	3	4	5	6	7	8	9	10	N/A
❏	❏	❏	❏	❏	❏	❏	❏	❏	❏	❏

Comments: _____

Analysis Skills: Uses facts and data to identify pattern and opportunities. Turns data into information. Good with numbers, data and computations. Sees the "data behind the data." Effectively determines root cause issues.

1	2	3	4	5	6	7	8	9	10	N/A
❑	❑	❑	❑	❑	❑	❑	❑	❑	❑	❑

Comments: _____

Conceptual Ability: Ability to fill in gaps when given an abstract topic and analyze more than just the facts. Sees the "big picture" through the entirety of context, content and patterns.

1	2	3	4	5	6	7	8	9	10	N/A
❑	❑	❑	❑	❑	❑	❑	❑	❑	❑	❑

Comments: _____

Strategic Thinking: Ability to come up with effective plans in line with an organization's objectives.

1	2	3	4	5	6	7	8	9	10	N/A
❑	❑	❑	❑	❑	❑	❑	❑	❑	❑	❑

Comments: _____

Listening: Pays active attention to what others have to say. Effectively understands the information people are conveying. People do not frequently need to repeat information to you.

1	2	3	4	5	6	7	8	9	10	N/A
❑	❑	❑	❑	❑	❑	❑	❑	❑	❑	❑

Comments: _____

Brings Solutions, Not Problems: Brings solutions in addition to identifying problems. Does not create problems. Is not the "Devil's advocate."

1	2	3	4	5	6	7	8	9	10	N/A
❑	❑	❑	❑	❑	❑	❑	❑	❑	❑	❑

Comments: _____

Pragmatism: Generates sensible, realistic, and practical solutions to issues and problems.

1	2	3	4	5	6	7	8	9	10	N/A
❑	❑	❑	❑	❑	❑	❑	❑	❑	❑	❑

Comments: _____

Negotiation: Effectively discovers common ground and reaches agreements to settle a matter or resolve a conflict.

1	2	3	4	5	6	7	8	9	10	N/A
❑	❑	❑	❑	❑	❑	❑	❑	❑	❑	❑

Comments: _____

Leading Edge: Represents the most advanced or innovative aspects of a profession.

1	2	3	4	5	6	7	8	9	10	N/A
❑	❑	❑	❑	❑	❑	❑	❑	❑	❑	❑

Comments: _____

Drive: Self-motivated; determined; striving vigorously toward a goal or objective.

1	2	3	4	5	6	7	8	9	10	N/A
❑	❑	❑	❑	❑	❑	❑	❑	❑	❑	❑

Comments: _____

Integrity: Do what you say you are going to do. Congruency of words and actions. Does not ethically cut corners. Does not manipulate data to prove a point.

1	2	3	4	5	6	7	8	9	10	N/A
❑	❑	❑	❑	❑	❑	❑	❑	❑	❑	❑

Comments: _____

Trustworthy: Able to be relied on as honest or truthful. Does not lie. Not deceitful. Maintains confidences.

1	2	3	4	5	6	7	8	9	10	N/A
❑	❑	❑	❑	❑	❑	❑	❑	❑	❑	❑

Comments: _____

Resourcefulness: Able to deal skillfully and promptly with new situations, difficulties, etc. Achieves results despite lack of resources.

1	2	3	4	5	6	7	8	9	10	N/A
❑	❑	❑	❑	❑	❑	❑	❑	❑	❑	❑

Comments: _____

Resilience: Ability to bounce back from setbacks and overcome obstacles. The capacity to recover quickly from difficulties; toughness.

1	2	3	4	5	6	7	8	9	10	N/A
❑	❑	❑	❑	❑	❑	❑	❑	❑	❑	❑

Comments: _____

Tenacity: Tending to stick to or adhere persistently to achieve a result.

1	2	3	4	5	6	7	8	9	10	N/A
❑	❑	❑	❑	❑	❑	❑	❑	❑	❑	❑

Comments: _____

Results and Track Record: Has a consistent track record of producing results and meeting or beating goals. No excuses.

1	2	3	4	5	6	7	8	9	10	N/A
❑	❑	❑	❑	❑	❑	❑	❑	❑	❑	❑

Comments: _____

Excellence: Sets and achieves high levels of performance for self and coworkers. Demonstrates low tolerance for mediocrity.

1	2	3	4	5	6	7	8	9	10	N/A
❑	❑	❑	❑	❑	❑	❑	❑	❑	❑	❑

Comments: _____

Political Savvy: Shows awareness of political forces in the organization. Recognizes how to get things done through both formal and informal channels. Does not have hidden agendas and is not self-seeking.

1	2	3	4	5	6	7	8	9	10	N/A
❑	❑	❑	❑	❑	❑	❑	❑	❑	❑	❑

Comments: _____

Selecting A Players: Choosing the best talent for the organization

1	2	3	4	5	6	7	8	9	10	N/A
❑	❑	❑	❑	❑	❑	❑	❑	❑	❑	❑

Comments: _____

Redeploying B/C Players: Moves or reassigns underperforming people to different positions.

1	2	3	4	5	6	7	8	9	10	N/A
❑	❑	❑	❑	❑	❑	❑	❑	❑	❑	❑

Comments: _____

Stress Management: Has grace under pressure.

1	2	3	4	5	6	7	8	9	10	N/A
❑	❑	❑	❑	❑	❑	❑	❑	❑	❑	❑

Comments: _____

Adaptability: Ability to alter plans according to changing circumstances or environments.

1	2	3	4	5	6	7	8	9	10	N/A
❑	❑	❑	❑	❑	❑	❑	❑	❑	❑	❑

Comments: _____

First Impression: How someone is originally portrayed.

1	2	3	4	5	6	7	8	9	10	N/A
❑	❑	❑	❑	❑	❑	❑	❑	❑	❑	❑

Comments: _____

Likeability: Puts people at ease. Builds and maintains trusting relationships. Does not turn people off. Not arrogant. Compassionate, friendly, genuine, and caring. Treats people with respect.

1	2	3	4	5	6	7	8	9	10	N/A
❑	❑	❑	❑	❑	❑	❑	❑	❑	❑	❑

Comments: _____

Self-Awareness: Being conscious of strengths and weaknesses. Works on areas for improvement for each. Minimizes "blind spots." Seeks 360-degree feedback.

1	2	3	4	5	6	7	8	9	10	N/A
❑	❑	❑	❑	❑	❑	❑	❑	❑	❑	❑

Comments: _____

Passion: Love of job.

1	2	3	4	5	6	7	8	9	10	N/A
❑	❑	❑	❑	❑	❑	❑	❑	❑	❑	❑

Comments: _____

Energy: Vigor. Adds dynamism, enthusiasm and vitality.

1	2	3	4	5	6	7	8	9	10	N/A
❑	❑	❑	❑	❑	❑	❑	❑	❑	❑	❑

Comments: _____

Customer Focus: Orientation towards serving customer's needs. Actively measures customer satisfaction.

1	2	3	4	5	6	7	8	9	10	N/A
❑	❑	❑	❑	❑	❑	❑	❑	❑	❑	❑

Comments: _____

Assertiveness: Confidence and directness in putting forward one's views without being excessively abrasive.

1	2	3	4	5	6	7	8	9	10	N/A
❑	❑	❑	❑	❑	❑	❑	❑	❑	❑	❑

Comments: _____

Ambition: Desire to add more value to organization through more responsibility. Not self-serving. Serves the company versus selfishly seeking promotion.

1	2	3	4	5	6	7	8	9	10	N/A
❑	❑	❑	❑	❑	❑	❑	❑	❑	❑	❑

Comments: _____

Communications-Verbal: Speaking in tone and manner appropriate for given situations.

1	2	3	4	5	6	7	8	9	10	N/A
❑	❑	❑	❑	❑	❑	❑	❑	❑	❑	❑

Comments: _____

Communications-Written: Conveys intent clearly, concisely, and professionally through writing.

1	2	3	4	5	6	7	8	9	10	N/A
❑	❑	❑	❑	❑	❑	❑	❑	❑	❑	❑

Comments: _____

Communicates Progress on Assignments: Keeps others up to date on work.

1	2	3	4	5	6	7	8	9	10	N/A
❑	❑	❑	❑	❑	❑	❑	❑	❑	❑	❑

Comments: _____

Team Player: Overcomes "we-they" situations. Leads team towards solutions that are best for the total company versus individual silos. Treats people with respect while holding them accountable. Cooperates with supervisors without being a "yes" person.

1	2	3	4	5	6	7	8	9	10	N/A
❑	❑	❑	❑	❑	❑	❑	❑	❑	❑	❑

Comments: _____

Team Builder: Ability to motivate employees to form a team that stays, and achieves together. Establishes collaborative relationships with peers that have open, honest communication. Shares credit.

1	2	3	4	5	6	7	8	9	10	N/A
❑	❑	❑	❑	❑	❑	❑	❑	❑	❑	❑

Comments: _____

Empowerment: Gives power, guidance, resources and assignments so others can grow and achieve results.

1	2	3	4	5	6	7	8	9	10	N/A
❏	❏	❏	❏	❏	❏	❏	❏	❏	❏	❏

Comments: _____

Coaching: Is coachable. Low "I Know" quotient. A people builder. Actively and successfully trains and develops people. Provides continual feedback. Helps people succeed.

1	2	3	4	5	6	7	8	9	10	N/A
❏	❏	❏	❏	❏	❏	❏	❏	❏	❏	❏

Comments: _____

Independence: Self-reliant; not dependent on others; can complete tasks and make decisions alone.

1	2	3	4	5	6	7	8	9	10	N/A
❏	❏	❏	❏	❏	❏	❏	❏	❏	❏	❏

Comments: _____

Planning Skills: Ability to set strategies to achieve goals within a set amount of time and ability to foresee future needs.

1	2	3	4	5	6	7	8	9	10	N/A
❏	❏	❏	❏	❏	❏	❏	❏	❏	❏	❏

Comments: _____

Meets Deadlines: Ability to complete tasks within given time frames.

1	2	3	4	5	6	7	8	9	10	N/A
❏	❏	❏	❏	❏	❏	❏	❏	❏	❏	❏

Comments: _____

Organization: Plans, organizes, schedules and budgets in an efficient, productive manner.

1	2	3	4	5	6	7	8	9	10	N/A
❏	❏	❏	❏	❏	❏	❏	❏	❏	❏	❏

Comments: _____

Prioritization: Effectively works on items in their order of importance or urgency.

1	2	3	4	5	6	7	8	9	10	N/A
❑	❑	❑	❑	❑	❑	❑	❑	❑	❑	❑

Comments: _____

Growth versus Fixed Mindset: Always looking for ways to get better versus "Know it All." Open minded to new ideas.

1	2	3	4	5	6	7	8	9	10	N/A
❑	❑	❑	❑	❑	❑	❑	❑	❑	❑	❑

Comments: _____

Diversity: Wide range of abilities, experience, knowledge, and strengths. Seeks a diversity of opinions and thinking. Can see through others' perspectives.

1	2	3	4	5	6	7	8	9	10	N/A
❑	❑	❑	❑	❑	❑	❑	❑	❑	❑	❑

Comments: _____

Effectively Runs Meetings: Keeps attention; doesn't waste time.

1	2	3	4	5	6	7	8	9	10	N/A
❑	❑	❑	❑	❑	❑	❑	❑	❑	❑	❑

Comments: _____

Vision: Idea of where the organization will be down the road.

1	2	3	4	5	6	7	8	9	10	N/A
❑	❑	❑	❑	❑	❑	❑	❑	❑	❑	❑

Comments: _____

Change Leadership: Ability to lead people through new situations.

1	2	3	4	5	6	7	8	9	10	N/A
❑	❑	❑	❑	❑	❑	❑	❑	❑	❑	❑

Comments: _____

Inspiring "Followership": Ability to gain supporters.

1	2	3	4	5	6	7	8	9	10	N/A
❏	❏	❏	❏	❏	❏	❏	❏	❏	❏	❏

Comments: _____

Conflict Management: Ability to resolve issues and find solutions.

1	2	3	4	5	6	7	8	9	10	N/A
❏	❏	❏	❏	❏	❏	❏	❏	❏	❏	❏

Comments: _____

Collegiality: Ability to discuss sensitive issues effectively and respectfully.

1	2	3	4	5	6	7	8	9	10	N/A
❏	❏	❏	❏	❏	❏	❏	❏	❏	❏	❏

Comments: _____

Empowers Others: Ability to delegate power or authority to others.

1	2	3	4	5	6	7	8	9	10	N/A
❏	❏	❏	❏	❏	❏	❏	❏	❏	❏	❏

Comments: _____

Creativity: Thinks outside the box; comes up with new ideas.

1	2	3	4	5	6	7	8	9	10	N/A
❏	❏	❏	❏	❏	❏	❏	❏	❏	❏	❏

Comments: _____

Appendix 4

TOPGRADING HIRING AND INTERVIEWING

"Create a team of high performers and you are likely to succeed, but keep a lot of low performers and you are likely to fail"
—**Brad Smart Ph.D.**, President & CEO Topgrading, Inc.

Topgrading is a hiring and interviewing methodology that is far more detailed and robust than standard interview processes. It has been shown to be extremely effective in improving success in hiring by significantly increasing the amount of A Players selected and reducing mis-hires of B and C Players. This hiring philosophy and process is detailed in the best-selling book written by Brad Smart, *Topgrading: How Leading Companies Win by Hiring, Coaching and Keeping the Best People.*

It follows 12 defined steps that are usually badly missed in a typical candidate interview process:

1. Measure Current Hiring Success
2. Create a Job Scorecard
3. Recruit From Networks

4. Screen Candidates with the Online Topgrading Career History Form and Topgrading Snapshot
5. Conduct a Telephone Screening Interview
6. Conduct a Series of Competency Interviews
7. Conduct the 4-Hour Topgrading Interview with at Least One Other Interviewer
8. Interviewers Receive Feedback and Coaching
9. Write a Draft Executive Summary on the Candidate
10. Ask the Candidate to Arrange Reference Calls
11. Coach Your New Hire
12. Measure Hiring Success Annually

Individuals who successfully pass through all 12 steps of the Topgrading process are considered A Players. To the A Player these detailed interview steps are very natural and not at all stressful, as their actual work accomplishments are in line with the information they provided in their Topgrading Career History Form. The hallmark of A Players in this interview process is they can provide very detailed and accurate descriptions of what *they* actually did to contribute to results. In addition to what they did, they can also provide specifics on *how* they accomplished it. Finally, they can easily provide very good references of prior managers during the interview, because there is very low risk of a prior manager referring an A Player.

Based on this methodology, candidates who do not exhibit A Player characteristics throughout the process should not be hired.

CPSIA information can be obtained
at www.ICGtesting.com
Printed in the USA
LVOW10s1353160117

521113LV00001B/85/P